PRAISE PAGE FOR A RANDOM POTPOURRI: AN ANTHOLOGY OF REMNANT SCRAWLS FROM A POLICEMAN'S DIARY

In *A Random Potpourri*, the author transcends the boundaries of conventional genres, creating a genre of its own. It's a literary symphony that harmoniously blends philosophy, science, spirituality and more. This work exemplifies the transformative power of literature to ignite intellectual curiosity and provoke introspection.

—Sam Paul,
Paulsons Group, Successful Entrepreneur

A Random Potpourri is a magnum opus of a profound intellectual exploration. The author's ability to seamlessly traverse diverse realms of knowledge is truly awe-inspiring. This book transcends time and place, offering a timeless reservoir of insights for generations ahead. It's a treasure trove for those who seek to broaden their horizons and deepen their understanding of the world.

—Dr. K. S. Vijay Elangovan,
Former Senior Editor, The Hindu

A Random Potpourri is a literary gem that delves into the intricacies of the human experience. The book's diverse themes and profound insights make it a captivating and thought-provoking read. With every turn of the page, it's as if he's uncovering the hidden stories of our lives.

—Dr Jayanthi Murali, IFS,
Chairperson, Tamil Nadu Pollution Control Board

Random Potpourri is a tranquil escape from the whirlwind of my entrepreneurial life. In its pages, I've discovered a wealth of wisdom that soothes my soul amidst the chaos. This book is a treasure trove of insights, a sanctuary where narratives explore life's nuances with exceptional storytelling.

As the leader of a vast industrial empire, my days are relentless, but this book has become a source of solace and inspiration. It whispers sage secrets, revealing life's intricate dance. It's a symphony of words that resonates deeply within, reminding me that wisdom can quench the soul's thirst even in the stormiest of times.

—Mr Rafiq Ahmed Jinnah,
Managing Director, Kothari Industrial Corporation Limited, Chennai

A Random Potpourri is a symphony of wisdom and enlightenment. It's a book that nourishes the soul and invites readers to explore the depths of their own consciousness. The chapter on "The Joy of Letting Go" resonates deeply with the principles of mindfulness. A valuable addition to the literature on well-being.

—Dhivya Kannan,
Mindfulness Life Coach, NI – Nurturing Institute, Chennai

A Random Potpourri offers a holistic perspective on health and well-being. The chapter on nutrition is a game-changer, guiding readers toward a healthier lifestyle.

—Dr. V. Kamatchi Selvam, DA., MSc (Psychotherapy and Counselling) (Gold Medal), MBA (HR), DAcu,
Head, Department of Anaesthesia, and Additional Chief Health Director, Southern Railway HQ Hospital, Chennai

In a world where our relationship with the environment is at a critical juncture, *A Random Potpourri* emerges as a clarion call for environmental stewardship. The chapters dedicated to nature and sustainability resonate deeply, serving as a rallying cry for those who champion the cause of our planet.

—Yogesh Singh, IFS,
Managing Director, Tamilnadu Forest Plantation Corporation Limited

A RANDOM POTPOURRI

AN ANTHOLOGY OF REMNANT SCRAWLS
FROM A POLICEMAN'S DIARY

K. JAYANTH MURALI
Director General of Police (Retd.)
Bestselling Author, Marathoner, and Peak Performance Coach

INDIA • SINGAPORE • MALAYSIA

Revised Edition 2023

ISBN
Paperback 979-8-89186-921-9
Hardcase 979-8-89186-923-3

In loving memory of Nila, my cherished mother-in-law,
whose spirit and love are woven into the very fabric of this book.

CONTENTS

Part II Health and nutrition

Part III Technology and social media

Part IV Policing and law

FOREWORD

SANDEEP RAI RATHORE, IPS
Commissioner of Police

Greater Chennai Police
No. 132, E.V.K. Sampath Road,
Vepery, Chennai - 600 007
Phone: 044-2561 5048
Email: tncopchennai@gmail.com

FOREWORD

As I sit down to pen this foreword, I am filled with an overwhelming sense of admiration and awe for the author of the extraordinary work I'm about to introduce to you – **"A Random Potpourri**: ***An Anthology of Remnant Scrawls from a Policeman's Diary."*** To describe this book as a literary marvel would be an understatement, for it is a symphony of words, a mosaic of thoughts, and a journey through the corridors of the human experience.

Before joining the Indian Police Service in 1992, I was an avid reader and an enthusiast of the written word. I am still a reader but I am unable to pour through literary works like I used to do before because of paucity of time. In my lifelong exploration of books and literature, I have encountered countless authors and their creations, but seldom have I come across a work as captivating, diverse, and thought-provoking as "A Random Potpourri."

The moment you embark on this literary odyssey, you find yourself immersed in a world where the author, with profound humility, extends an invitation to delve into the treasure trove of his musings and reflections. It's as if he opens the door to his diary, beckoning readers to explore the vast tapestry of his mind.

What sets this book apart and indeed elevates it to a realm of its own, is the sheer diversity of topics it encompasses. From the intricacies of policing and law enforcement to the nuances of health and nutrition, from the wonders of technology to the depths of spirituality, this book is akin to a grand banquet of ideas, where each chapter is a delectable dish, carefully prepared to tantalize your intellectual palate.

One cannot help but marvel at the author's ability to seamlessly navigate between these multifaceted subjects, providing insights that are as enlightening as they are informative. He defies the constraints of categorization, embracing the "random" nature of life itself, and in doing so, he mirrors the very essence of existence, where unpredictability and diversity are the norm.

As I devoured the contents of this book, I was particularly drawn to several impactful chapters that left an indelible mark on my mind. Among them is the chapter titled "The Joy of Letting Go." In a world where we often cling to our worries, grievances, and attachments, the author gently reminds us of the profound liberation that comes with letting go. His words resonate with wisdom and offer a guiding light toward inner peace and freedom.

In "What You Seek is Inside You," the author delves into the depths of human introspection. He beautifully articulates the notion that the answers to our questions and the solutions to our problems often lie within ourselves. It's a powerful reminder of the boundless potential that resides within each of us, waiting to be harnessed.

Another chapter that left an indelible impression is "Growth Begins at the End of Your Comfort Zone." Here, the author celebrates the art of pushing boundaries, taking risks, and embracing discomfort as a catalyst for personal growth. His insights are a rallying cry for anyone seeking to break free from the shackles of familiarity.

As I moved through the pages of this book, I found myself immersed in a chapter titled "The Heart of the Matter." In this profound exploration, the author underscores the importance of addressing the root causes of our problems rather than merely treating the symptoms. It's a reminder that true solutions lie in understanding the core issues, whether in our personal lives or within society.

In "High-Value Man" and "High-Value Woman," the author delves into the qualities that define individuals of exceptional character. His insights into confidence, ambition, and success resonate as beacons of guidance for anyone seeking to enhance their personal and professional lives.

The author's exploration of technology and social media is both enlightening and thought-provoking. In chapters like "The Emerging Future of Firearms in Law Enforcement" and "Hacking as a Service," he navigates the ever-evolving landscape of technology, shedding light on its potential benefits and pitfalls. Deeply insightful are also the sections dedicated to policing and law, offering invaluable perspectives on topics like cybercrime risks, mindfulness, and spirituality in law enforcement. It is a testament to the author's dedication to his profession and his commitment to improving the lives of those he serves.

One cannot discuss "A Random Potpourri" without acknowledging the author's exceptional writing style. His prose is a tapestry of eloquence, clarity, and accessibility. He possesses the rare gift of conveying complex ideas with simplicity, making even the most intricate subjects accessible to readers from all walks of life. His writing is a testament to the belief that profound knowledge need not be shrouded in jargon but can be shared with grace and humility.

As I read through the pages of this book, I couldn't help but marvel at the author's ability to present diverse topics in a format akin to a menu in a world-class restaurant. Readers are invited to savor the chapters as they would savor culinary delights, choosing what appeals to their intellectual appetite. This approach mirrors the inclusivity of the book, ensuring that it resonates with readers of varying tastes and backgrounds.

In conclusion, "A Random Potpourri" is a literary masterpiece that transcends the boundaries of genre and subject matter. It is an eloquent testimony to the power of the written word to inspire, educate, and transform lives. The author's humility, wisdom, and boundless curiosity shine through every page, inviting readers on a journey of self-discovery and enlightenment.

I extend my heartfelt gratitude to the author for sharing his insights, experiences, and wisdom with the world. May this book find its way into the hands of countless readers, inspiring them to embrace the diversity of life, seek answers within, and embark on their own journeys of self-discovery. "A Random Potpourri" is not just a book; it is a beacon of intellectual and spiritual illumination. As I go back to re-read a few chapters, I am reminded of the words of Marcel Proust: "The real voyage of discovery consists not in seeking new landscapes, but in having new eyes." Through "A Random Potpourri," the author gifts us with new eyes through which we may view the world, our lives, and ourselves.

Yours Sincerely,

5.9.23

SANDEEP RAI RATHORE, IPS.,
Director General of Police/
Commissioner of Police,
Greater Chennai Police.

To

Dr. K.Jayanth Murali, IPS.,
Director General of Police, Retd.,
Patio Flat, No. E-1, Door No. 22/10,
Rutland Gate 4th Street,
Nungambakkam, Chennai-6.

ACKNOWLEDGEMENTS

In the ethereal realm of literary creation, where words dance and thoughts mingle, I humbly extend my profound appreciation and unyielding gratitude to the luminous souls who have woven their essence into the fabric of this book, A Random Potpourri: An Anthology of Remnant Scrawls from a Policeman's Diary. Like radiant stars adorning the midnight sky, their contributions have illuminated my path, infusing this endeavour with an iridescent brilliance.

Foremost among them is my cherished companion, my beloved wife Jayanthi, whose presence has been an exquisite symphony of unwavering support and boundless patience. In the tapestry of my existence, she has been the steadfast thread that has fortified my spirit, shouldering my burdens with grace and selflessness. To you, my dearest, I offer a cascade of gratitude, an ocean of appreciation.

To my revered parents, whose footsteps carved the foundation of my being, I am forever indebted. Their wisdom, tender love and unwavering guidance have sculpted the very contours of my soul. In their nurturing embrace, I found the seeds of integrity, diligence and resilience that have blossomed into this literary offering. To my dear father and mother, words fail to capture the depth of my appreciation.

Enraptured by paternal love, I extend my heartfelt thanks to my treasured daughters, Tanya and Sonya, whose radiant presence has painted vibrant hues on the canvas of my existence. Your affection, unwavering support and tender encouragement have been nourishment for my creative spirit, igniting a fervent passion within. With each beat of my heart, I am eternally grateful for the gift of your love.

To my dear siblings, Ashok and Priya, you are the celestial companions who have embarked on this extraordinary odyssey with me. Your unwavering belief, camaraderie and inspiration have been the gentle winds that propelled this book to majestic heights. With heartfelt reverence, I extend my deepest thanks for the unique threads you wove into this tapestry.

A resplendent beam of appreciation illuminates the path of Vidhya, whose unwavering enthusiasm, unparalleled dedication and meticulous eye for detail have rendered invaluable contributions to this literary opus. Her resolute pursuit of perfection kindled an eternal flame of gratitude within me. To her, I offer an effusion of heartfelt thanks.

Amidst this symphony of support, I encounter the unwavering friendship of my dear Rafiq Bhaiya, an unwavering pillar of strength through tumultuous tides. In the realm of uncertainty, your presence has been a beacon of hope and solace. And to Bhaskar, a wellspring of inspiration, whose unwavering belief in my abilities has transformed doubt into determination. To both of you, I extend my deepest appreciation and gratitude.

With reverential awe, I bestow my sincere gratitude upon the entire constellation of souls at Notion Press, most importantly luminaries like Ms. Surekha Thamannan who painstakingly worked on my manuscript under the visionary leadership of Mr. Naveen. Their orchestration of efficiency, commitment to excellence and dedication have propelled this project to soaring heights, where dreams manifest into tangible reality. I am forever indebted to their stellar contributions.

To my cherished team, Murali, Govindan, Suresh, and my steadfast drivers, Thiygarajan and Arun Prasad, you have been the unyielding pillars that fortified the scaffolding of this literary venture. Amidst the whirlwind of countless moving parts, their support and tireless dedication was big a boon in completing the project.

With profound appreciation, I humbly extend my deepest gratitude to all who have contributed, knowingly or unknowingly, to the kaleidoscope of inspiration that graces the pages of this book. Your presence is etched upon its very essence, forever intertwined with its narrative tapestry.

Lastly, I offer my heartfelt thanks to the readers, those cherished voyagers who embark upon this literary voyage. It is through your eyes that these words come alive, and your hearts resonate with their melodies. Your presence, dear reader, completes the alchemical equation, transforming mere ink and paper into an immersive experience, a transformative journey of the soul.

INTRODUCTION

It is with great humility and gratitude that I address you – my readers – for your outpouring of support and encouragement received in response to my previous literary endeavours. It is your patronage that has emboldened me to embark upon this fourth project, titled *A Random Potpourri: An Anthology of Remnant Scrawls from a Policeman's Diary*. This book is truly a jumbled mix of writings on a variety of topics, ranging from the concerns of nutrition and health to the intricacies of policing and law enforcement.

I never had this idea of compiling the blogs I had published over the years and my writings which did not find their way into my earlier books. I was goaded into it by my friends who believed that there is tremendous value for readers to gain from my sundry writings. And that it would be a pity if all my writings remained confined to my blogs and scrapbook. I am glad I listened to them, as I have enjoyed the process of compiling this book. In this book, I have tried to put together some of my thoughts on policing and law enforcement along with nutrition and health issues that are uppermost in our minds today. My ideas are by no means new or original, but they are based on sources which are freely available for anyone who cares to look for them. I have also tried to present these topics in an easy-to-understand style so that even those not conversant with the different aspects of these subjects can easily understand what they are about.

A common question that people ask is why should a senior police officer dabble in writing when he already has to spend most of his work time preparing reports and pushing files. What inspired me to write is that I grew up feeling that I didn't fit in the world in which I existed. I felt voiceless as a kid, and I felt isolated. Eventually, as I grew older, I realised I could find my power and voice through writing. Then, in 2017, I decided to write for the *Deccan Chronicle*. The resident editor Mohan was kind enough to earmark a weekly column in the paper for me. I could contribute a 1800-word article every Monday for my column. Thus began my writing journey. The first article I wrote was on police suicides, which, however, generated unnecessary controversy within my organisation and reprimands from my seniors. While quoting stats about the status of police suicides in India, I happened to mention truthfully, according to the situation prevailing at that time, that Tamil Nadu was witnessing the highest number of police suicides in the country. Coincidentally, the Tamil Nadu Legislative Assembly's budget session was underway around the same time. During the Police Vote on Account, the opposition leader began criticising the ruling party, quoting stats from my article, which put the Home Secretary and the Director General of Police in a spot. The Director General of Police was furious at me. Seething with anger, he blurted out that I would have to face the consequences for violating the conduct rules, which stipulate disciplinary action for criticising the government in power. Fortunately for me, nothing of that sort actually happened as the budget session ended on a positive note for the ruling party, and because of the smooth passage of the session all the anger that had built against me was forgotten and transmuted into feelings of exuberance and joy. But my first adventure in writing taught me a valuable lesson, that is, to veer away from controversy. Despite being scared and having second thoughts, I continued writing. To steer away from controversy or threat to my job, I decided that I will contribute articles on subjects that would not stir the hornet's nest. I thought technology, health and nutrition, law and so on were a safe bet; so I started contributing articles every week to the *Deccan Chronicle*. After I had contributed 42 articles consecutively over the 42 weeks, I decided to publish them in the form of a book. This is how my first book, *42 Mondays*, came about.

After writing for more than a year and a half to the *Deccan Chronicle*, my contract with them ended. Next, I began writing for *DTNext* once a fortnight. After I had accumulated enough materials that would go into two books, I approached Thomson Reuters with some of my select writings on technology and policing. The vice president of the publishing group after perusing the manuscript soon agreed to publish my anthology of selected writings. That's how my second book, *Soliloquies on Future Policing: An Anthology on Emerging Technologies, Cybersecurity and Law Enforcement*, came about.

Besides writing, the thing I love most is running. For a long time, I had nursed a secret desire to write a training manual on long-distance running.

As I approached 50, to commemorate the day, I ran my first half marathon with both my daughters. And three months later, in February 2013, I ran a full marathon at Auroville. Soon I was running half and full marathons in different towns across India. There was a demand from many friends, colleagues and subordinates that I conduct training programmes for them to run marathons. As I did not have adequate time to write a full-fledged training manual, I created a website (www.jayanthmurali.com) where I began writing blogs on running. Many members of my community started to follow my blogs and began looking forward to them though I posted them sporadically. I had accumulated about 20 blogs by the time *Soliloquies on Future Policing* was out for printing.

Soon I felt I was experiencing a weird sense of vacuum after I had finished the work connected with the publication of *Soliloquies*, and to overcome the emptiness that had engulfed me, I decided to write *Enkindling the Endorphins of Endurance: Your Ultimate Go to Guide for Running Your First 5k, 10k, Half and Full Marathon*, which would become my third book. I decided this book would not just serve as a training manual but would also be a motivational book for runners. I began writing it in October 2021 and completed the 40-odd chapters by February 2022. The printed copies found their way to the bookshelves in July 2022. Now, having completed my three books, I had emptiness staring at me again. Although I was still writing blogs and contributing articles to newspapers, I could feel the void inside me growing. After three books, I had probably grown addicted to the adrenalin rush I would feel when having to work with deadlines or sitting for meetings with my publishing agent and publishers. The withdrawal symptoms after my third book became so intense; it seemed as though I might go mad if I didn't get my fix again soon. The cravings became unbearable, and to fix them I desperately needed to write again. My mind began to go in circles, and I was unable to decide the subject on which I should write the fourth book. Ideas began zooming in and out of my mind; some of them were bizarre and outright absurd, and some that initially seemed good met with internal resistance, scepticism and imposter syndrome. I stepped up my running to counteract the uneasiness of the withdrawals I was experiencing from the cessation of activities connected with publishing. My friends at this point suggested that I compile all my unpublished writings into a book. Running more marathons did not seem to help me with my strange hankering. But when the writing itch became uncontrollable and the insistence of my friends became louder,

I started to look for ways and means to overcome it. Out of sheer desperation, I finally decided to act on the idea of my friends of stringing together some of my remnant articles into a new book. I had about 30 such articles on hand and I decided to write 30 more to turn them into a new book. I approached my publisher again with this new idea and was pleasantly surprised when he immediately welcomed it. That then in short is the story behind the birth of *A Random Potpourri: An Anthology of Remnant Scrawls from a Policeman's Diary*.

The book is titled *A Random Potpourri* because its contents are truly random. Random means lacking a definite plan, purpose or pattern. It suggests a lack of method or system, as in jumping from one thing to another; it emphasises accidental occurrence without prearrangement or planning, like a chance encounter; it applies to that which occurs or is done without a careful choice or aim; and it applies to that which is done, made or said without regard for its consequences, relevance and so on, and therefore stresses the implication of accident or chance. It also connotes nonchalance or haphazardness. While reading the book, one will meet all the attributes of randomness in the riff of topics, their content, a mix of articles and the subjects chosen for this book. The word 'potpourri' derives from the French 'pot pour', the literal meaning of which is 'putrid pot'. The purpose of potpourri, which is a mixture of dried natural fragrance materials in a decorative bowl, is to provide a gentle natural scent in our living places. Similarly, potpourri in literature means a collection of miscellaneous literary extracts, especially of unrelated objects, subjects and so on. This book fits the bill of potpourri as it is an assortment, medley, miscellanea, miscellany, mixed bag, mixture, motley, salmagundi, smorgasbord and a hodgepodge of pieces on topics as diverse as spirituality and quantum mechanics to extreme ownership and AI. The intention behind compiling this book is to give the readers a whiff of literary fragrance on a diverse range of matters. Since this is a compilation of articles that couldn't find their way into my earlier books, not because of quality but because they did not fit into the themes of my earlier books, they are remnants of my diary.

The book is also a potpourri of informative, analytical and descriptive writing. Although written by a police officer it has lots to offer to people from all walks of life. It may help those who want to understand what policing is all about, what people expect from us and how we think and operate. Even those who are not connected with policing will find this book quite useful. I have tried my best to make this book interesting for all kinds of readers irrespective of their educational background! Readers can treat this book like a menu in a restaurant. They can treat themselves to whatever they want and skip the chapters that do not seem appealing to them. They can read the chapters in whatever order they want or skip some chapters altogether if they wish to. It won't matter if they choose to have the dessert first and the main course later. For example, if you are interested in losing weight but don't have the time or money to go to the gym, then you can go to the chapter 'Weight loss plan without exercise during a lockdown (pandemic)'. Similarly, if you are feeling stuck in life and don't know why you are holding on to negativity, then you can jump to the chapter 'The joy of letting go' and learn how to let go of all the things that you are holding on to.

In this book, as already mentioned, I have covered a diverse range of topics such as technology, health, nutrition, law and many more. Each of these topics represents a different aspect of our lives in the society, and each one has the power to shape our future in different ways. I have tried to present each topic in an honest and unbiased way, providing readers with information they need to make quick judgements. Throughout the book, I have shared my personal experiences, insights and reflections on the topics to make the reading more relatable and engaging. I believe the book offers something for everyone, and I hope it will be a valuable resource for readers. I would like to thank all the readers for picking up this book and for taking the time to read it. It has been an honour and privilege to share my thoughts and experiences with you. I hope this book will be a source of inspiration and a catalyst for positive change. In the first part, readers will come across topics of general interest such as 'the joy of letting go', 'life happens for you', 'what you resist persists', 'law of diminishing intent' and similar ones for inspiration and motivation. Given below is a list of chapters and a gist of the subject each chapter deals with.

Description of Chapters

1. **The magical powers of forest bathing**: Forest bathing is the art of spending intentional time with nature and is practised throughout the world to increase health and restore well-being. More and more people are turning to forest bathing as an evidence-based way to unplug, relieve stress and anxiety and spark creativity.
   In this chapter, I discuss the numerous health benefits of spending time with nature and how it can improve physical and mental well-being.

I believe in the healing and rejuvenating powers of nature and have personally experienced the benefits of forest bathing. Spending time with nature, surrounded by trees and greenery, has helped me reduce stress, improve my mood and boost my immune system.

2. **How to create a life that feels good on the inside, not just one that looks good on the outside**: I share tips on how to create a fulfilling and satisfying life that goes beyond external appearances and focuses on inner well-being. Through this concept, one can strive to create a life that feels good on the inside, rather than one that just looks good on the outside. This has helped me focus on cultivating inner happiness, well-being, healthy relationships and positive habits.
3. **Mood follows action**: In this chapter I explain how our actions and behaviours can greatly influence our mood and emotional state, and how we can use this understanding to improve our mental well-being. I wrote this chapter because I always found that my actions can have a direct impact on my moods and emotions. Whenever I made an effort to take positive actions such as exercise, meditation and gratitude practice, I discovered that this led to an improvement in my mood and overall well-being.

   Goals can be helpful if they're aspirational, but they can also be unproductive if they're too rigid and unattainable. It's important to remember that small steps matter just as much as large ones. The best way to take small steps and create momentum towards your goals every day is to start by acknowledging that our mood follows our actions. If we want to feel happier, there are things we can actively do every day that will create the right mood and build sufficient momentum.
4. **The hidden healing power of meditation: why painting is a form of meditation and mindfulness:** I discuss the meditative benefits of painting and how it can be used as a tool for self-expression and stress relief because I found painting to be a relaxing and meditative activity that allowed me to focus on the present moment and express my creativity. It helped me reduce stress and anxiety and improve my overall well-being.
5. **The joy of letting go**: I explore the benefits of letting go of negative emotions and attachments and how it can lead to greater inner peace and freedom because I experienced the power of letting go of things, people or events that were causing stress or negative emotions in me. It is a tool that has immensely helped me in my personal growth and inner peace.

6. **The heart of the matter**: I delve into the importance of understanding and addressing the underlying issues that cause problems in our lives, rather than just treating the symptoms. This chapter came about because I believed in getting to the core or essence of something. Whether it's understanding the underlying cause of a problem or the key principles of a subject, whenever I focused on the heart of the matter I had the answers.
7. **Life happens for you, not to you**: When something unexpected comes up, instead of being annoyed that your plans have to change, think of it as something that you were meant to do. Not everything in life happens for a reason, but everything in life happens for you. In this chapter, I discuss the idea that the challenges and difficulties we face in life can ultimately serve as opportunities for growth and self-discovery. I believe that challenges and struggles in life can be opportunities for growth and personal development. I, therefore, want my readers to have a positive attitude and experience the potential for growth in difficult situations.
8. **What you resist persists, and what you accept dissolves!!** I explain the concept that what we resist persists and how acceptance and surrender can lead to greater inner peace and ease. In this chapter I want my readers to understand that by resisting change or negative situations, we are holding on to them and prolonging the problem and that we must try to accept and let go of situations to move on and find a resolution.
9. **Law of diminishing intent**: I discuss the idea that the longer we put off taking action towards our goals, the less likely we are to achieve them and the importance of taking action promptly. We should become aware that the more time that passes after a decision or action, the less committed we become to it. We must try to act on our intentions quickly and stay committed to our goals.
10. **We can make Tamil Nadu the carbon champion of India**: I discuss the potential for Tamil Nadu to lead the way in reducing carbon emissions and promoting sustainable energy practices. I believe that by taking steps to reduce carbon emissions and promoting sustainable and environmental-friendly practices, Tamil Nadu can become a leader in this field and help in reducing its carbon footprint.
11. **Can we eradicate corruption?** I examine the potential and the steps that can be taken to reduce corruption. Corruption is a complex issue that requires a collaborative effort from individuals, organisations

and the government to address. Transparency, accountability and legal framework can be effective tools to combat corruption.

12. **How and why extreme ownership can be life-changing**: Extreme ownership is the belief that we are fully responsible for our actions and their outcomes. This means taking ownership of our mistakes and learning from them, rather than blaming others. It also means being proactive in finding solutions to problems. I believe in taking full responsibility for my actions and their outcomes. It also means being proactive in finding solutions to problems.
13. **The conundrum of human–wildlife conflict**: The conundrum of human–wildlife conflict is a complex issue that requires a balance between protecting wildlife and preserving the livelihoods and safety of local communities. It is important to find sustainable solutions that benefit both humans and animals. This is a complex issue, and I try to find sustainable solutions that benefit both humans and animals to address this problem.
14. **What you seek is inside you!** This means that the answers to our questions and the solutions to our problems can often be found within ourselves. It is important to trust our intuition and to have confidence in our abilities.
15. **The problem of illegal organ trafficking**: The problem of illegal organ trafficking is a serious and growing issue that has devastating consequences for both donors and recipients. It is important to raise awareness about this issue and work towards finding solutions.
16. **Self-discipline is at the heart of marathon training**: It is important to set goals and stick to a training schedule to be successful. This requires a great deal of willpower and determination. We must understand that self-discipline is important for marathon training and cultivate it to successfully cross the finish line of a marathon.
17. **Be so good that they can't ignore you**: This means that by working hard and becoming an expert in your field, you will be impossible to ignore and will be able to achieve success.
18. **Growth begins at the end of your comfort zone**: This means that true growth and personal development occur when we push ourselves out of our comfort zones and take on new challenges. In this chapter, I explore how we can achieve our goals in life by only getting out of our comfort zones.

19. **How to apply Disney's motto to your life**: 'Where Dreams Come True'. I believe in the power of imagination and dreams, and this motto resonates with me.
20. **High-value man**: A high-value man is confident, ambitious and successful. He is someone who can attract and retain the attention of others. Please read and learn how you can transform yourself into a high-value man.
21. **High-value woman**: A high-value woman is confident, ambitious and successful. She is someone who can attract and retain the attention of others. Any woman can be a high-value woman.
22. **The law of assumption**: Here I explore the idea that when we assume something to be true, it becomes our reality. It is important to be aware of our assumptions and question them.
23. **The power of 'Om' chanting**: 'Om' is a sacred sound and symbol in many Eastern religions and spiritual traditions. Chanting 'Om' is believed to bring inner peace and spiritual enlightenment. I discuss the benefits of incorporating this practice into our daily routine.
24. **The power of silence**: Silence can be a powerful tool for self-reflection and inner growth. It allows us to quieten the noise of the outside world and focus on our thoughts and feelings. I explain the importance of quietening the noise of the outside world and the immense benefits of practising silence.
25. **The soul is stronger than its surroundings**: This means that our inner strength and resilience are greater than any external challenges or obstacles we may face. I explain the importance of cultivating inner strength and resilience and how one could surmount any obstacle one would confront in their life.
26. **When you blame others**: This means that when we blame others for our problems, we give away our power to change and improve our situation. It's important to take responsibility for our actions and choices. I discuss the importance of taking full responsibility for one's actions and choices.

The second part of the book is on health and nutrition. The reader will find some interesting articles on how to lose weight, an interesting article on how to take care of our skin without using artificial cleansers and others.

27 In '**A dirty secret to a healthy skin**', I share a secret for healthy skin that may surprise you. It's a simple yet effective method that will leave your skin feeling rejuvenated.

28. In **'Weight loss plan without exercise during a lockdown (pandemic)'**, I delve into how one can lose weight during lockdowns without any exercise as the gyms would remain closed.
    Lose weight during a lockdown without exercise – part 1: In this section, I discuss the first step of the weight loss journey during the lockdown, focusing on the importance of setting specific and realistic goals.
    Lose weight during a lockdown without exercise – part 2: In this section, I share the second step of the weight loss journey, emphasising the importance of tracking your food intake and making healthy food choices.
    Lose weight during a lockdown without exercise – part 3: In this section, I discuss the third step of the weight loss journey, which includes the importance of staying hydrated and getting enough sleep.
    Lose weight during a lockdown without exercise – part 4: In this section, I share the final step of the weight loss journey, including tips on how to stay motivated and maintain the progress made during the lockdown.
29. **Mind-blowing benefits of tree-hugging**: I share the mind-blowing benefits of tree-hugging and how spending time with nature can improve our mental and physical health.
30. **Healing powers of grounding**: In this chapter, I discuss the concept of grounding and how practising it can improve our overall well-being.
31. **Why sprinting is the best anti-ageing exercise**: I explain why sprinting is the best anti-ageing exercise and how it can improve overall health and fitness.
32. **Are exogenous ketones beneficial for endurance runners?** In this chapter, I share my thoughts on the benefits of exogenous ketones for endurance runners and if it's worth considering as a supplement.
33. **Which is the best fuel for running? Sugar or ketones?** In this chapter, I discuss whether sugar or ketones is the best fuel for running and the pros and cons of each.
34. **Coronavirus genetic vaccine is a medical miracle**: Here I share my thoughts on the recent advancements in the coronavirus genetic vaccine and how it's a medical miracle that can potentially save lives.

35. **A concise guide to a plant-based diet**: In this chapter, I discuss how one can adopt a plant-based diet and the benefits it can have on their overall health.
36. **Berberine: A supplement with multiple benefits**: Berberine is a supplement with multiple benefits. In this chapter, I discuss the multiple benefits it can provide for overall health and wellness.

The third part of the book is about technology and social media. It covers topics such as why social media is a low-hanging fruit for cybercriminals and also topics such as cybercrime as a service (CCaaS), hacking as a service (HaaS), criminal robots and drones, Internet of Things (IoT)-based crime investigation and much more. Here is an overview of chapters.

37. **How 5G tech can enhance the bandwidth of policing in future**: I explore in this chapter how 5G will revolutionise law enforcement agencies by improving response times substantially and enhancing the efficiency of patrol cars, drones, virtual reality (VR), augmented reality (AR) and face recognition technologies.
38. **AI can revolutionise traffic management in Indian cities**: In this chapter, I discuss how AI is slowly entering and about to revolutionise traffic handling by helping police identify traffic hazards, reduce traffic congestion, control emissions besides helping design and manage transport systems and analyse travel demand and pedestrian behaviour.
39. **Hacking as a service**: In this chapter, I discuss the concept of HaaS and the potential dangers it poses to businesses and individuals.
40. **Cybercrime as a service**: I examine the growing trend of CCaaS and its potential impact on cybersecurity.
41. **A comprehensive look at policing in 2050**: I explore the potential future of policing and the technological advancements that may shape it.
42. **The potential of AI to transform the future of policing**: I discuss how AI can revolutionise policing, including improved crime analysis and prediction.
43. **Immortality through mind uploading**: I examine the concept of mind uploading as a potential path to immortality and the ethical considerations surrounding it.
44. **Quantum mechanics and consciousness**: I explore the relationship between quantum mechanics and consciousness and the potential implications for our understanding of the mind and reality.

45. **IoT-based crime investigation**: I share my thoughts on how IoT can be used to improve crime investigation.
46. **Should police departments use robotic interrogators?** I examine the pros and cons of using robot interrogators in police department and the ethical considerations surrounding it.
47. **Spooky mind-reading technology**: I discuss the potential of mind-reading technology and the ethical implications of its use.
48. **Criminal robots and drones**: I explore the potential use of robots and drones in criminal activities and their implications on law enforcement.
49. **Battling the weapons of mass distraction**: I discuss the negative impact of technology on our attention and the importance of disconnecting from weapon of mass distraction (WMD) and fostering mindfulness.
50. **Reclaiming our analogue heritage in the digital era**: I explore how to balance the benefits of technology with the importance of preserving our analogue heritage in the digital era.
51. **The emerging future of firearms in law enforcement**: I examine the potential advancements in firearms technology and their potential impact on law enforcement and society.
52. **What does ChatGPT hold for the future?** I discuss the potential of large language models like ChatGPT and its implications for customer service and content industries.
53. **Challenges and benefits of deepfakes in law enforcement**: I examine the potential dangers of deepfake technology and its implications on crime, politics and society.
54. **Voice biometrics as a critical technology for fighting frauds and cybercrime**: I explore the potential of using voice technology to detect and prevent fraud, including voice biometrics and voice-based authentication.

    The fourth part of the book deals with policing and law. The reader will find articles on cybercrime risks of non-fungible tokens (NFTs), mindfulness and spirituality for policing. Here is a brief description of what each chapter explores.
55. **The growing cybercrime risks of NFT explosion**: I examine the potential risks and vulnerabilities of the growing NFT market and its impact on cybercrime.
56. **Can the police live by bread alone?** I discuss the importance of spirituality for law enforcement officers and its potential impact on their well-being and job performance.

57. **Can spirituality bear the cross of the police?** I explore the potential of spirituality to provide emotional and mental support to law enforcement officers and the impact it can have on their well-being.
58. **Mindfulness for mindful and humane policing**: I discuss the benefits of mindfulness and its potential to improve decision-making and reduce stress in law enforcement officers, promoting a more humane and empathetic approach to policing.

Throughout the book, I share my personal experiences and reflections, offering a unique and valuable perspective on various facets and aspects of life. From delving into the depths of technology and its impact on society to exploring the intricacies of health and nutrition to discussing the nuances of the law and its application, this book is a diverse and comprehensive exploration of various topics. It has been a privilege to share my perspectives and insights on these subjects, and I hope the readers will find the book informative. I hope this book will entertain and amuse readers and help them gain valuable insights on the topics I have chosen to write on, besides assisting them in improving and enriching their lives with my thoughts and reflections.

So *A Random Potpourri* is a thought-provoking and insightful collection of musings, reflections and observations from my career in policing and law enforcement. I hope my unique background and wealth of experience will make this book entertaining for anyone.

In conclusion, the chapters in *A Random Potpourri* are a reflection of my journey and the lessons I learnt along the way. It is a reminder that no matter our profession, we all have a story to tell and a unique perspective to share. *A Random Potpourri* is a testament to the power of the written word and the impact it can have on both the writer and the reader. Writing this book has been a labour of love, and I am deeply grateful to have had the opportunity to share my ideas and thoughts through this book. I look forward to continuing to write and explore new subjects in the future, and I thank the readers for joining me on this journey. I hope you will enjoy reading the book as much as I have enjoyed putting it together for you. I wish you happy reading – and happiness.

Part I

GENERAL

Chapter 1

THE MAGICAL POWERS OF FOREST BATHING

Last week after a long run at the IIT Madras campus, I decided to venture into the forest area after leaving my mobile phone behind in my car. I let my mind guide me, and I wandered into the woods at a tortoise's pace. I slowly felt nature enter me through my ears, eyes, nose, mouth, hands and feet. My ears took in the melodic sounds of the birds singing and the breeze rustling in the leaves of the trees as my eyes gazed at the trees' varied greens while the sun's rays danced and filtered through the branches. My nose inhaled the fragrance of the forest and the natural aromatherapy of phytoncides. I placed my hands on the tree's trunk and felt the tree's life force mingle with mine as I felt a pleasant tingle rip through me, filling me with a sense of joy and calm. The serenity and bliss of the woods were all that I needed to unfasten my senses to the power of the forest and establish a connection with it.

The exhaustion of having just run 42 km and all the stresses and problems hanging over me evaporated instantly, enabling me to relax, eliciting a new perspective which allowed me to view the negatives of my life positively. I felt my energy come back miraculously, refreshing and rejuvenating me with unknown vitality. Being in nature felt so good. The screeches of the grove, the aroma of the trees, the rays of the sun playing through the leaves and the fresh, clean air gave me a sense of comfort and a feeling of peace, unknown.

Have you ever been to a forest? Have you spent time there? Did your time there feel like heaven on earth? Do you often yearn for the peace of the woods? Do you ever feel like you're constantly running on a hamster wheel? Like you can't escape the same old things, people and routines? So much in this world feels out of our control. But what if there was a way to make a change in your life that is in your control. What if you could relieve the stress of your day, refresh your mind and rejuvenate your soul all in one go? Forest bathing is just that for some people.

If your answer is yes to some of the questions posed above, you probably need a forest bath. Forest bathing is just being in nature and connecting to it through our senses of sight, hearing, taste, smell and touch. In Japan, people practise forest bathing or *shinrin-yoku*. *Shinrin* in Japanese means 'forest', and *yoku* means 'bath'. Hence, *shinrin-yoku* means bathing in the forest setting, or drinking in the wilderness through our senses. The word 'bathing' is associated with dirtiness and uncleanliness. However, this is not the case with forest bathing because people do this type of bathing in natural surroundings. The natural surroundings make the bathing experience seem so much more spiritual as it helps people reconnect with nature because it involves mindfulness. You can achieve a state of mindfulness through various meditation forms and forest bathing. During forest bathing, like during mindful activities, you deepen your senses, suspend judgement and focus on the 'now', which connects you with your consciousness or soul.

Forest bathing, a form of spending time with nature, has immense benefits for one's physical, mental and spiritual well-being. If you spend time in the woods, you might have noticed that you feel more alert, refreshed and grounded. Spending time with the natural elements of the woods, like trees and streams, or living near a forest or going to green space has many benefits for your physical, mental and spiritual well-being. But forest bathing isn't a new concept. It's been with humanity for thousands of years. It's a practice that dates back to at least the early 1900s. A forest bathing session is an intentional act where people go to reconnect with nature, get some fresh air and get their minds and bodies back into balance. It's also a type of exposure therapy that helps people beat the stress and pressures of life by giving them a chance to experience the natural environment. It's no wonder that people are getting drawn to this practice in this age of technology. People find this practice incredibly inspiring besides experiencing a plethora of health benefits.

Stress and anxiety can affect your life and your relationships. Stress can hurt your health and your day-to-day life. Many people find that stress and anxiety can suddenly creep into their lives without warning. If you're feeling stressed or anxious, it might be time to think about how you might be able to have a healthier, more stress-free lifestyle. Forest bathing is a green lifestyle. It's a way of thinking, feeling and spending time with nature to reconnect with ourselves and become more in tune with the natural world. Forests act as natural air purifiers, filtering out harmful elements and releasing oxygen into the environment. While we breathe in the fresh air, we breathe in phytoncides – airborne chemicals that plants give off to protect themselves from insects. Phytoncides have antibacterial and antifungal qualities, which help plants fight diseases.

One Japanese study illustrated that participants averaged a massive 50 per cent rise in natural killer (NK) cell activity after a three-day camping excursion in the forest. Hence, science reveals that forest bathing boosts immunity, reduces cancer risk and enables you to recover from illness faster. One study showed that even glancing at trees through a hospital window decreased time to recovery for gallbladder surgery patients. Further, walking through the woods also increases your body's adiponectin levels and reduces the risk of heart attack due to its anti-inflammatory impact on blood vessels. D-limonene found in some forest air may reduce lung inflammation. People with breathing troubles due to asthma and COPD have exhibited improvement after forest bathing due to high oxygen levels in the forest, which consequently reduces inflammation.

There are many benefits of forest bathing: stress reduction, relaxation and improved mental health and cardiovascular functions. It is proven to lower stress hormone generation, heighten feelings of happiness, free up creativity, lower heart rate and blood pressure and boost the immune system to accelerate recovery from illness. It also supports positive social interaction and physical health and creates environmental consciousness. Being in nature gives us a sense of calm, but it's also a great way to reconnect with ourselves, our loved ones and community. When you go into the forest and breathe fresh air, it positively impacts your body. You can relax, and your stress levels go down. You can reset and cleanse your mind, so spending time in a forest is a beautiful way to relax, unwind and rejuvenate.

Chapter 2

HOW TO CREATE A LIFE THAT FEELS GOOD ON THE INSIDE, NOT JUST ONE THAT LOOKS GOOD ON THE OUTSIDE

Are you tired of living a life that feels empty on the inside? Do you think your life is just a performance rather than who you are? Do you feel like there's something more to life but cannot find it, no matter how hard you look? If this sounds like you, then read on. Because you are about to discover how to create a life that feels good on the inside and not just one that looks good from the outside.

When you feel good inside because you live right and do what makes you happy – mentally, physically, emotionally and spiritually – it will show how good you feel on the outside. When you live right and feel good inside, people will see it on the outside. We only have one life. It's not worth wasting it to gladden others; if people don't love and regard and respect you for that, you don't need them. Please don't forfeit your happiness over it.

When society judges you based on your appearance, finding happiness cannot be easy. Even if you have the world's perfect house, car and wardrobe, none of that matters if you don't feel good on the inside. We all want to live a happy life. But in our constant pursuit of success and fame, we sometimes forget what matters. It's not about how many followers you have or how many likes you get on Instagram. Instead, it's about finding a sense of inner peace with who you are and how you choose to live your life each day. It's about living a life that feels good on the inside and not that looks good on the outside.

What Does It Mean to Lead a Life That Feels Good on the Inside?

A life that feels good on the inside is one where you feel connected to your true self and your authentic desires. It is a life where you feel like you are being yourself and thus experiencing pure joy and contentment, which contrasts with a life where you constantly try to fit in and please others. While a life that feels good on the inside is different for each person, it denotes the following:

- Finding your purpose – You have a clear sense of why you are here and what you are meant to do. That can range from making a difference in the world to something as simple as making a difference to one person you meet in your life.
- Finding your passion – You are passionate about what you do and are driven to make it an integral part of your life. It is not something you do out of necessity but something that is a part of who you are.
- Finding joy in the little things – You are grateful for whatever life gives you and find joy in the little things. You appreciate what you have while striving to improve yourself.
- A sense of connection to others – The people in your life feel like family to you, and you feel connected to them, which can range from close loved ones to the people you meet daily. You are compassionate and empathetic towards others.

Why Does Creating a Life That Feels Good on the Inside Matter?

If you lead a good life, you can tap into your potential and find meaning in whatever you do. You will also positively impact the people around you and help improve the world. Moreover, a life that feels good on the inside will help you avoid burnout and find long-term happiness. You will be able to find joy in what you are doing, even if the task seems complicated now. You will know that you are doing what you are meant to do and fulfilling your purpose in life. This will be a source of happiness and fulfilment. Therefore, if you create a life that feels good on the inside, you can lead a fulfilling life and be happy simultaneously.

Four Steps to Create a Life That Feels Good on the Inside

There are many ways to create a life that feels good on the inside. However, the following steps are the most effective:

Step 1: Identify what your life would look like if it felt good inside – What would you do? Who would you surround yourself with? What would your environment be like?

Step 2: Identify the beliefs and mindsets currently holding you back – What self-limiting beliefs do you have? What thoughts do you keep having that hold you back? What fears do you have?

Step 3: Make changes in your life to eliminate the above – What changes can you make to eradicate those beliefs and mindsets?

Step 4: Create a daily ritual that supports your goals – What can you do every day to support your goals? What can you do to make your life feel good on the inside?

An attitude of gratitude could be a key to creating a life that is good on the inside. I had the habit of glamorising others' lives and downplaying my own until it dawned on me that comparison is a thief of joy. I am yet to meet a successful person who is happy with their life. I have met successful people who continue to blame others for their failure or talk negatively about others or who feel that their life, despite crores, is not fulfilling because they are yet to acquire that red Ferrari, or successful dads who think that others' kids are doing better in studies than their own, and some who are deeply dissatisfied because despite owning several businesses, as they are unable to become an Adani or an Ambani. And several single friends who truly believe 'all the good girls have been taken'. But there are a few whom we can count on our fingers who see life through the lens of gratitude. Even though everyone has a 'story', it's those who flipped the switch on the perspective and adopted an attitude of gratitude that have come out swinging and feeling damn good regardless of life's circumstances. People who dwell with an attitude of gratitude for the thousands of blessings that come their way daily in the form of little things cannot help but feel overwhelmed and beautiful inside, which is palpable when we come across such beautiful souls.

Conclusion

Creating a life that feels good on the inside – and does not just look good on the outside – is no easy feat. When you are busy with work, school, family and everything in between, it can be hard to make time for yourself. Finding the motivation and energy to do things you love can also be challenging. After all, whoever said life was easy. The world around us is constantly evolving and growing as more people become interested in living more enriching lives. Whether your interests lie in mindfulness, nutrition or another self-help topic, there are countless ways to explore what makes you happy. If you're ready to ditch the old habits that aren't serving you anymore and embrace new ones that will bring out your best self, you could change your life forever.

It is an exercise in self-love and self-awareness that will help you tap into your potential and find joy and meaning in your life. Furthermore, it is an exercise in being kind to yourself and treating yourself with the same respect, love and care as you would treat others.

Chapter 3

MOOD FOLLOWS ACTION

I woke up on a beautiful Sunday morning feeling sore all over my body. I live in an area called Nungambakkam in downtown Chennai. Downtown Chennai is as picturesque as it gets in any other Indian city. With its narrow alleys and lanes, the area has always been a hive of activity. And, with the onset of a new day, the activity only intensifies. Coffee shops sprout their heads here and there and a steady stream of office workers pour into their respective destinations. The streets are filled with honking autorickshaws, heavy-duty trucks and cabs. The din is so deafening that not even the birds seem to notice. If you're an early riser, the city comes alive at around 6:30 a.m. If you live anywhere near the city centre, you know what that means: you'll have to get out of bed if you want to avoid missing any of the action.

It doesn't get much better than waking up to the smells of freshly brewed coffee and the sight of your favourite cat stretching on the windowsill. There's nothing quite like the smell of a new morning in Chennai city. Not the stale, impersonal fragrance of a metropolis, nor the fractured notes of a suburb, but an altogether different one, a city that still breathes, an unfussy one that will offer you just enough freshness and colour to lift your spirits and make you feel as if the day is yours to begin. You ask yourself what's so special about this moment and you realise that you're in a city that feels like home. You've made friends, found your passion, and you've found your forever home, too.

Located at the southernmost latitude of the country, Chennai enjoys a climate that is both temperate and warm. This makes it one of the best cities in India to live in if you're looking for a balance between a warm, languid summer and a refreshingly chilly winter. In addition, it is also one of the most densely populated cities in the country, with a population of almost 8 million people. This makes it one of the most complete and bustling cities in South India. Settling down in Chennai can be a tough decision for many people, but once you get used to the hustle and bustle of the city, it can feel like a home away from home. The city is home to a diverse and lively community, with people from all walks of life living, working and playing together. It's not every day that you feel lucky in such a beautiful city, so savour this one. Even if you aren't a romantic, the sight of a new day is enough to make you appreciate it. So, it was with me on that morning. I had been looking forward to this day for a long time. And, yes, it was going to be a beautiful one. Or so I thought as I headed off to the IIT campus.

Every Sunday, my teammates and I do a long run there. The previous evening in my eagerness to outdo my friend who had accompanied me to the gym, I had exerted myself like crazy, and the delayed-onset muscle soreness which had set in was so brutal and painful that I knew there was no way I could undertake the long run. But, being a leader of my team, the notion of letting them down felt downright terrible, so I showed up despite the gloomy mood. After showing up, I accompanied the boys for a short distance before resting and waiting for the team to finish. But, once I got going, I didn't feel like stopping and did the entire length of 40 km, which left me feeling great, as though I was on top of the world. The cascading endorphin surge within me left me beaming with joy and a sense of achievement in the end.

It was then that the realisation dawned upon me that one doesn't have to feel great to act. Just showing up is enough to see one through. You don't have to feel good to act. The behaviour or action we take on the spur of the moment makes us change our mindset and gets us out of the stuck rut and builds the required momentum. Taking action despite feeling gloomy is what creates motivation automatically.

My laptop bag was messy and cluttered. I wanted to organise it for a long time, and I kept putting it off to do it on a better day when I had more time on my hands. And that better time never seemed to arrive. That time kept stretching. I didn't realise the strange perturbation and feeling of unhappiness emanating. Whenever I encountered my laptop bag, I detested myself for procrastinating and not ferreting out time to organise my stuff. I reached a point where it got unendurable, and I recalled the Nike slogan, 'Just do it!' I arranged my bag instantly and experienced a joy unknown.

Clutter wreaks havoc on our mental health. Decluttering might not solve all our problems, but it brings us close to peace and happiness. It's crazy we associate much of our unhappiness with our habits and lifestyle. We rarely realise how our outer world reflects our inner world. Decluttering our physical surroundings is a good place to start, but you need to declutter every aspect of your life to see actual change. Once we have cleaned our wardrobes and tables, emptied the junk and donated our old clothes, our moods will climb from dullness and gloom to lightness and joy. The same holds good for our minds; when we declutter our minds of all unwanted thoughts and beliefs, that's when the dark clouds hovering over and inside your mind get cleared away and give way for pure light to filter into your consciousness and fill you with the genuine joy of life.

Harvard psychology professor Dan Gilbert has through research established that mood follows action. It means we often feel worse before feeling good, and to feel better, we need to do something that leads to better feelings. It can be anything from eating a piece of chocolate or watching your favourite movie. Mood follows action is a crucial concept in human behaviour. No matter what mood you are in, if you don't act on it, you will stay stuck.

The same goes for mood in response to stimuli. If you show up at a particular time daily with your companion, your brain will associate that time with joy and start developing a favourable response to that time slot. Various studies have proved this point, with fascinating results. For example, one research has found that people who work out for 15 minutes before work are in better moods and more productive than those who don't do any exercise during the day.

As mood follows action, if you want to be confident, act like a confident person. If you're going to be motivated, then show up and do things that encourage you. For example, writing is one of the most common ways to make money online. When people write, they also practise their writing skills and improve their grammar and vocabulary. They're having fun while building up a portfolio of work before they apply for jobs or become serious writers down the road.

It's not just about making money from a passion; it's about doing something that is motivating and establishing good habits. Once we show up and get done, our mood improves because we have accomplished something.

I frequently don't feel motivated enough to go to the gym. Even when I don't feel like it, I get the work done if I show up and act like I love working out. It's hard to get motivated to go to the gym, but once you're there, you feel better. I can say the same for writing when it feels like all your energy has drained. Showing up and writing for a few moments makes me feel better and more energised. Many people have trouble showing up and getting things done, whether going to the gym or writing. But what they don't realise is that when they show up, they get their work done. Feelings of accomplishment and pride replace feelings of guilt and shame. We all know that showing up is one of the essential things in life. Not just for physical health but also for mental health.

We all have days when we don't feel like doing anything. But, if you want to get the work done, you need to show up. The first step is to find out what your motivation is. Why are you not feeling like it? Is there anything you can do to make you feel more motivated? Once you figure it out, take a deep breath to make you feel better about yourself. When I feel less motivated to work, I always remind myself that showing up is essential. Going to the gym can be a great way to get back on track. I know that when I don't feel like writing, I need a break from my computer screen. Taking a walk outside or getting some fresh air can help me clear my head and come back with renewed energy.

For instance, sometimes the feeling of not wanting to do something can be intense. It can feel like the world's weight is on your shoulders, forcing you to stay stuck, like the despair of getting stuck in quicksand. But what if I told you it's possible to take action despite feeling jammed sometimes like the brakes in your car. You might ask, 'How is that possible?' Well, it all boils down to how we think about things. When I sat down to write a few weeks back, I experienced an overwhelming writer's block. I could not put even a word on the paper, although I realised I had been staring at a blank page for over 20 minutes. It's not always easy to take action when we don't feel like it. Sometimes, we may have to pause and infer why we may feel stuck. Could it be because of a lack of sleep? Or worry about some upcoming event, or could it be because of the overwhelm of the current workload?

I took a break. I walked over to the kitchen and made myself a cup of coffee. And gazed at the potted plants on my balcony, admiring the green leaves and the lovely blossoms shimmering and playing in the sunlight. Slowly, I noticed my mind drift away from the book as my senses took in the crisp taste of the energising brew and the incredible herbage of the freshly watered potted plants. I realised that taking this small break was perhaps the best thing I did. When I got back to write, I found the words flowing like the stream of a gushing river filling up page after page as though some strange presence was doing the writing through me.

We all have those days when we don't feel like doing anything. It's easy to get caught up in the 'I don't want to' cycle and let that feeling defeat us. But there are ways to break out of it.

Here are some tips on how you can take action despite not feeling like it:

- Do something that you enjoy, which could be a hobby such as painting or cooking.
- Find something important for you and do it.
- Think about your end goal and take one step towards it.
- Take care of yourself by eating healthy food, getting enough sleep and drinking needed amount of water.

In her TED talk, writer Brené Brown discusses how the practice of showing up is a key to success. She believes we can be a part of something bigger than ourselves when we show up. Brown's words are especially relevant to writers who often feel like they are spinning their wheels. She says, 'If you're not showing up, you're not doing the work. And if you're not doing the work, then all the rest of this stuff doesn't matter.'

Chapter 4

THE HIDDEN HEALING POWER OF MEDITATION: WHY PAINTING IS A FORM OF MEDITATION AND MINDFULNESS

Did you know that painting can be a form of meditation and mindfulness? If you're not already aware of the benefits of painting, this article is here to change your mind. Painting can help you destress and focus. It can help you regain your balance and find inner peace. It allows you to clear your mind, quiet your thoughts and relieve stress. With so many benefits, it's no wonder so many people paint.

Painting can also help you lower blood pressure and improve your immune system? Or that it can reduce the symptoms of stress, depression and anxiety? But it's true! Painting is more than just a hobby – it's an art form with therapeutic benefits. When you create art, you tap into your inner self and express your emotions. When you're painting, your mind is free to wander and explore beyond the boundary of limits. It's also a great way to know yourself and accept your emotions.

Further, have you ever wondered why so many people enjoy painting? Or why painting is among the most fulfilling activities people engage in? Perhaps you've considered painting a hobby, but aren't sure if it's the right fit for you. Or maybe you've considered attending painting lessons but have been hesitant to commit to it. After I started painting a few years ago, I discovered that painting anchors me in my pursuit for a more profound peace and awareness of the world around me, so painting has become a meditative pastime and an aid to well-being. Painting helps me to cut myself out all the noise and distractions and teaches me to love the small things around me.

Neuroscience Research Reveals Painting Is Akin to Meditation

Creating art is similar to meditation, as both target the same brain regions. When we paint, we experience flow states much like meditation, which can thus help us reach our creative goals. Neuroscience has found that creating art activates the prefrontal cortex, hippocampus, parahippocampal cortex and visual cortex, all of which play a role in self-reflection and creativity goal setting. The art you create can be your self-expression, something you've never done before, or a way to explore your emotions.

Why Is Painting a Form of Meditation and Mindfulness?

First and foremost, painting is a meditative activity. It's a mindful way to connect with yourself, your emotions and your creative side. It allows you to momentarily let go of worries – after all, you're only focusing on one thing: your brush or pencil (or whatever you're painting with). By meditating on your art, you're also considering the context of what you're painting, which leads to more profound thoughts and a more holistic perspective on your work. It also helps you create more nuanced work, as you're not just relying on your visual senses. With meditation, you're also tapping into your creativity, something everyone can use more in their lives.

Painting Is an Artform of Mindfulness

Painting is a form of mindfulness because it connects you with your emotions and helps you accept them. Painting enables you to explore your feelings and express them through creative work. It's also a great way to destress. When you paint, you're not focusing on the small things that stress you. Instead, you're taking your focus off of your work and relaxing into the act of creating art. Painting is a type of mindfulness that allows you to settle into your emotions and voices in your head. You can listen to these voices, ignore them or choose to paint over them. The choice is up to you. You can also use your art to connect with others and share your feelings.

Self-care is a big subject. It seems like everyone is constantly battling stress and exhaustion in our fast-paced world. But taking time for yourself isn't always easy. The last thing you feel like doing is sitting still and focusing on something that might make you feel uncomfortable. But the benefits of painting extend beyond the walls of your home. It can provide you with a sense of calm, healing and even mindfulness. Painting is a great stress reliever – it's fast, cheap and requires little to no setup.

Painting Gets the Brain into a Flow State

Painting is a flow state type, which happens when you focus on an activity and experience a natural high. You're in a calm state of mind, and your brain is getting the benefits of a workout. Science proves that getting your brain in a flow state can reduce stress, lower blood pressure and improve immune function. Getting into a flow state can also make you more creative, benefiting your work as an artist. Research has also shown that flow states can help you reach your creative goals. When you're in a flow state, you're less distracted and more likely to achieve your goals. Your creativity will improve, making it easier to develop new ideas.

Painting Is Therapeutic – It Heals and De-stresses

As any therapist will tell you, art is therapeutic and can help heal and destress. How? First, by creating art, you're tapping into your creativity. You're also connecting with your emotions and letting them flow through you. These two aspects of the invention are what all therapists find most beneficial in therapy. When you connect with your creativity, you'll connect with your emotions. You're expressing yourself and releasing the pain you're feeling through your art. Painting can also help you destress, as it's a form of creative expression that doesn't require follow-through. You're not doing anything with your hands, so there's no pressure to make things perfect.

Conclusion

When we think of art and painting, we tend to think of it as an activity reserved for the more artistic minds among us. That is a significant misconception, as artwork touches on many different facets of our personality. Not only does it engage our senses, as it requires us to observe, analyse and synthesise colours, but it also helps boost our emotions and mental faculties. Art is a critical component of mental wellness, as it is a means of self-expression with the potential to impact anyone who engages with it positively. The practice of painting is no exception, as painting has many therapeutic benefits. It is a form of self-care that allows us to escape from the pressures of the outside world and reconnect with our inner creativity. When you immerse yourself in painting, you realise the tremendous healing power of painting and how it can help you find inner peace and balance. Painting can also be a form of meditation and mindfulness as it enables you to connect with yourself and lets you express your emotions, relax and destress.

Chapter 5

THE JOY OF LETTING GO

After reading Gretchen Rubin's *Outer Order, Inner Calm*, I launched myself into packing my bags for a New York trip in the second week of November 2022. As I started to dig into my wardrobe, I realised I had accumulated an awful lot of stuff over the years. I realised that I hadn't missed any of the untouched stuff which I have not used during the pandemic. So I decided to ask myself the three questions which Ms Rubin lays out in her book *Do I Use It? Do I Need It? Do I Love It?* If the answer to all three was no, then I must get rid of the stuff. And that's how I ended up making four sacks loaded with old clothes, old books, old mobile phones, wires, old files and papers. Doing that proved to be a liberating experience for me. I still have so much more stuff to let go, but I realised it was fear that I would need it at some point, or the thought of the item developing some magical future use which was making me cling to it. In the process of cleaning up my closet, I discovered a metaphor. Just like the physical stuff we hold on to, we in our minds hold on to the stories we tell ourselves, old identities that we don't identify with anymore, toxic relationships and so on. That may be taking mental space and is most likely not serving us.

Hence, I started journaling to examine the things holding me back, which I had to let go of. A quick look at the inventory of my mental space disclosed that I had unconsciously rented my mental real estate to three things and some old beliefs which I had to let go of as they were probably holding me back. The first thing that showed up during the analysis was that a few current life circumstances – like the recent death of my pet dog and the collapse of the wall on my beachside property – had compelled me to stay focused on the negative a great deal.

My predicament was akin to the story of three men with sacks that I had read long ago. The story goes about three men named Raja, Saji and Ram lived, each of whom had two sacks, one tied in their front and the other at their back. When Raja was asked to describe his sacks, he replied that he had filled the sack in his back with all good and pleasant things while the bag in the front had all the negative things that had happened to him. Now and then, Raja would open his sack in the front, examine his dark negative life and think about it. Because he focused on the negative, Raja's life was full of unhappiness.

On the other hand, Saji had all the good things in the front sack and all the mistakes and wrongs on the back sack. When Ram was asked about his sacks, he replied that he kept all the good deeds and blessings of the people in his front sack and the back sack was empty as he had cut a big hole at the bottom. Therefore, all the bad things that went into his back sack fell out, so there was no weight. As Ram's mind was delinked from negative and focused on blessings, his life was joyful and blissful. To lead a happy, joyful life, I decided to identify with Ram and remember all the gifts while acknowledging and letting go of negativity and judgement towards others – like the back sack of Ram.

The second revelation that popped up during the self-analysis was that I held resentments and was bitter due to recent events, which I had to let go of. My plight was something analogous to the story of two monks, which goes that, while returning to the monastery, two monks came across a stream that a beautiful young girl feared crossing. Noticing the predicament of the pretty girl, the elder of the two lifted her and swiftly carried her to the other side. Both continued their journey afterwards to the monastery. Later at twilight, the younger monk came to the older monk and demanded how a monk could touch a woman. The elder monk smiled at him and replied that he had left the woman by the riverside long ago. But the younger monk was still carrying her in his mind. In life, we all have unpleasant situations that can fill us with resentment or irritate us, but despite such circumstances, we should not carry the hurt in our minds; we should, like the senior monk, drop such baggage and let go of it as soon as possible.

The third thing that came up during journaling was that my mind was consuming loads of mental energy to cling to my current story. I decided to stop clinging to my little story and allow myself to embrace the larger story of which I was part. I decided to draw inspiration from the tale of a dew. A beautiful dewdrop that lay shining like a pearl atop a leaf all of a sudden slid down to the edge of the leaf. It was terrified of falling and getting smashed, so it desperately tried to hold on to the leaf. But, unable to cling on, it surrendered to gravity. And then the fear transformed into deep joy as the tiny dewdrop merged with the vastness that was the pond. Now the dewdrop was no more. No, it had not got destroyed. It had become one with the whole.

We have attached ourselves to things and people so much that we cannot let go of them. We often get attached to things such as cars or people and believe they make us happy. A man enchanted by a woman believes he derives happiness from his partner, and life would be miserable without her. Therefore, he feels he can never let go of his attachment because he is unaware that his attraction stems from a desire to fill the void within him, which prompts and prods him to seek joy outside of himself. All the attachments and cravings will drop once he relies on his inner resources and his inner emptiness is filled from within.

We are always full of desires. We want to go to exotic places, meet new people, eat gourmet food and have abundant wealth and good things in life. We tend to mistake desires as needs. Cravings are potent when we allow them to ruin our lives. Desires, when unfulfilled, make us miserable. But when we examine the desires properly and learn what they are, letting go of them becomes easy.

Chapter 6

THE HEART OF THE MATTER

At 58, Rajesh Kumar, an old classmate of mine of undergrad times, had worked his way up to become an agro-entrepreneur whom many admired and envied. Even his competitors, who disliked his drive and ruthless ambition, had to concede that they respected him. When I met him recently, he came across to me like the enigmatic Elon Musk with a dash of Jeff Bezos in him. But, on a summer afternoon, while at work, he felt uneasiness creep into him, and a feeling of total paralysis swept him. His eyes teared up, and his hands turned clammy. His heartbeat climbed like the roar of an aircraft engine taking off into the skies. Pain in his chest felt excruciating as he toiled to breathe. His lungs despaired for a whiff of oxygen. As he continued to gasp for air, he felt a sharp shooting pain rise from his chest and radiate down to his arms. His pounding chest felt as though an enormous elephant was trampling and tearing his heart away. Suddenly, his world turned black as he helplessly watched himself get sucked into a dark abyss. Soon, he lost all consciousness. Later, in the evening, when he opened his eyes at the nursing home, he realised he had just been through a heart attack.

Making millions and winning the best exporter award had become his obsession and passion. His father had taught him to be fiercely passionate about his enterprise. Taking his father's advice seriously, he immersed himself in work and gradually forgot to slow down and mindfully enjoy the little things in life. Most of us tend to do so, but not to the outrageous extremes resorted to by him. For instance, during my ADGP L&O days, my office overlooked a vast expanse of the oceanfront with a beautiful lawn bang outside. But, I can't recall a single occasion of having taken a hiatus to drink in the breath-taking view my office offered to all.

Conversely, babies, Zen monks and some individuals can tune out of the chaos around them and have beauty surrounding them all the time. Even a mundane activity like taking a stroll in the busy street fills them with joy and happiness rather than stressing them. By appreciating little things and being grateful for them, we can alter the stressful, hostile environment lurking inside us into one of peace and joy. We live in a magical world packed with marvels of God's creation, and it would be a sheer disservice to let them pass by unseen just because we are focused and hell-bent on creating an impact in life.

Most people who navigate through such hard times undergo some emotional scarring. But the positive mindset helped my friend find new meaning and purpose in the face of adversity. He felt gratitude for life because of the good that came out of it. The catastrophe taught him not to take life for granted. His bond with family and friends deepened, little things lighted up his day, and life began feeling like a celebration.

While skimming channels on my TV, I recently came across a scene in an animated movie in which a small fish swims across to a bigger and older fish and asks her to show her the ocean. The older fish informs the small fish that they are, in fact, in the ocean. But the little fish yells back, 'No, this is just water; I want the ocean.' The import of this parable is that despite living amidst joy and bliss, we create suffering and unhappiness in our lives – striving to scale some Mount Everest that we have created and embedded in our heads. We appear to have painted that peak as the perfect destination that will enable us to discover happiness. For Rajesh, his Mount Everest was to scale his company into a Fortune 500 company.

In the corporate world and bureaucracies, we see a similar propensity manifest in the hierarchy as a clamour for plum posts. The intense desire in some to garner top posts generates extreme stress and suffering because of an erroneous belief that binds their self-worth to the coveted job. When the unmet desire lingers over extended durations, the frustration springing from it often manifests as a psychosomatic disease. Hence, we can circumvent unfulfilled desire from taking a toll on health by accepting and surrendering to 'What is' and not longing for an external designation or tag that can never fill or replenish the lack within. Because true joy emanates from the formless dimension inside. And when we honour our inner space and live from there, the outer circumstances automatically lose the power to torment us.

Accepting is what has helped my friend flip his life and make it meaningful. Rather than dwelling in the past or experiencing anxiety about the future, it would do us a world of good if we took the time to look into what lies within. The spirit within us is more important than our past or the future. It may not matter where we came from because we can change our identity by going within and altering the story or meaning we have assigned our lives. Similarly, we may anticipate a particular future but eventually suffer a setback and experience a different outcome. At which time it's our reliance on our inner self that can lift us and steer us out of the storm. We have a vast cosmos of consciousness inside each one of us that we must endeavour to access through spiritual tools like prayer, meditation, journaling, inner conversations or just by observing silence.

Chapter 7

LIFE HAPPENS FOR YOU, NOT TO YOU

In London, in April 2018, I picked the gauntlet of attending Tony Robbins' flagship seminar, *Unleash the Power Within*. I experienced my life improve for the better after the four-day workshop. One of the several essential lessons I learnt at the seminar was that life happens for us and not to us. We may call this a law of attraction, or brain reticular activating system. When we believe and focus on life as being benevolent, providing us with whatever we need, life gets more manageable. But, if we see life as some vengeful avenger, it will become a veritable hell. Ponder back on your life, and you'll see that this has always been true.

Recently I was in the vortex of a choppy life, and suddenly, too many things appeared to be coming about simultaneously. It seemed as though I was being caught off-guard. Recently our dog Coco died after a long and slow decline; I remember making eye contact minutes before his demise; he flashed a winsome look as he blissfully drifted off to heaven. Following this, an overpowering sadness gripped me, and the days of grieving began stacking up. Further, circumstances added other simultaneous occurrences to my woes, including an unexpected transfer.

When pain grips us, we can either dwell in it and suffer it, or accept it and glimpse the good it has created in our lives. All of them may seem to be awful. But we must understand that circumstances hand us the pain to serve us and help us tap into the resources we hold within us and become the persons we need to become. We usually tend to blame someone for the anguish they have caused in our lives without looking at the good that came out of it. When we decide to blame someone for the mess they have created, we must be ready to give credit for the good that has permeated our lives. My teacher once told me that we should never say 'why me?' When good things happen, we don't pose the same question as when bad stuff happens to us.

Sometimes I have noticed things happening when we aren't living up to our true purpose or capabilities. The universe then decides to yank us out of our comfort zones and wiggle us up. This awakening is where the opportunity to grow spiritually occurs. It forces us to look within and seek answers for things that seem to be unfolding in our lives. The simple reason is that we can only control our feelings, thoughts and behaviours because trying to influence others would be akin to controlling the weather. We discover the silver lining if we sincerely surrender to the universe and seek the answers to the questions.

The universe or source then starts offering situations and circumstances that foster growth, and hence when we believe that life happens for us and not to us, we can work miracles at any moment. And we move away from feeling angry, hurt or sad to feeling good. We start recognising the testing moments as a lesson, a trial or an opportunity, so we always win. As we understand our emotional health, we build resilience to cope with so-called bad things positively without the numbing emotions. Contrarily, if we react, we might end up feeling as though the universe were conspiring against us.

When we develop a feeling that the universe is conspiring against us, we stay stuck in the same place because our beliefs that we will never have enough, never be competent, never be successful or confident start manifesting as reality. But once we flip the idea that we have everything we need, our life dramatically changes; we become successful and receive everything we need in abundance. Further, when things happen, the choice of labelling the situation we are in is entirely up to us; we can look at a half-filled glass of water as half full or half empty. We can either dwell on the disaster or find the silver lining. Stepping back and seeing the big picture is imperative because it can help us zoom out and detach ourselves from feeling all wound up.

Besides, Eleanor Roosevelt once remarked, 'No one can make one feel inferior without one's consent.' How people treat an individual is their karma, and how the individual reacts is his karma. We cannot litter negativity and wonder why life is so crummy. When we become capable of embracing change, everything will start to happen for us, as we will ride the wave and receive the best in life.

We don't always understand why things happen the way they do, but when we gain some space, time and perspective and reflect on the significant events of our lives, we can see how the universe led us there. If we get lucky, we can even find moments where we found ourselves exactly where we were supposed to be. I have been able to connect the dots numerous times in my own life. I can discern one particular dot that led me into civil services out of several dots there. Had I not fallen into bad company and disgraced myself while pursuing my undergraduate studies in agriculture at Hyderabad, I would not have forced myself to seek my postgraduate and PhD programmes outside Andhra Pradesh. As Delhi happened to be a hub for preparation of civil services exams, pursuing my PhD programme at Delhi and my induction into the university quiz team paved the way for my entry into the civil services in September of 1991.

Steve Jobs, CEO of Apple and Pixar Animation Studios, delivered a powerful commencement address on 14 June 2005 to a graduating class at Stanford University. On lines similar to mine, Jobs elucidated how the nastiest points in his life – dropping out of college, being overthrown from Apple and contracting cancer – served as portals to a higher level of creativity and insight. The lecture delivered an intimate peek into what inspired this successful, iconic man, and Jobs' advice is timeless. In the same speech, Jobs also famously said: 'You can't connect the dots looking forward; you can only connect them looking backwards. So you have to trust that the dots will somehow connect in your future. You have to trust in something – your gut, destiny, life, karma, whatever. This approach has never let me down, and it has made all the difference in my life.'

Finally, if there were only beautiful sunny days, we would take the sun for granted, but we also need thunderstorms and rains to break the monotony and wash things anew. For instance, if things never went wrong in our lives, we would know when they are going right. If we never experienced loss, how would we experience gain? How would we know how beautiful being perpetually in love feels without getting jilted. We all have to play a part in the game called life. We will all have things happening in our lives to do the work, explore the silver lining and never let go of it once we find it.

Chapter 8

WHAT YOU RESIST PERSISTS, AND WHAT YOU ACCEPT DISSOLVES!!

I was once a smoker. I picked up the habit early in life. When my classmates lit up during recess, I sometimes bummed a couple of drags from my buddies who were puffing away. That's how it began. What I relished most was the instantaneous dopamine rush chaperoning the whacks delivered to the receptors in the brain by nicotine. And the concurrent sense of relaxation. However, things took a twist for the worse after I enrolled myself for a PhD degree in microbiology in New Delhi. The long working hours and the fast-approaching deadlines left my mind craving nicotine to soothe my nerves and spark my brain. I battled, resisting the temptation to light up, but what I combated persisted, and soon, I reached a point of no return where I started lighting up all by myself. The smoking habit stayed after my PhD through my police training days at the National Police Academy in Hyderabad until my third posting as Superintendent of Police in 1999 when my eldest daughter, five then, rebuked me and resisted my hugs because she detested the sharp odour of tobacco, which swaddled me like a raucous aura. Her pleas and evasive attitude wrenched my heart and spurred me to kick my habit cold turkey. I had made more than a dozen previous attempts to end smoking. However, I was unsuccessful as I probably had disregarded the natural law of the universe of 'What You Resist Persists!' I had possibly failed because I had energised the smoking habit by focusing on quitting. That created resistance in the process, making it more challenging to shove my nicotine dependence. The moment I concentrated my energies on gaining the love and affection of my daughter, things flipped, and kicking the habit became a child's play. Ever since I made this shift 20 years ago, I have never restarted nor resumed smoking.

The eminent Swiss psychiatrist Carl Jung (1875–1961) advocated that whatever you resist persists. Meaning that whatever we resist, we attract more of it towards us. He asserted that when we resist anything in our lives, we try to think about it all the time to either avoid or expel it; in the process, we entice more pain and suffering for battling the resistance that keeps building. Also, when we resist, we enable things to persist because we tend to focus on what we don't want in our lives and attract more of it. We dissolve the inevitable pain when we acknowledge the resistance and embrace it by consciously accepting it.

For instance, when we encounter pain and suffering, we want to resist it and refuse to accept it because it's not our nature to embrace the pain. A young woman in her mid-thirties lost her husband, who was approaching his forties, to a sudden massive cardiac arrest. Abruptly, the beautiful world of the wife turned upside down. Initially, she couldn't deal with it and found herself in perpetual grief and depression. Soon realisation dawned upon her that it was counterproductive to wallow and endure indulgent self-pity over the loss. Gradually, she accepted the loss as the will of God and picked up the threads of her life, primarily to perpetuate the dreams and vision of her beloved late spouse. Her departed husband had yearned for her to do her PhD. While alive, he had divulged that nothing in life would give him more happiness and joy than watching her complete her PhD. He was also a devoted social worker and a business strategist. Deciding to fulfil her departed husband's vision and ideals, she immediately resumed pursuing her PhD, which she once discontinued. To eke out a living, she accepted to work as a business strategist for a handful of companies. Simultaneously, she also hurled herself into a life of service for the deprived in society. She had recently come across an initiative called 'Covidwidows', launched by an NRI for the women who lost their husbands to the coronavirus. On similar lines, she decided to serve the vast majority who were suffering under the onslaught of the pandemic by connecting the philanthropically minded citizens with the deprived. She created a website and approached an influential agency to execute her plans to achieve this mission, making it a grand success. Amidst all this, she suddenly realised that her life had become incredibly meaningful and purposeful. Her idea soon became a roaring success as she could disburse relief of over Rs 50 lakhs to hundreds of beneficiaries within a month, bringing her immense joy and happiness. Throughout this experience, she could constantly feel the presence and guidance of her husband in everything she did, which filled her heart with joy and a new zest for life. So, just by letting go and not resisting her husband's demise, she could bring meaning and purpose back into her life.

I also find this law showing up when we fight or rebel against something or someone. I have often noticed that anti-war rallies often end in violence, or harmless protestors often get arrested. Because when we focus on what we don't want, we continually attract that into our lives. We often hear people or authorities declaring war on whatever turns out to be a menace or problem. We have an ongoing war against terror, a war against drugs, a war against poverty, a war on coronavirus and so on. Despite the launching of war and taking desirable steps, the battle most times never gets won. For instance, despite launching a fight against coronavirus, we could not contain its spread and advancement into the second phase, which proved deadlier than the first phase. We have been waging war against poverty since Independence, but we have not eradicated it. It's believed that it is for this reason that Mother Theresa refused to attend anti-war rallies. However, she was always willing to participate in peace rallies. She presumably knew that if the protestors agitated for what they wanted or focused on what they needed, they probably would achieve their goals.

When we resist what is, we experience suffering. We suffer when things turn out to be different from how we intended them to be. Think of a time when you felt uneasy, resentful or unhappy; you will invariably discover that you were resisting the moment. The way to find inner peace is to develop an awareness of whatever we may be unconsciously resisting and make a conscious choice to let it as it is. If we acquire the ability to say yes to every experience, we may have circumvented suffering. The deeper problem could be fear, insecurity, uncertainty and so on. When we resist pain, we nourish and nurture the deeper problem. Buddha preached that the mind creates everything, so something lurking within us is causing the pain, and there is nothing external responsible for it. Pain inside us or the deeper problem is what manifests as superficial pain.

Most times it's not the experience that causes us pain and suffering but resistance to the experience. Humans tend to classify, categorise and label everything as good, bad, right, wrong and so on. When we are feeling sad, we may label the experience as bad. Any experience in the absence of a label is just a feeling. A feeling may be uncomfortable, but it is not a problem in and of itself.

The way to find inner peace is to develop an awareness of whatever we may be unconsciously resisting and make a conscious choice to let it as it is. If we acquire the ability to say yes to every experience, we may have circumvented suffering,

For example, most people losing a limb in an accident or some part of the body go on a self-victimising trip of 'why me?' Instead, let go of the loss and find ways of living with the disability. For instance, a friend who suffered an accident a few years back refused to accept the fact and kept dwelling on it, questioning why he had to lose his leg while his other co-travellers were sparred. As he remained stuck there, he attracted more negativity into his life. After that, he began to suffer from depression and hypertension. Much later, when he changed his mindset and made peace with God by filling his heart with pure gratitude for having spared his precious life with a mere loss of a limb, he was able to rediscover beauty, peace and joy again in his life.

Thus, holding on to resistance is like trying to change life after something has happened. It's a futile pursuit. You add more energy and power to what you don't like as you resist what has happened. And when you do that, you are bringing more of it at a furious rate. The event or circumstances can only get more prominent because that is the law of attraction. When we experience pain and suffering, we want to resist it because it's not in our nature to embrace the pain. Pain is not the cause of the problem. It's the consequence of a deeper problem: fear, insecurity, uncertainty and so on. When we resist pain, we nourish and nurture the deeper problem. Buddha preached that the mind creates everything, so something lurking within us is causing the pain, and there is nothing external responsible for it. Pain inside us or the deeper problem is what manifests as external pain.

Chapter 9

LAW OF DIMINISHING INTENT

Our brains are an idea-generating machine. Ideas may pop into your mind when watching a movie or TV show, having a shower, talking to someone, daydreaming, jogging/working out, making love and so on.

Sometimes when I go to a hotel and see something mundane, I get an idea of setting up my office in a particular style. And occasionally, while attending a conference, I get some fantastic insight while watching a presentation. Sometimes, ideas and opportunities unexpectedly appear in our minds from thin air.

When the ideas arrive, we most often fail to take action, i.e. to either note them down or implement them immediately. We postpone action under some pretext or the other. For instance, we often come up with justifications such as I will do it when I have more time or money, when necessary resources arrive or when I find the right opportunity. The longer we postpone an idea under such pretexts, the more massive the chances of it not getting accomplished.

We can explain this by a law enunciated by great Jim Rohn, called the law of diminishing intent, which states, 'The longer you wait to do something you should do now, the greater the odds that you will never actually do it.'

For me, it happened two years back. I decided to create valuable content on YouTube by conducting and publishing interviews of outstanding leaders from all walks of life. I made a list of prospective people I would interview and purchased essential equipment to produce the content. I commenced by carefully preparing the questions and fixing an appointment with Legendary Walter Isaac Dewaram IPS (Retd). The shoot went off phenomenally well. After some brisk editing, I had the content uploaded on YouTube, where it continues to be available. Soon after, I was transferred and posted as Additional Director General of

Police (Law and Order). It was a tough assignment, and I always found myself neck-deep in work. The equipment I had purchased began to gather dust, and the hobby I had embarked on went into long dormancy.

After a year and a half, I found myself reposted as Director Vigilance and Anti-Corruption and had all the time in the world to revive my YouTube channel, but I couldn't take it forward. Something had happened during the intervening time; doubt and laziness had crept in. Every time I tried to recommence, feelings of incompetence and thoughts of putting it off to a better day derailed me. After my first video, over two years had drifted by, and the idea of having squandered valuable time tormented me. The agony and guilt got to a point where I couldn't tolerate myself and my procrastination anymore.

Exasperated and fed up with me, I decided to go ahead and make a video no matter what. But, there was a lockdown due to the raging pandemic, and no guests were available for interview. I still pressed on and recorded a video and shared it with my family. I mentioned in the video that though it was not perfect, the message was so important that I couldn't wait to share it with them. I was so happy and relieved that I had broken the logjam and unlocked the creativity that had been rotting, rusting and destroying my insides.

So, the key take-away from this is that 'if one waits for perfect conditions, nothing will get done'. So we have to go out and take action no matter what and stop the law of diminishing intent right on its tracks.

To illustrate this point, let me narrate how Richard Branson created Virgin Airlines. When Branson arrived at the airport to fly to the British Virgin Islands, he received information from the airline staff that they were cancelling the flight because of insufficient passengers. Branson immediately hired a flight and began selling the seats right then and there. Boom! Right then, Virgin Airlines was born. There was no stopping Richard after that. What better example can there be for us of the magic of taking immediate action.

We should therefore never pay heed to doubts and adverse inner voices that keep screaming at us that we are either not good to go or not smart enough to accomplish the task. There are no limits to achieving when one stifles the negative inner voice.

Remember, we have a lot of potential in us, and whenever an idea strikes our mind, we should pursue it aggressively like a wildcat that pursues its prey and hunts it down. So please read books, blogs and watch YouTube videos to teach yourself how to silence your negative voice and launch yourself into action immediately without wasting a minute.

Our mind often comes up with great ideas that we can pursue all the time. So seize such opportunities and take action ASAP. The great ideas that flash into your mind have a purpose of benefiting us and the entire humankind, so take action to defeat all the resistance building inside you and bring the idea to fruition. Best of luck!

Chapter 10

WE CAN MAKE TAMIL NADU THE CARBON CHAMPION OF INDIA

The 26th edition of the United Nations Conference of Parties (COP), which commenced at Glasgow on 1 November, concluded on 12 November. India's Prime Minister Mr Modi, while addressing COP26, pledged to cut carbon emissions to net zero by 2070. Earlier, the US and EU had announced achieving net zero by 2050, while China had aimed at net zero by 2060. The world's fourth biggest emitter of carbon dioxide – after China, the US and the EU – is India. Carbon emissions are responsible for the greenhouse effect and climate change.

Today, we are witnessing adverse weather events such as flash floods and storms due to heavy rains, periodic droughts, abnormal seasonal patterns, wildfires, cyclones and so on, costing human lives and creating enormous economic burden on the state. New emerging studies link the COVID-19 pandemic to increased deforestation and invasion into animal habitats. We have so far carried on with our lives, ignoring climate change and its power to cause economic loss and cost human lives. Now, the world realised that climate change is real and affects everyone. We may indict the capitalistic mindset and indiscriminate industrialisation for global warming, but humans are at the nucleus of the crisis.

Honourable TN Chief Minister M. K. Stalin, since assuming charge, has repeatedly emphasised the importance of environmental protection and has been taking proactive steps in this direction. Recognising climate change as a severe catastrophe facing mankind, the Climate Change Mission, under his leadership, has been set up at a budget of Rs 500 crores. The objective of the Climate Change Mission is to focus on climate change adaptation and alleviation activities. And for the first time, the minister of environment has been additionally assigned the climate change portfolio. Besides, the other excellent initiatives launched by the honourable CM are the Tamil Nadu Wetlands Mission and the Green Tamil Nadu Mission. The Green Tamil Nadu Mission aims to increase TN's total forest and tree cover area to 33 per cent of the state's land area. At the same time, the Wetlands Mission, at Rs 150 crore, has been set up with the objective of restoring ecological wetlands in Tamil Nadu.

Now that our honourable PM has committed at COP26 to achieve net zero by 2070, all Indian states would have to immediately take steps in that direction. Tamil Nadu is already leading the race and can achieve the spectacular mission of net zero way ahead of other states if it decides to become a 'Zero Carbon State'. The TN police force could also endeavour to become a 'Zero Carbon Police Force' by adopting energy-conserving practices. Specifically, the city of Chennai could commit itself to becoming the world's lowest carbon footprint city by 2050.

The measures to accelerate our prospects for emerging as a carbon champion in the country would involve developing a sound strategy and road map to achieve carbon neutrality through the adoption of energy-efficient appliances (such as LED lights), conservation measures to curtail electricity and water consumption in buildings and solar energy initiatives for home water heating. Other actions such as extending solar roof-tops across all government and police buildings by 2040, deploying electric vehicles and fuel/route optimisation for all government and police vehicles would reduce carbon emissions.

Transforming the government fleet of vehicles into hybrid vehicles through green procurement, water-conserving practices and digitalisation would reduce carbon emissions significantly. The success of this initiative would lie in setting up a solid framework to implement the endeavour and raise awareness. We would have to create an internal governmental culture of energy conservation through education and awareness.

India today has more than 200 central and state legislations to deal with environmental violations. A plethora of laws has become an impediment to enforcement. A single comprehensive and integrated law on environmental protection is the need of the hour. The Pollution Control Boards need more powers. They cannot punish violators; they can only launch a prosecution. In our constitution, Article 51A imposes a duty on every citizen to protect the natural environment, including forests, lakes, rivers and wildlife, and show compassion to all living creatures. But only industries and organisations get prosecuted for violations. Citizens who are harming the environment are going scot-free. The net zero target of 2070 for India means we would have to have Green Police/Environmental Police to book and punish violations committed by individuals. For the long-term future, climate change represents a fundamental security challenge. Hence, police may have to reorient policing towards adapting to environmental transition because policing in the future will have to react to societal pressures that extreme weather episodes create.

Today, we are facing climate change head-on. At this point, we may argue that it's the government's job to tackle climate crisis, but we should remember that we are equally responsible, too. We should take action towards energy conservation and more responsible consumerism. Although capitalism and markets are a boon to our economic growth, we must balance by consuming just what is needed sustainably. As consumers, we wield great power; we can help the state to become the country's 'Carbon Champion' by turning into citizen conservationists through education and awareness. Finally, as citizens, we must pledge to leave behind a planet that we inherited in all its pristine glory for our children and grandchildren. That's the greatest and best gift we can leave behind.

Chapter 11

CAN WE ERADICATE CORRUPTION?

There is, of late, a revival of interest in Sardar Vallabhbhai Patel. Just a couple of days ago, the world's tallest statue with a height of 182 metres, the 'Statue of Unity', befitting the leader, was unveiled. I found myself enraptured in my school days when my fifth-grade Anglo-Indian teacher taught a lesson titled the 'Ironman of India'. Enthralling stories of Patel's leadership during the Farmers' Movement in Kheda and Bardoli and the iron hand with which he merged India by integrating 600 native states captivated me to no end. Sardar Patel was one of the greatest leaders of our freedom struggle. Patel remained the treasurer of the Indian National Congress till his death. When it came to managing the funds, his honesty was unimpeachable. As a deputy prime minister of India, he regularly contacted the chiefs of provincial Congress committees on phone. Still he always paid the telephone bill from his pocket, depleting more than half of his salary on it. Such was the honesty and uprightness of Sardar. Commemorating his integrity, the 'Vigilance Awareness Week' is observed in India every year during the week Sardar Patel's birth anniversary falls in October. This year we are observing the Vigilance Awareness Week from 29 October to 3 November 2018 on the theme 'Eradicate Corruption – Build a New India'.

Corruption is the use of public office for private gain. It flows from the basic human tendency of greed. Corruption in India is a phenomenon that permeates every level and walk of life. Corruption being anti-national, anti-development and anti-poor are taking its toll by eroding the moral fibre of our country and eating into its very vitals.

Corruption is like cancer. Just as cancer's uncontrolled proliferation devastates the systems of the human body, corruption wreaks dysfunction and anarchy by destabilising the strategies of governance and the rule of law.

Transparency International's 2017 Corruption Perception Index ranks India at 81st place out of 180 countries. A study conducted by Transparency International in 2005 recorded that more than 92 per cent of Indians had at some point paid bribe to a public official to get a job done, and about 50 per cent of Indians had first-hand experience of paying bribes. In the recent Asia Pacific Global Corruption Barometer survey, the perception of India was that of a country having the highest bribery rate of 69 per cent, which means about seven out of ten persons have to pay bribe to get their work done. An assessment by the agency reveals that the lost opportunity caused by corruption in terms of investment, growth and jobs for India is over $50 billion a year.

The reasons for corruption in India include:

- Profuse regulations;
- Byzantine tax and licensing systems;
- Manifold government departments with opaque bureaucracy and ill-defined discretionary powers;
- A monopoly of government-controlled institutions on certain goods and services delivery;
- The lack of transparent laws and processes.

History has constantly demonstrated that human nature is unchangeable and human heart corruptible. For instance, on questioning some people 'what they would do if they found ₹50,000 bundles on the road?' 90 per cent answered they would pick it up. On rephrasing the same question, 'what if there is CCTV watching, would you still pick the money bundle?' 80 per cent replied they wouldn't. Human nature is such that 10 per cent will be honest come hell or high water, 10 per cent will be dishonest no matter what, while the remaining 80 per cent will modify their conduct as per the situation. That only shows that a supervisory system or laws are imperative to curb corruption.

India has enacted several anti-corruption laws under which public servants can be penalised or imprisoned for several years, such as the amended Prevention of Corruption Act 1988, Indian Penal Code 1860, the Lokpal and Lokayuktas Act 2013, the Black Money (Undisclosed Foreign Income and Assets) and Imposition of Tax Bill 2015, the Prevention of Money Laundering Act 2002, the Companies Act 2013, Whistleblowers Protection Act 2011 (yet to be notified) and so on. India is also a signatory to the United Nations Convention against Corruption since 2005.

Policing, policies and laws cannot eradicate corruption. Changing the mindset, attitudes and values of people is the best antidote. Corruption will decline once society starts valuing wisdom and soul culture as success/superior goals, compared to money and material advancement.

Chapter 12

HOW AND WHY EXTREME OWNERSHIP CAN BE LIFE-CHANGING

Extreme ownership means owning everything in your world to an extreme degree. It means you are accountable for not just those tasks you directly control but all those that happen in your reality for which you may not think you are responsible. It may be a road accident while on your way to work. The fault may not be yours, but taking ownership for events and happenings caused to you but not by you.

For instance, the Hollywood movie *The Shawshank Redemption* catalogues the experiences of a formerly successful banker as a convict in the gloomy jailhouse of Shawshank after being found guilty of an offence he did not commit. Bank merchant Andy Dufresne, an innocent man after getting a conviction for slaughtering his wife and her lover, takes full responsibility for it and eventually earns the respect of his fellow inmates, especially long-time convict 'Red' Redding, a black marketeer, and comes to be influential within the jail. Ultimately, Andrew achieves the end on his terms. Taking full responsibility for the crime he did not commit shifted the life of prisoner Andy Dufresne, eventually earning him redemption.

Leadership skills are vital in almost every position. Any job, whether small or menial, requires you to step up and take ownership of your actions. The thing is that most of us tend to struggle when the pressure's on because we feel like we have so much to lose. Fear of failure, an unwillingness to put ourselves out there and other limiting beliefs often hold us back from developing our true potential as a leader. But that can change if you understand the concept of extreme ownership. If you haven't heard about it before, 'extreme ownership' is a leadership philosophy that has been gaining more attention in recent years thanks to its ability to help people succeed in all areas of life – not just at work but also outside the office.

Extreme ownership is a simple but powerful principle that every leader and team member should understand. It's a simple idea with a complex meaning; as leaders, we can take ownership of everything in our organisation, club, team or business. Anything that goes wrong is the result of faulty leadership at some level. If you are reading this, you are probably already an effective leader who can lift the performance of your team members. The next step is moving from being an excellent leader to becoming exceptional by taking extreme ownership of your actions as a leader. Ownership is significant because it involves trusting others to be just as accountable as you are and care for one another. It is a safety net against stress and overwork. It supports tremendous efficiency because everyone figures out what they're singly and collectively supposed to do.

What Does Extreme Ownership Mean?

Extreme ownership is a concept popularised by Jocko Willink, a former navy seal and current CEO of the military training company Echelon Front. Many recommend that you take ownership of your life and share responsibility, but what does that mean? For starters, extreme ownership differs from simply 'owning your mistakes'. Some use this phrase to forgive someone for their mistakes and get them back on track without judgement, but it's not necessarily a good thing. When you own your mistakes, you don't accept that you made a mistake; you acknowledge that you also got caught in the process, which is not the same thing as taking extreme ownership, as this suggests that you accept responsibility for your mistakes and learn from them.

How Can Extreme Ownership Help You?

The ultimate goal of extreme ownership is to let go of your fear and anxiety so you can excel both as a leader and in life. If you can confront your fears, own your mistakes and step up to share your opinions without hesitation, then there's no obstacle you can't overcome. Extreme ownership will help you walk the walk and lead by example if you're leading a team. Let's say one of your employees made a mistake. If you're a powerful owner, you'll immediately own up to that mistake and communicate the steps you will take to ensure it doesn't happen again.

Three Steps to Help You Take Extreme Ownership of Your Life

For many, extreme ownership may seem far-fetched or like something too difficult to achieve. But by following these steps, you can take ownership of your life and walk away as a better leader, no matter your challenges. These three steps can help you take extreme ownership of your life:

- Define what 'success' means to you – Success doesn't have to mean climbing the corporate ladder. It can mean anything you want – even if it's something small, like finishing a project on time. Once you know what you want to achieve, you can focus your energy on those goals instead of worrying about what might go wrong.
- Step 1: Take 100 per cent responsibility for everything in your life – Let's face it: we're all human and bound to make mistakes. But instead of letting your mistakes hold you back and keep you stuck, take ownership of them and use them as a learning experience. That doesn't mean you should beat yourself up for making a mistake, but you should accept responsibility for the mistake and decide not to repeat it.
- Step 2: Decide what's most important to you – Let's say you're in a relationship, and your significant other is pushing you to move in together. You're not ready for that step, but they want to take it now. If you decide what's most important to you, you can say 'no' to that decision and be happy with your choice.
- Step 3: Commit fully to your decisions and don't waiver – When you make a decision, don't change your mind just because something new comes along. If you've decided to take on a project and it's going to take longer than you expected, don't give up and start looking for an excuse to quit.

Bottom Line

Now, these are just a few of the benefits of extreme ownership, but by now, you should have a better understanding of why the concept can be life-changing. If you want to be a better leader, take ownership of your life and let go of your fears so you can excel regardless of the pressure on you.

CHAPTER 13

THE CONUNDRUM OF HUMAN–WILDLIFE CONFLICT

It was daybreak. Saumitra and his friend were lazily strolling nearby the wooded areas in the periphery of their village when they came across a herd of elephants approximately 200 feet away. He could see roughly 15 or 16 of them, half juveniles and half adult females grazing the way they do, ripping branches off trees and gnawing them down. He had seen several herds of elephants doing this frequently, but he smelled some eerie hostility in the air this time. Before he could react, he suddenly saw a massive male elephant spin around, put his trunk in the air with his ears extended out, ululating and charging at them. Terrified, they tried to flee, but there's no outrunning a seething rogue elephant. As he stood transfixed, Saumitra could see the grey, the hair follicles, the eyeball, the trunk, the tusk, the foot – the whole thing. The next thing Saumitra knew was that the elephant had hurled him into the air and then slammed him to the ground. Excruciating pain followed as the elephant's tusk pierced through his left thigh, goring it and ripping it out sideways. After a pause, the elephant lifted its leg and transferred its six-tonne body weight on the helpless 60 kg man lying on the ground, crushing his ribs and snuffing out his life instantaneously, just the way we unknowingly trample small insects under our feet when we step on them.

Wild animals can become more horrifying than even the most dreaded terrorists, like Osama bin Laden, when we put a growing squeeze on their habitat. Expanding human and animal populations, shrinking forests and the proliferation of invasive species are evolving into a confrontation that has potential to develop into a full-blown battle. The terror unleashed by the elephant that killed Saumitra earned him the name Osama bin Laden as a barb to the dreaded terrorist. He was a rogue bull elephant liable for at least 27 deaths and devastation of property in the jungles of the Sonitpur district in the state of Assam. After its two-year rampage from 2004 to 2006, the authorities shot the elephant dead.

Likewise, Avni was a six-year-old tigress suspected of having killed 13 people over two years in the hills of central India. The authorities hired a hunter to tranquillise the tigress with a dart. But when the tigress began charging at the hunter despite the dart, the hunter yanked the trigger of his gun and brought the beautiful beast down. Just a day after they exterminated Avni, another tigress in Uttar Pradesh was run over and beaten to death by furious locals after she mauled a 50-year-old man. A few days later, another majestic tigress Sundari, suspected of killing a woman in Orissa, was relocated to Nandankanan Zoo.

Is it right on our part to call Avni a man-eater? Because man-eaters don't transgress into our habitats, it's we who trespass into their habitat. Tigers are solitary and require vast territories – Are we not supposed to respect and honour their territories? When we dishonour and trespass into their environments, they have no option but to attack humans. We have lost 95 per cent of tigers since the twentieth century started. We now have only 3900 tigers left. Now the tigers require us more than ever. If so, is it not our responsibility to respect their territories, let them live in peace, protect them and not trespass into them as tourists or as hunters to poach them?

Elephants and tigers are slaying one person a day in India as humans constrict their habitat. According to the ministry of environment, 1144 people got killed in attacks in 1143 days between April 2014 and May 2017. And man is slaughtering a leopard a day as the man–animal struggle for space is growing to enormous proportions as India continues to forfeit vast swathes of wooded areas to urbanisation, pushing animals into human-occupied zones.

When we get down to Tamil Nadu, the predicament is no different. Whenever the West Zone Inspector General of Police routinely gives the daily situation report to me, I get to hear at least two to three cases of human–animal conflicts every week in which they kill or maim a human, especially in the Nilgiris. Most of them are because of elephants entering farmer's fields. The forest department attributes this to a shift in land use patterns and crop cultivation close to reserve forest tracts.

Likewise, we see a rise in human–animal conflict during droughts and summer as water scarcity drives the animals to the periphery, bringing them into conflict with humans. Increased cultivation of animal-enticing cash crops such as sugarcane heightens the contest, which we can observe near Sathyamangalam Tiger Reserve and Rajapalayam. Frequent forays of humans into the wilderness seem to have familiarised these animals far too much with humans.

When wildlife ravages the crops or human habitats, making sounds of screaming, wailing, howling, bursting firecrackers, beating drums, bonfires and letting ferocious hounds do not seem to have much impact. Wild animals continue to plummet into wells; elephants continue to trample humans; wild boars continue to cause havoc in agricultural farms; leopards continue to maul cattle and humans with rising regularity due to the infringement of wildlife corridors, making migration of animals along the traditional corridors impossible or fragmented.

Data from the state forest department and the ministry of environment, forests and climate change of India contend that in Tamil Nadu alone, the human–animal conflict has claimed at least 185 human lives and the lives of over 132 elephants and tigers between 2013 and 2016. This data does not include monkeys, leopards, rabbits, deer, bears and other animals regularly entering into conflict with humans.

One explanation why the Nilgiris region has seen a rapid increase in human–wildlife conflict is that the area has witnessed the proliferation of invasive plant species. Invasive plants have been introduced from various parts of the world and thrive at the cost of native diversity. Eleven of the world's 100 harmful invasive species now found in India – such as *Lantana camara*, *Parthenium hysterophorus*, *Prosopis juliflora* – have mushroomed inside protected tracts, causing negative consequences such as the banishment of native species on which local herbivores such as elephants, gaur and wild boar depend on for food. All three exotic species are inedible, and some, such as the *Parthenium*, are harmful to herbivores. *Prosopis* can be toxic and cause severe indigestion and tooth decay to wildlife. Traces of *Prosopis* have been detected in elephants that reportedly died of starvation at the Mudumalai Tiger Reserve and in another dead elephant found near Thengumarahada.

Hence wild animals stray into planter's fields more often because of a lack of better fodder in the wild. Most invasive species create a dense, rough and thick undergrowth in the forest, as these species, particularly *Lantana* and *Parthenium*, grow as thickets with hardly any space between them, which thus impedes the movement of large animals, both herbivores and carnivores, and obstructs their access to both ancestral activity corridors and food sources.

Furthermore, plantations of the forest department have been further aggravating this effect. Species such as *Acacia* and *Eucalyptus* have been decreasing the water table levels, further benefiting exotics that get better adapted to drier environments. A resin-like substance that trickles from such foreign species renders the soil acidic, hindering the growth of any other plant species. The raising of vast plantations of eucalyptus and wattle in the past by changing grasslands and shola forests has led to the devastation of the original habitat of the Nilgiri Tahr.

Further, the ban on cattle grazing also appears to have contributed to the undergrowth and a loss of dung and cattle manure, which can be a source of nourishment for native species. Therefore, the situation emanating from the lack of edible plants inside forests and hampering movement inside the woods has compelled carnivores and herbivores to move outside of jungles in search for food. Under such circumstances, farming fields have become very attractive to large herbivores such as deer and elephants as they find the fields crammed with edible plants. Predators, in turn, pursue the herbivores out of the wilderness; as a result, the latter come into conflict with the humans. Presently, the Indian bison visits the Kodaikanal town in Tamil Nadu because of the non-availability of fodder and the extensive plantations of alien species.

Therefore, human–wildlife conflicts have enormous consequences. Such confrontations have given rise to hostility, vexation, resentment and alienation. Most families are suffering crop losses from wildlife invasions. The animals that most often obliterate crops are elephants, deer, pigs and monkeys. Pigs mainly raid root vegetables and subterranean crops. Most of these animals attack crops at night; hence defending crops against destruction can be difficult. To protect the crops, the farmers have to stay awake at night. Farmer's families resort to rotational guarding of fields, with substantial health impacts such as sleep deprivation or disruption in daily schedules. Suppose animals overrun the agricultural areas when the crop is ready for harvest, destroying several months of work. Not just crop losses, livestock losses also happen frequently in such areas. Such losses have higher impact than crop losses because cows, goats and buffaloes embody several years' worth of investment or savings. And antidotes for such losses veer around steps like fences, guarding and so on to diminish wildlife entry into human habitation or fields, or 'compensation' for those affected, injured or killed by wildlife. Those most affected by human–wildlife conflict seem to be forest dwellers or farming communities that live near forests.

The forest department extends peanuts as compensation to the victims of crop loss. The compensation ranges from a meagre Rs 5000 to Rs 10,000. To avail the benefit provided by the forest department for crop loss because of pillaging animals, one has to go through a long-winded bureaucratic procedure. The authorities process claims only after claimants furnish a certificate by the village administrative officer and the agricultural officer. Compensation for death or permanent disability is more straightforward, though. It varies between Rs 20,000 and Rs 1 lakh for disability and Rs 3–5 lakhs in case of death. Wildlife attacks are one rationale for migration. When an elephant trampled the breadwinner of a family in the Nilgiris, the remaining family members shifted to Coimbatore shortly afterwards.

The human–wildlife conflict is a feature of almost all forested landscapes in India. The cause behind most conflicts, as we have seen, is the burgeoning population of both humans and animals, resulting in enormous competition for land. India, at the moment, would do well if it handled the conflict by engaging the affected communities and vigorously safeguarding the existing habitats of animals from human interference. The measures we are taking to curb it are ineffective as it is reactive. A proactive step, such as engaging the community, would portend well for diluting the conflict.

A more straightforward, cost-effective warning system (SMS alerts) as used in Valparai for notifying the presence of elephants could get replicated in other parts of India to ease the way to coexistence. To tackle the problem of human–animal conflict, governments may have to undertake a rapid modernisation of forest departments. Bigger budgets and better infrastructures will strengthen the hands of the forest department to ward off attacks with the help of modern techniques such as GIS, drones, lasers, scanners, DNA fingerprinting, infrared sensors, 3D sensing and imaging. Deployment of drones and the use of AI could predict animal movements accurately. We should also contemplate using robots to chase or guide wild animals into safe directions.

Chapter 14

WHAT YOU SEEK IS INSIDE YOU!

Everything we are looking for is within us, but as a culture, we have developed this tendency to seek answers outside of us constantly. We do this by seeking advice from parents, mentors, teachers or counsellors, by googling the internet for answers, by reading self-help books or by listening to podcasts or attending personal development seminars. We seek not only happiness but also love, permission, satisfaction and validation from others. In the end, we meet with disappointment because none of them has the power to fill the void we experience within us. Because joy, happiness, pleasure, suffering, sadness, agony, torment and ecstasy happens inside us. Not realising this, we always try to find joy and satisfaction from the outside. The outer may provide the signal or trigger, but the real feelings stem from inside of us. Our tendency to seek answers from outside has created a billion-dollar self-help industry where coaches, gurus, personal development seminars, spiritual retreats, astrologers and so on are capitalising on the inclination of individuals to find answers outside of themselves. When in actuality, everything we seek is already within us. Validation, permission, joy, happiness, love, satisfaction and so on are all within us, and we can access this from within. We can give it to ourselves; as per the law of attraction, when we do this, we are likely to attract the same from others.

As a kid, I always sought validation from my parents. I would study hard and be a good boy because I wanted them to praise my behaviour, and I always strove to score over my brother. My daughters are unlike me. They have chosen courses in colleges which appealed to their inner selves, but never because we as parents validated their choice. Most kids today never strive to seek validation, but go by the intuition of what feels good to them and their conscience. Trusting one's intuition and living by one's hunch is living from within. Such individuals are generally happy and more responsible for their lives because they have made the decisions themselves and have not relied on anyone outside when choosing the path of their lives.

Sometimes most of us wait for permission to write, sing, act or play a sport, but we fail to realise that we are today living in a world where we don't need anybody's permission to write; we can turn into an author by self-publishing our books on Amazon, or sing and record our songs on iTunes, or reveal our acting or speaking capabilities to the world through YouTube videos. We no longer have to go outside seeking to be an author, a singer, an actor or a podcaster. We can be any of these by simply using the internet.

When we feel lonely, we look for love. Love is the thing most of us seek outside of ourselves. We think love has to do with someone else. But it's not about someone else; it's everything about us. When one feels lonely and goes looking for love, it's the loneliness that awaits him most and not the love. When an individual is bubbling with love inside him, more love will come chasing after him. Love is your quality; it's like offering the person who loves you a key to open up what's inside you. You can love yourself even if the person you are in love with is not with you. We don't have to look outside – at our parents, friends and romantic partners – for love, though all of them seem to offer reassurance that we are loved. We look for love most when we don't enjoy our own company. When you enjoy or love being in your own company, love will come calling to you.

Other people can't fill our hearts or make us feel whole and complete. When we expect those things from others, we put too much pressure on them as we enter situations in our lives from a place of lack and deficit. If you want to get love from others, you must first learn to love yourself, have dates with yourself and feel entirely comfortable in your own company; only then will you be able to attract and keep love in your lives.

Further, when it comes to life's problems, the answer to all our problems is within us. It's just a matter of finding it, pulling it out and using it. But the truth is that everything we seek is already inside us. All we need to do is recognise what it is and then bring it into the light to use it to your advantage. The only thing standing between you and your goal is yourself. If your goal is to have a better relationship with your partner, you first need to work on your relationship with them. It might seem an obvious solution, but sometimes we don't see the forest for the trees. Once you start taking action and making progress, you'll be amazed at how quickly things begin to change for the better.

No matter what your desire for change is, you are already at the place of fulfilment. Instead of searching outside yourself for a solution, take a look inside and focus on what you can manifest within your reality. No greater power exists than the energy of the universe. It is only through connecting with this energy that we can indeed manifest what we desire. By acknowledging that all things are already in our world and trusting that they are there to help us, we can choose to step into our power. The key is to move from being an observer into a participant.

As already mentioned, there is no greater power than the energy of the universe. Only through connecting with this energy can we manifest what we desire, which is evident in the movie *The Secret*, which illustrates how we can manifest anything we want. The secret is that we are connected to an all-powerful source of energy. There are no limitations. The trick is learning how to tap into it and use this energy. By visualising what you want and connecting with the universal energy, you can start seeing positive changes in your life.

The movie also illustrates what happens when you don't believe in yourself or others. The universe is a mirror that reflects your thoughts at you, so if you think negative about yourself or others, that's what you will get back from the universe – negative experiences. After watching this movie, I was able to connect with my inner source of power to change my life for the better, and I am sure many people who care will be able to do the same and learn how powerful they are!

The movie also teaches us about karma; karma is simply an action/reaction process where if we do something good for someone else, something good will happen in return for us (and vice versa). This concept is very effective when trying to manifest what we want because we can use it as a way of connecting with others and realising that everyone has their karma which may be different from ours, so it's important never to judge anyone based on their actions

Your purpose and desire for change are here to stay, so don't let another day go by without following your inner calling to manifest your desires into reality. Don't let fear hold you back. You have the power within you, and it is time to connect with it. By acknowledging that all things are already in our world and trusting that they are there to help us, we can choose to step into our power. The key is to move from being an observer into a participant.

While the universe is vast and infinite, what you seek is always within reach. It's just a matter of opening yourself up to new possibilities. Everything you desire is already inside you. It's just a matter of realising it and accepting it. The key lies in finding the confidence to pursue your dreams and reaching out for what you want. Well, what do you want? What brings you joy and fulfilment? What would make your life more abundant and fulfilling? What makes your heart sing? Those are the things that truly matter. Pursue these things with all your might. Surround yourself with people who will support and encourage you along the way. When you find what brings you joy and fulfilment, let nothing stop you from pursuing it using everything you've got. When the world tells you that dream is out of reach, tell them where to go – your goals are always within your reach!

We must quiet our minds and focus on one thing to connect with this vibrational frequency: your breath, a mantra or a positive thought. Once you are relaxed and at ease with yourself, you can open your mind and invite the universe in. You can do this by asking the universe for what you want or need. You can also do it by simply allowing things to happen. Trust that the universe has your best intentions. Embrace the unknown and let go of any expectations.

To do this, we must be mindful and present in each moment, accept what is happening around us and focus on the things that bring us joy. By doing so, we can positively impact the energy of our thoughts and actions, and in turn positively move the energy of our world. The more you are in tune with this energy and its vibrations, the more you open yourself up to receiving its benefits. There are many ways to practise this form of energy work, and the more you do it, the stronger your connection will become. This form of energy exists in everything, but some things are naturally richer in it than others. For example, blueberries and dark chocolate are both healthy foods, but dark chocolate has far more of this energy than blueberries. That's not to say you can't benefit from eating blueberries, but you will get more out of eating dark chocolate.

We must be open to receiving this energy and let go of any resistance we might have to it and must be available to the fact that what we want may not look exactly the way we originally envisioned. When we manifest with intention, we open ourselves up to receiving the best possible outcome for our highest good. The more we are in tune with this universal energy, it is easier to receive what we want in life.

What are the signs that you have got connected with this universal energy? You might feel like everything is happening by chance, or you might feel like you are working hard but not getting anywhere. One of the most prominent signs that you possess universal energy is you feel comfortable and at ease with where you are in life. If you feel stressed, anxious, worried or if life doesn't seem to be working out for you, then you are probably not in sync with this universal energy.

No matter what your desire for change is, you are already at the place of fulfilment. Instead of searching outside of yourself for a solution, take a look inside and focus on what you can manifest within your reality. No greater power exists than the energy of the universe. It is only through connecting with this energy that we can indeed manifest what we desire.

Chapter 15

THE PROBLEM OF ILLEGAL ORGAN TRAFFICKING

In the novel *Coma* written by Robin Cook and made into a movie by Michael Crichton, a quizzical physician (Genevieve Bujold) discovers that nefarious seniors are drugging healthy patients into a comatose state, killing them and selling their organs to wealthy patients in desperate need of transplants. She confronts her avaricious doctor lover (Michael Douglas) and gets behind the sinister conspiracy. Similarly, in the book *The Baby Train*, written by Jan Brunvand, a subject wakes up in a hotel bathtub to discover that one of his kidneys is missing.

Not just in fiction, this has been playing out in real life, too; for instance, in January of 2013, Kendrick Johnson, a Georgia teen, was found dead in his school under mysterious circumstances. Initially, it seemed like a freak accident of death due to suffocation resulting from convoluting a gym mat. Exhumation of the body six months later led to the discovery of a corpse stuffed with newspaper inside. The brain, heart, lungs and liver of the boy were missing. FBI investigation into the matter led to stunning revelations.

Recently in China, a missing six-year-old boy was found weeping in a field, with both eyes removed, presumably for the corneas. In China, organ brokers mainly target young people in internet forums with slogans such as 'Donate a kidney, buy the new iPad.' In April 2011, Wang Shangkun's mother in Anhui, Central China, discovered that her 17-year-old son had sold his kidney and bought an iPad and iPhone with the money. Wang now suffers from decreased kidney function and other complications.

Similarly, in India, a scan taken after a four-year-old girl underwent surgery in 2015 to remove an infected kidney in a reputed hospital in Delhi left the girl's father shell-shocked when it revealed the disappearance of the other organ. Whatever the reasons for the missing kidney, the incident focuses on the business of illegal transplants and organ trafficking.

Three major kidney-trafficking rackets extending through several states and neighbouring Nepal got busted in India in June 2016. Two of them involved staff of a major private hospital in Delhi, while the third, a fake doctor and his family, operated one of India's most notorious rackets. The lynchpin of the most unparalleled racket was Amit Kumar, 65, who, with no training in medicine or surgery, along with another person, performed 50 illegal transplantations in three months before being nabbed.

One of the leading causes behind the demand for organs appears to be the lifestyle shift, which has introduced type 2 diabetes mellitus, obesity and metabolic syndrome in epidemic proportions.

An estimated 98 million Indians are likely to have type 2 diabetes by 2030. Untreated diabetes leads to organ failure, necessitating a transplant. With lifestyle diseases affecting people at younger ages, the country is witnessing widespread prevalence of chronic diseases with concomitant organ failure.

But there are not enough donated organs to go around. As of 2018, according to reports, about 114,000 people are waiting for a new organ in the US. An individual has to wait three-and-a-half years for an organ to become available for transplant.

And so, the underground trade continues to persist. It has indubitably decreased, but it is still there. About 3–3.5 lakh patients need transplants in India at any given time.

Tamil Nadu alone accounts for around 3500 patients with end-stage kidney failure on the waiting list for a transplant, with another 400 patients waiting for a liver transplant. In 2007, Tamil Nadu was considered the hub for illegal kidney transplant racket when a scandal rocked the state.

Hence, there is a flourishing and macabre black market for body parts worldwide. The World Health Organisation estimates that an illicitly obtained organ is sold every hour through underground networks. The kidney is the most commonly sought-after organ, and kidneys can fetch up to $2,000,000. Reports estimate that 75 per cent of all illegal organ trading involves kidneys.

The liver trade, though prices range from $4000 to $157,000, is less common due to a difficult postoperative recovery period that hinders donors. Hearts are available for $1,200,000, skin a mere $10 per square inch, a shoulder for $5500 and a pair of eyeballs for $1500.

Diabetes and hypertension are the most significant causes of kidney failure in our country, accounting for 40–60 per cent of chronic kidney disease. Around 200,000 people need a kidney every year in India, but only approximately 3 per cent of the demand gets met. There is thus a demand and supply problem.

Cadaveric donations and brain-dead victims of road accidents could help bridge the demand for organs in a big way. More than 148,000 people die annually from road accidents; close to 65 per cent are from severe head injuries, which translates to around 90,000 people in hospitals with 'brain death' each year.

According to figures published in the *Indian Journal of Anaesthesia* in 2013, of the 205 patients declared brain-dead at the AIIMS Trauma Centre, only ten became potential organ donors in the past five years.

Before 1994, India was one of the largest kidney transplant centres in the world as low cost and high availability brought in recipients from around the globe. In 1994, the country passed the Transplantation of Human Organs Act (THOA), banning organ commerce and promoting posthumous donation of organs.

The above Act allows only a 'near relative' to be a living donor. It also allows 'swap' donations and permits donations from 'affection or attachment towards the recipient or any other special reason'.

China, since the 1980s, has obtained the bulk of its transplanted organs from executed prisoners. One source estimated that China killed at least 4000 prisoners in 2006 to supply approximately 8000 kidneys and 3000 livers for foreign buyers.

Iran is the only country with no waitlists for kidney transplantation as it is the only country that allows organs to be bought and sold for money, which has been hailed as the safe organ-trading model by many.

Within the European Union, member states regulate organ donation. As of 2010, 24 European countries have some form of presumed consent (opt-out) system, with the most complex and limited opt-out procedures in Spain, Austria, Belgium and Wales yielding high donor rates. The UK, on the contrary, has decided on an opt-in system. India could borrow from the Spanish system of organ donations.

Spain leads the world with 35 organ donors per million people, compared to Britain's 27, US' 26, Australia's 11 and India's miserly 0.16.

The Multi-Organ Harvesting Aid Network – MOHAN Foundation – was established in 1997 in Tamil Nadu by a group of practising medical professionals and their friends to promote 'organ donation'. It has been tirelessly working as a support group and doing an excellent job coordinating organ donation, retrieval and transplantation.

The funds so raised could help the foundation run its activities smoothly and equip it with drones to swiftly transport donated organs to hospitals without relying on a green corridor. The foundation has also been advocating the inclusion of the 'clause of organ donation in the driving licence', which could save many lives.

According to the Transplant Authority of Tamil Nadu, the state has led the nation in organ donation, with 4938 organs transplanted in the past eight years. Tamil Nadu is also the first Indian state to make certification of brain death compulsory, successfully create a green corridor for organ transport and initiate discussions about organ donation in society.

The total organ donations in our country have been surging as well, and it has gone up from 1149 in 2014 to 2870 in 2017, including a two-and-a-half times increase in kidney and liver donations, not to mention a whopping 6.5 times rise in heart donations.

Lastly, the use of body parts to benefit others is deeply embedded in Hindu mythology. The earliest depiction of xenotransplantation is the case of Lord Ganesha, wearing an elephant head. Besides, our scriptures tell us that our body is mortal and soul is eternal. If so, by donating one's organ, one's body takes on an eternal quality. The organs of our body continue to live on after we die. Even if we are ill or old, we all have the gift of life to give it to another one. We can provide a more excellent gift than we ever can when we were alive. It's by far the ultimate spiritual gift we can offer.

CHAPTER 16

SELF-DISCIPLINE IS AT THE HEART OF MARATHON TRAINING

According to Kenyan long-distance runner and Olympic marathon champion Eliud Kipchoge, 'self-discipline is not a one-night affair'. One develops it step by step. You can't step into a gym for a day and build muscle. It takes time to build muscle. Similarly, to train for a marathon, you must make a training plan and follow it for months before adapting to withstand the rigours of a marathon race.

The word 'discipline' comes from the Latin *disciplina*, which means teaching or learning. Self-discipline is 'the capacity to regulate one's emotions and behaviour' or 'self-control'. Discipline is the foundation of success in any endeavour.

A study published in *Frontiers in Psychology* has found that self-discipline is a better predictor of success than IQ or socioeconomic status. It also found that people with high self-discipline have better life outcomes, such as higher grades, more employment opportunities and lower levels of substance abuse.

In the world of running, too, couch potatoes through self-discipline can become marathon runners. While it's not always easy to get up and move around every day, many couch potatoes find that they can achieve fitness goals by breaking up long periods of sitting with short bursts of activity. If you're a couch potato, try to get up every 30 minutes and do some light walking or stretching. Or, if you have access to a gymnasium, go for a quick workout (e.g. walking on a treadmill). The key is to get moving every once in a while, even if you don't feel like it, to improve your overall fitness level and keep you from gaining too much weight.

Breaking the addiction of sitting for long hours can help build strength in the core and improve posture, thus helping to keep an active mind. You may struggle with this. It would be best if you started slowly and gradually increased your speed. If you are new to running, start walking for short distances before gradually increasing your time on foot. You should also stretch after every run and take rest on days when needed. Over time, you will see improvements in your running form and endurance. Running is an excellent means of losing weight and building strength while keeping the mind fit. Running goes beyond physical health as it also helps to maintain a healthy lifestyle. A sedentary lifestyle can lead to weight gain and other health problems such as high blood pressure, diabetes and heart disease. By incorporating running into your daily routine, you can prevent these health issues and feel better overall. The 36-year-old Janine Joubert was a couch potato who lived in Hamilton, New Zealand. She was depressed, on medication, overweight, unfit and sick with asthma and high blood pressure. In May 2014, she ran her first marathon in Rotorua. If she could do it, there is no reason why you should not do it.

In the film *Brittany Runs a Marathon*, Brittany is a mid-twenties party girl battling her weight, finances and toxic relationship. Quite broke to join a gym and too hesitant to ask for support, Brittany attempts to reshape her life with the once-unimaginable goal of running the New York City Marathon. Unhappy with her weight, diet and overall daily undisciplined life, Brittany takes baby steps with the eventual goal of running a marathon. The movie ends with Brittany crossing the finish line after a long, agonising build-up to the race, which comes from self-discipline.

Run Fatboy Run is another flick based on running that tells the tale of Dennis, a paunchy middle-aged man who sets out to run a marathon to win back his ex-girlfriend Libby, whom he had left at the altar five years ago. Meanwhile, Libby meets Whit, an athlete planning to run a marathon and gets engaged to him. To prove to Libby that he too can run and win her, Dennis, who has no previous marathon training, trains from scratch battling blisters, chafing and fatigue to run a marathon. The movie is a story of self-discipline, the triumph of the human spirit over sloth and indiscipline. Towards the movie's end, Dennis collapses near the marathon finish line and cannot get up, but upon seeing Libby calling to him, he gets up, sprints to the finish and slumps in her arms. So the final message of this feel-good film is that every goal we set is attainable.

Many celebs who started as couch potatoes became self-disciplined runners. One of the most famous is Steve Prefontaine, a runner from the University of Oregon. In 1975, he worked as a carpenter when he decided to try out for a local track team. He never made it onto the track team, but that didn't stop him from running. He would practise by jogging on the nearby track and then run along the beach at night. Eventually, his workouts paid off, and he made it onto the track team at the University of Oregon. There, he started to be known as 'Pre' because of his short stature and speed on the track.

As his career progressed, Prefontaine continued to find ways to push himself further. He set long-distance records for both men and women, won several gold medals in international competitions and even set an American record for indoor mile running at the Oregon Trials in 1973. Of course, these achievements would not have been possible without hard work. And even though Prefontaine started as a lazy couch potato, he eventually became one of the most famous runners in history because he worked hard to become a self-disciplined runner.

All the discipline and hard work Steve puts in is evident in *Without Limits*, a powerful Hollywood movie that tells the story of Steve. The film also brilliantly cuts live footage of his famous attempt to win a gold medal at the Munich Olympic Games in 1972. In the rock-and-roll world or other realms, for a person to earn the title of a 'legend', they would have to be controversial, have disdain for authority, be blessed with immense talent and, most importantly, have a life that ends too soon. The life of American distance runner Steve Prefontaine flawlessly had it all. The flick reveals how Prefontaine delighted in almost rock-star status due to his running ability and defied the conventions of the time – dragging the sport into a new era. Steve once said: 'I don't run to see who has the best endurance, I run to see who has the most guts. I know that is me.' One can develop mammoth confidence in Steve if one cultivates the self-discipline and determination to demolish whatever goal is in front of them.

Another world-famous long-distance runner who went from being a couch potato to a 2014 British Championship 100 km race in a record time of 6:19:20 at the age of 39 is Steve Way. He began running seriously in 2007 to overcome lifestyle-related health issues, and he weighed over 100 kg and smoked 20 cigarettes a day. But by 2014, he had run the London Marathon under 2:20 four times and also broke the qualifying time of 2:17 for the Commonwealth Games for the first time.

Another inspiring story of a famous runner who became great through self-discipline is that of Stephen Kiprotich. He was born in Uganda, and his uncle seeing his unusual talent for running decided to sponsor his running. Soon, Stephen became the first Ugandan to win the New York Marathon and also the first Ugandan to win Olympic gold. Stephen himself attributed his success to solid self-discipline and commitment to training, which he developed through his early years of running while working hard to earn money for himself and his family. Self-discipline allows us to make the right decisions by aligning them with our values and helps us discover our purpose. Working on our purpose with self-discipline builds confidence and resilience to face setbacks and emerge victorious in whatever field we pursue.

I want my readers to take to running because running is a great way to build self-discipline, a key component of success. Running can motivate people to be healthy, lose weight or get fit for a marathon. For someone not interested in fitness, running can seem like a huge challenge. We have seen some famous people who started as couch potatoes becoming accomplished runners through self-discipline. They all started slow and got the hang of it, but eventually through commitment and persistence went on to become accomplished runners. So, when you run and get into good shape, your confidence will skyrocket, and you'll start feeling better about yourself. You'll also be able to make decisions confidently, leading to tremendous success in all areas of your life. In addition to building self-discipline, running can help you manage stress and depression, improve memory and even prevent diabetes. All this makes running a win for everyone! So if you decide to take up running and are enthusiastic about it, there is no better day than today. But before you embark on running, here are some aspects that you should bear in mind:

- Start slow; walking is always an option if you're getting used to exercise.
- Remember that it takes time to build up stamina; even the most experienced runners need time to build up their endurance.
- Ensure you're eating correctly and taking the time to rest when needed.
- Running is hard work, so make sure you have time for rest days too!

There are many ways to become a great runner. Some people find success through genetics, while others rely on dedication and perseverance. Whatever path you take, one thing is sure: self-discipline is necessary for success. An overabundance of self-discipline can be a real asset in the running. Without it, runners risk burning out before they ever get started. Self-discipline allows runners to stay committed to their goals and remain motivated on the long journey ahead. I find that all successful runners have some things in common. First, they are highly focused individuals who know what they want out of life. Second, they are committed to their goals and do whatever it takes to reach them. Third, they consistently practise self-control: eating well, getting enough sleep and staying hydrated when needed – in short, being self-disciplined means that you take care of your every step so that you can achieve your goals and reach your full potential.

Once you become a runner and start loving it, you can set your eyes on running a marathon. For a runner to turn into a marathoner, self-discipline is again a prerequisite. Training for a marathon needs a tonne of mental strength to wake up at 5 a.m., jump on the treadmill for an hour before heading off to work or school and then come home after 9 p.m. Running a marathon is an exciting challenge; it takes commitment, focus and determination. Athletes need to establish clear goals and a robust support system around them. One can develop self-discipline through dedication, hard work and constant practice. A marathon aspirant must develop self-discipline early in their training regimen – especially if they have never set these goals. Self-discipline is also vital for any athlete who wishes to compete at an elite level. The ability to stay focused and keep a long-term goal in mind can help athletes push through difficult times and reach their full potential.

Further, marathon aspirants need to control their actions and behaviours in the face of temptation. They should develop the ability to resist short-term gratification in favour of long-term goals. In many ways, self-discipline is the opposite of impulsivity. Impulsivity is an inability to delay gratification, which is crucial for long-distance running. That said, self-discipline is a skill that needs to be learned and developed over time. Long-distance runners need to learn how to practise delayed gratification. They need to know how to train their willpower muscles and make it a habit, not just a temporary act. They can achieve it through mindfulness meditation, yoga and other forms of meditation or by taking some time out each day to focus on their goals and commit themselves to those no matter what.

A marathon aspirant must also develop the ability to recognise their emotions and learn how to manage them. People who are good at noticing how they feel can calm themselves down or adjust their behaviour and generally achieve their goals. A marathoner with self-discipline can control his emotions and behaviours when needed, staying focused on their goal. Self-discipline is also about setting priorities and ensuring that you spend time doing important things rather than spending all of your time striving to train for a marathon. It would help if you worked on self-discipline daily; the more you practise it, the better it gets.

Why Self-Discipline Is at the Heart of Marathon Training and Running

Self-discipline is one of the biggest challenges to anyone's running routine, let alone a runner's training schedule. Regarding training for a long run, staying on track with your runs and not devolving into painful self-flagellation is about as much fun as being spanked with a wet noodle. Nevertheless, staying disciplined in your training requires just a tiny bit of effort, and the good news is that once you understand the why and how of self-discipline, you can build up your inner strength over time. Self-discipline isn't easy because it means making choices daily to say 'no' to things that would make us happy or comfortable instead of saying 'yes' to what we need most to succeed. And this is why self-discipline is at the heart of marathon training and running itself.

Self-discipline is a critical component of a successful long-term commitment to any endeavour. It's the ability to prioritise your goals over other temptations and distractions. Self-discipline is the ability to delay immediate gratification in favour of long-term goals. It is a complex combination of habits, attitudes and values that influence everything we do, including our health and fitness goals. To train for a marathon, you must have self-discipline. It would help if you remained committed to your training schedule no matter what life throws your way, which requires both self-awareness and self-control. Self-awareness involves recognising your strengths and weaknesses to compensate for them when necessary. Self-control is the opposite of self-discipline; it's the ability to do what you want without giving in to temptation. Without these two qualities, it isn't easy to stick with a long-term goal such as training for marathons.

Why Is Self-Discipline at the Centre of Marathon Training?

One word that best describes the running lifestyle is perseverance. It's a word that can be associated with anything you set your mind to, whether it's an Olympic gold medal, writing a book or completing a marathon. Running is no different. The key to success is finding something you enjoy doing and sticking with it long enough to see results. It takes a lot of hard work and determination to become a great runner, but anyone who has taken the first steps on their journey will tell you there is no other feeling like it.

In our early twenties, self-discipline may not be a problem at all. It may be one of your most vital qualities. But as you wander track, self-discipline becomes much more of a problem. Why? It's because as we get older, our brain starts to change a little, and what works in your twenties may not help in your thirties or forties. Another reason self-discipline becomes much more difficult as we get older is that other things compete for our attention. In our twenties, we may be very focused on just getting to the top, but in our thirties and beyond, we may have the goal of having a stable income or career. These things add up to make self-discipline will not be much more of a challenging in our thirties and beyond.

Decide When You're Going to Run, Not When You Can?

If you have a fondness for running, you can become a dedicated runner. If you want to get serious about marathon training, it's also critical that you learn to make the most of your time so that you know exactly when you will run and that you do not 'wander track' yourself. The best way to do this is to decide when you're going to run and stick to it, even if that means running when it's raining or when no one else wants to be out running. Also, when deciding when to run, you must fix and desist from procrastination. Once you determine when to run, getting out of doorsteps will be much more challenging.

What Will Keep You Accountable and on the Path? What Will Help You Succeed?

The first step to building up self-discipline as a runner is to decide with your running buddies that you will stick to your running schedule. For marathon training, you'll need to commit to being out on the road every day because that will help you succeed. How? As runners, we often feel like the ones who 'should' be accountable because we are out on the road. We are not 'supposed' to be out there doing what we love to do. We may feel guilty for not being 'ready' for our runs or for not being disciplined enough to get out on the road. If you expect to get more out of running, however, you have to learn to feel accountable for being out on the road, which means feeling like you are keeping yourself on track and responsible for your success.

How to Develop Self-Discipline in Your Running Routine

Self-discipline is something that one can develop over time. The key is gradually challenging yourself to engage in activities you have not yet done. For example, if you have never run a 5k, then first run a 5k, then run a 10k, then run a half marathon and finally run a marathon; you have now completed four different types of running events. Keep challenging yourself to complete new activities, and you will naturally develop self-discipline as you become more and more comfortable with the idea of doing new things.

As runners, we know that a long run is essential to training for a marathon. But how can you train effectively? Running a long distance isn't easy. It takes a lot of focus and self-discipline to grit your teeth and keep going at the same pace for the hours it takes to complete a run. If you're ready to take your running to the next level and run faster than ever, you need to add more self-discipline into your training. It would help if you also worked on adding more variety to your runs by mixing in shorter intervals with hills or speedwork.

Race Day Self-Discipline

Race day self-discipline is the final frontier of self-discipline, and if you want to achieve your best marathon performance, then this is the most critical aspect of self-discipline you will need to practise. You have a choice regarding how you want to feel on race day and how you want to perform. You can choose to feel excited and optimistic, or you can choose to feel anxiety and dread. The key is to decide how you want to touch on race day and then focus on the aspects that will help you succeed in those chosen feelings. Your race day self-discipline should be twofold: First, you must mentally prepare yourself for the event by either visualising yourself performing well or by writing down what you want to accomplish in your run. Second, you need to physically prepare yourself so that you don't slow yourself down by taking too much time to get to the starting line or not eating enough before the run.

Self-Discipline for Training

As you train for your first marathon, gradually introducing new types of running into your training is a key to building up your self-discipline. For example, the first type of running you will want to introduce into your workout is 'interval training': running at an intensity that is slightly harder than what you're used to on your long runs but not so hard that it causes you to break a sweat. Interval training helps you to gradually increase your pace and thus your pace security. Interval training is also ideal for building up your self-discipline, as it focuses on pushing yourself to run harder, but not so hard that you start feeling 'out of control'. As you pull into your training schedule, you'll want to gradually start incorporating 'speed work': running at a pace between your long runs but still slightly slower than your marathon pace. Speed work helps you to progressively increase your pace security.

How to Build Up Your Training Intensity over Months

As you build up your training, you'll want to gradually increase your training intensity, always staying slightly below what you're used to on your long runs. How do you do this? You keep track of your training and ensure you don't do too much too soon. For example, if you're used to running 20 long runs per year, you'll want to keep your long run distances close to that, but don't go out and run 20 consecutive long runs. Keeping track of your training is essential because your training intensity is a good indicator of how well you can keep yourself disciplined. The more disciplined you are in your training, the harder you'll want to push yourself during your training runs, but still make sure you're not pushing too hard. Gradually increase your self-discipline over time as you slowly build up your training intensity.

What To Do if You Come Short of Your Goals?

You must learn from your mistakes if you fall short of your goals. One of the better ways to do that is to make a detailed list of what you did wrong during each training run or race, then make a clear plan to correct those mistakes on your next training run or race. For example, if you forgot to eat enough before your last run, then make sure you eat enough before your next run. If you run too slow on your previous run, then make sure you run bit faster on your next training run.

Self-discipline is also an essential aspect of being successful. It's a trait that varies from person to person and depends on the situation. For instance, under pressure, someone might show self-control by pulling all-nighters to finish a project, but the same individual might struggle to stay organised at home and have issues keeping up with their chores. While it can be challenging to maintain self-discipline in certain situations, we often find ways to make it easier.

Conclusion

Self-discipline is the ability to govern one's actions and maintain a strong sense of commitment to a goal. One can acquire self-discipline through practice, but one can also learn by modelling successful people who demonstrate self-control. Self-discipline is an essential aspect of any long-distance training regimen. By maintaining healthy eating habits, drinking plenty of water, getting enough sleep and logging miles on the road or trail, marathoners can improve their chances of reaching their goal. In addition to physical fitness, self-discipline allows marathoners to stay committed to their goals and train hard day in and day out. Long-distance running is not known for its forgiving nature. Anyone who takes on this challenge needs to have strong self-discipline to endure physical exertion and stay motivated and committed to their goal.

Chapter 17

BE SO GOOD THAT THEY CAN'T IGNORE YOU

When comedian Steve Martin was quizzed about why he was successful in his career, he immediately replied: 'Be so good they can't ignore you,' which flies in the face of conventional wisdom by suggesting that it should be a person's talent and skill – and not necessarily their passion – that determines their career path. Trying to find what drives us instead of focusing on areas in which we naturally excel may be ultimately harmful and frustrating to job-seekers. Former Apple CEO Steve Jobs, in his famous Stanford University commencement speech, urges idealistic grads to chase their dreams or passion, which is contrary to Steve Martin, who believes that one's career success depends on finding out what one does well and where one has built up his 'career capital' and then put all of one's efforts in that direction. But if you look at what Jobs did: he didn't follow his passion for Zen Buddhism. If Jobs had followed his love, he would have become a teacher in a Zen monastery. Instead, the Apple founder had several stops and starts – including famously dropping out of Reed College and travelling to India in search of enlightenment. Steve Martins cautions against taking 'follow your passion' as the lesson from Jobs' life – he points out that the vast majority of careers have equally odd stops and starts and that 'follow your passion' is reductive and quite useless as a guiding principle.

In his new career strategy book, *So Good They Can't Ignore You*, Cal Newport asserts that the passion hypothesis is forcing a decline in job satisfaction. If you believe you should follow your passion and then by finding a job that conforms to that passion, you're setting yourself up for a failure. People with unrealistic expectations about passions in their career will discover themselves chronically job-hopping and continually discontented with whatever job they have.

Newport thinks the passion hypothesis is also fundamentally blemished for several other reasons. The first reason is that passion is rare. In 2002, a study team led by Canadian psychologist Robert J. Vallerand distributed a comprehensive questionnaire to a group of 539 Canadian university students. They found that most of them had hobby-related passions like cricket, hockey, video games and so on, not career passions. Newport argues that this is suggestive that you can't follow a passion for your career if you don't have job-related passions to pursue.

The second reason the passion hypothesis is poor advice is that passion takes time to build. For instance, Amy Wrzesniewski conducted a study of college administrative assistants and discovered that the strongest predictor of an assistant calling upon her work as a calling was the number of years spent on the employment. In other words, the more experience the assistant had, the more probable they would love their work.

In today's world, you must make noise if you want to get heard. You can no longer wait for the right opportunity or a perfect moment to present yourself. You must take the bull by its horns and find your ways of introducing yourself. People in this world succeed not because they're the smartest or most skilled but because they are so good at becoming what they do that people can't help but notice them. We call these people 'stand out' professionals, and one of their secrets is learning how to be so good that people can't ignore them despite all the noise around them. Here are some ways to be so good that people can't ignore you.

Commit to Constant Improvement and Learning

Successful people are always searching for new ways to improve themselves and their skills, even if they've been doing their job for decades. If you commit to constant improvement and learning, you'll never settle for your current skill level. You'll constantly look for new ways to better yourself, your expertise and your skills. This continuous improvement will make you stand out from the crowd.

Network Like Crazy

There's no better way to get your name out there than networking. Whether attending or hosting a networking event, broadcasting your contact information or finding ways to get involved in your industry's social media groups, getting your name out there in the world can be a very effective way of getting noticed. Networking is all about connecting with people who have a common interest as you. You'll have access to potential mentors, collaborators and life-long connections through networking. You'll also have access to individuals in positions to hire you, promote you and give you a leg up in your career.

Develop a Signature Skill

One of the easiest ways to make yourself stand out amongst your peers is by developing a signature skill. That doesn't necessarily mean you must become a skillful surgeon or an elite athlete, which means you need to find out what you're good at, what you have a particular talent for or what you love doing so much that you can't help but dive headfirst into it. This signature skill can be anything from cooking to designing to creating music. The key here is that you're so incredibly good at it that people can't ignore you. Calport encourages people to develop a 'craftsman mindset'. The craftsman mindset is that you should concentrate on gaining rare and valuable skills since this is what guides to good career outcomes.

Show Up – a Lot

The best way to stand out is to show up – a lot. You need to engage with your industry in every way possible. It would be best if you could attend industry events, conferences and seminars. It means you must make it your business to be at the forefront of your industry and make yourself accessible to everyone you meet. It means you need to make it such that people will be sorry if they don't get to know you and your work.

Be Proud of Who You Are and What You Have to Offer

One of the best ways to differentiate yourself from the rest of your industry is to be proud of who you are and what you offer. It's easy to get wrapped up in what everyone else is doing and trying to be just like them. It's easy to fall into the trap of comparing yourself to others and becoming a loser, which is a sure-fire way to make yourself unappealing to people and make them want to ignore you and your work. Instead, learn to be proud of who you are and what you have to offer. Be proud of your background, your heritage and your upbringing. Be proud of your struggles and your journey. Be proud of the fact that you have something to offer the world.

Give People Something to Talk About

If you want to make yourself stand out amongst your peers, give people something to talk about yourself. That means that you need to be creative in everything you do. You need to create such a memorable experience or product that people can't help but want to talk about it. You need to be so creative in everything you do that it leaves a lasting impression on your audience. You need to be so creative and original that it becomes something that people will talk about long after you've gone.

Conclusion

For an employee, being good at their job is one of the essential qualities. You won't be employed for long if you're not a good worker. However, being a good worker doesn't always mean you'll succeed in your career. While being a good worker is crucial to staying employed and keeping managers happy, it doesn't have much impact on whether or not people will want to work with you again after they leave your company. To get people to want to work with you again, you need to focus on becoming so good they can't ignore you. If you're reading this article and thinking, 'Who would ever ignore Steve? He is very famous indeed. We've got some excellent news for you! Becoming so good they can't ignore you isn't as hard as it sounds.

Use the strategies for making your company or enterprise suitable so that your customers or clients can't ignore your company's products. Keeping an eye on the competition is an integral part of any business. It's even more critical in a crowded industry, where the attention of potential customers is at the highest premium. The key to staying ahead of your competitors is to understand their business and find ways to set yours apart from theirs. You should position your company as being distinct from your direct competitors. If you follow such strategies, your company will rise above the noise of the crowded marketplace and become something special to your target audience.

It would be best if you made yourself known amongst your peers and industry leaders. You can do this in several ways, including committing to constant improvement, networking like crazy and developing a signature skill. You can make yourself stand out in many ways, but they all begin with a commitment to excellence in everything you do.

Chapter 18

GROWTH BEGINS AT THE END OF YOUR COMFORT ZONE

I grew up a lazy boy shunning discomfort whenever it presented itself. I was extremely happy to stay in my comfort zone. I was not too fond of physical activity and loved eating and sleeping. This crept into my life even after I joined the Indian Police Service. I was deeply ensconced in my comfort zone. As a result, I started developing a pot belly. It looked awkward when I wore the uniform. But still, I couldn't drag myself to the gym. But, after some time, when people started staring at my paunch, I couldn't stand myself, broke free from my comfort zone and started running. Once I stepped out of my comfort zone and started running, I started feeling good, my confidence returned and I rapidly started reducing weight.

Similarly, I had always wanted to acquaint myself with the crypto world, but I remained within my comfort on the pretext that I didn't even possess basic knowledge of it. I, therefore, hesitated to challenge myself to master it. Eventually, when I saw an ad for a DeFi course on YouTube, I stepped out of my comfort zone. I registered for the DeFi accelerator course the London Real Academy offered. I had to shell out nearly 2.5 lakh rupees for a four-week course. But I am happy that I didn't allow resistance in the form of my comfort zone to stop me from doing so because I completed the course successfully, and now I know a great deal about the crypto world. So, getting out of one's comfort zone may seem daunting initially, but once we stir ourselves out and show up, we eventually succeed in growing out of it and gaining momentum in life.

Have you ever felt like you weren't achieving your full potential? Everyone can realise their dreams, but it often requires leaving their comfort zone. Growth begins at the end of your comfort zone; it's a place of unknowns and self-doubt, but it's also the birthplace of success. It's where you can push yourself to try something new, take risks and create a new path. It's a place of growth, self-discovery and potential. It's a place where you can challenge yourself to become the best version of yourself. So, if you're ready to reach new heights and unlock your potential, it's time to venture out of your comfort zone.

There is a saying that comfort is the enemy of progress. When we are content with a certain level of success or knowledge, we tend to stay in that space and avoid the risks that come with pushing ourselves to the next level. However, growth only turns on at the end of our comfort zone. When we challenge ourselves to go beyond what we already know and do, we open the door to new possibilities and opportunities. By taking risks associated with leaving our comfort zone, we can discover strengths and abilities we never knew we had and develop skills that will aid us in future endeavours. By pushing ourselves further, we can become more confident and resilient and hone our creativity and problem-solving skills. Ultimately, growth begins at the end of our comfort zone. Only when we leap into the unknown can we realise our full potential.

Growth is an essential part of life, and it can be challenging to achieve growth without pushing ourselves out of our comfort zone. We often find ourselves stuck in our routines, unable to break away from the relaxed state we've created. However, the rewards can be invaluable if we are brave enough to step outside of our comfort zone. By leaving the safety of the familiar and embracing the unknown, we open ourselves to a world of possibilities and new opportunities for personal growth.

Everyone has a comfort zone, but sometimes getting stuck is easy. Stepping out of your comfort zone is hard, but it's necessary for success and growth. It requires a shift in mindset – you must stop being afraid of failure and start embracing the challenge. Taking risks and pushing yourself beyond the familiar is hard work, but the rewards are worth it. When you bust out of your comfort zone, you open yourself to new experiences and possibilities. You can develop new skills, create valuable connections and discover hidden talents. You'll also gain confidence and self-esteem, which can lead to even more opportunities. So if you're feeling stuck, take a step back and ask yourself how to push yourself to do something that scares you. Whether speaking up in class, starting a new business venture or anything else, pushing yourself out of your comfort zone can lead to excellent results.

Growth Begins at the End of the Comfort Zone

Whether you're in the midst of a significant life transition or just taking stock of your life, there's no denying that growth begins at the end of your comfort zone. However, it's not always easy to recognise where this zone lies. You might find yourself limiting your growth or allowing discomfort to prevent you from taking risks. Here are some tips to help you identify where you're at.

Defining Your Discomfort Zone

Defining your discomfort zone is a challenging process. There are some things you can do to help you get started. The first thing you need to do is make sure you understand how you feel about discomfort. Some people get afraid of uncertainty, and it can be terrifying. Understanding the difference between being scared and feeling uncertain will help you deal with uncertainty. Another thing to remember is that discomfort is a normal part of life. It depends on how we wire our minds and body to handle stress. The good news is that discomfort can lead to growth, too. You can get more comfortable with the discomfort by practising and experimenting.

One of the best ways to get comfortable with discomfort is to start small. It may be something as simple as driving a rental car. You can know your tolerance level and learn to adjust your performance. You may experience anxiety and doubt when you do something new, which can be good, but you must remember to stay comfortable. It can be scary to step out of your comfort zone, but it can also be an exciting opportunity. If you are in a career that is not fulfilling, you may be reluctant to change. You might be afraid of failure or disengagement. However, if you want to improve your career, getting a master's degree within five years can help. To expand your comfort zone, you need to write down your goals. You can then set S.M.A.R.T. goals – or Specific, Measurable, Achievable, Realistic, and Timely. You must also set aside time to write and think about what you want.

Fear of Failure Is Just Another Word for 'Lessons Learnt'

Even though most people are terrified of failure and equate it with discomfort, it is still an essential part of the human experience. Failure is an inevitable part of life. It's a good place outside your comfort zone. Fortunately, it is also an opportunity to learn and grow. For instance, failure is an opportunity to learn about your strengths and weaknesses. It can teach you what not to do, how to ask for help and how to deal with frustration. It can also force you to realise your priorities, eventually leading to success. One way to overcome your fear of failure is to focus on the lessons you learnt from your mistakes. If you can learn from them, you will have a stronger foundation to build upon. The other important thing is finding people who will help you move on. The next time you have a problem, you should reach out to someone you trust and ask them for help, which will get you back on track and keep you from sabotaging yourself. If you are afraid of failure, you will probably never do anything you've always wanted to do. Your fears may stop you from taking risks, leading to increased depression and anxiety. The most important thing to remember is that failure is part of the human experience. You can learn from it and succeed, but you cannot avoid it. Failure is a signal that your dreams are worth pursuing. The best way to conquer your fear of failure is to focus on the opportunities it presents. In short, failure is the mother of all successes.

Making the Most of Your Comfort Zones in Your Life

Getting out of your comfort zone can be difficult, but it's crucial to personal growth. People often stay in their comfort zones because they feel safe and experience low stress levels. However, they miss out on new experiences and risks. Getting out of your comfort zone can help you expand your horizons, build confidence and better understand yourself. When you are afraid to step out of your comfort zone, a mindset of fear and uncertainty may be holding you back. The programme in your brain may be assuming the worst. However, considering the best-case scenario, you can move forward with your goals. One of the most compelling reasons to push boundaries is that it increases flexibility. As you get used to challenging activities, they become more natural, allowing you to respond better to life's stressors. You will also be more adaptable, which can lead to a greater appreciation of life.

Another reason to step outside of your comfort zone is that it will make you more creative. As you push yourself to do strange things, you will release a store of untapped knowledge and resources in your mind. Getting out of your comfort zone can also help you develop leadership skills. If you're afraid of public speaking, you may want to start attending a local Toastmasters club. This way, you will practise speaking up during meetings and see if you can master it. Other examples of getting out of your comfort zone include taking a new route to work or trying a new restaurant. These small changes can make a big difference in your personal and professional life.

To Grow You Have to Get Out of the Comfort Zone

Having a growth mindset means stepping out of your comfort zone and working through any tension points you might be experiencing. You'll learn how to start networking in a way that is comfortable for you and how to avoid the things that break you down.

When it comes to success, sometimes it's necessary to push yourself beyond your comfort zone. That doesn't mean taking unnecessary risks but taking calculated risks and stretching yourself to grow. When you step outside of your comfort zone, you open yourself to new opportunities, experiences and perspectives. It also forces you to confront your fears and doubts, which can be daunting but ultimately rewarding. Of course, having the right mindset is essential when pushing yourself outside of your comfort zone. It's not easy, and you're bound to face obstacles and failures. But with hard work and determination, you can overcome these challenges and succeed. It's also important to stay focused on your goals and not be deterred by any setbacks. Ultimately, pushing yourself outside your comfort zone is the only way to grow and reach new heights of success. So if you're looking for a challenge, why not push yourself a little. You may be surprised by what you can achieve.

Everyone has a comfort zone they like to stay within, whether it's the same routine, job or even place. But if we stay in our comfort zone for too long, we can become stagnant, missing out on opportunities to grow and succeed. That's why pushing ourselves to step outside of our comfort zone and take risks is essential. Stepping out of our comfort zone can be daunting, but it's often the only way to reach our full potential.

It would be best if you had the right mindset to break out of your comfort zone. It's important to remember that it's okay to make mistakes and that failure is a part of the learning process. You must also be willing to put in the hard work and dedication to reach your goals. With the right attitude, you'll be able to take on any challenge and see it through to the end.

The rewards of pushing yourself outside of your comfort zone are worth it. Not only will you be able to reach your goals and find success, but you'll also have a more positive outlook on life. So why not challenge yourself today and start getting out of your comfort zone? You never know what amazing things you can achieve!

Chapter 19

HOW TO APPLY DISNEY'S MOTTO TO YOUR LIFE

There's nothing more magical than a visit to Disney. The company's theme parks are full of fairy-tale castles, talking animals and characters who make dreams come true. If you've ever visited one of the parks, you know there is something special about every aspect of them. There is a specific saying at Disney called 'The Disney Way'. It's a guiding principle for employees everywhere, regardless of their position. New employees get a copy of the motto on their first training day to ensure everyone understands the slogan.

Disney's motto is 'Keep Moving Forward' – something the company believes we should apply to every part of life. Let's explore how we can apply Disney's motto to our life.

What Does Disney's Motto Mean?

There are many different ways a person can live their life: they can be kind, they can be cruel, they can be generous and they can be selfish. Disney's motto is a way of living that promotes kindness, generosity and optimism. It is a motto to follow if you want to be a good person. It's a motto of optimism and perseverance that people can use in many situations or life challenges. It is not just about trying harder but also about trying smarter. It's almost always looking for ways to improve yourself and the world around you. It's about being optimistic and taking the best possible action in any situation. It calls for us always to move forward in life and make the most out of every day.

How to Apply Disney's Motto to Your Life

We can apply Disney's motto to all aspects of our life. We can use it to make better decisions, work towards our goals and even help ourselves stay healthy. Disney's motto is a great way to come up with new ideas for ways you can improve your life. You can also use it to help you stay motivated and focused on your goals. For example, if you're trying to lose weight, you can use Disney's motto to help keep you motivated. You can remind yourself to keep moving forward and that simply trying harder is not enough. As such, you can try new things and experiment with different ways of staying healthy. If you're trying to get ahead at work, you can use Disney's motto to help you make better decisions. You can remind yourself that you can't stop moving forward no matter what happens during the day. As such, you must ensure you're always making the best decision no matter how challenging the situation. If you're trying to become more positive, you can use Disney's motto to help you stay positive regardless of what life throws at you. You can remind yourself that you must keep moving forward and that nothing can stop you from trying to be your best self.

Remain Confident in Your Abilities and Decision-Making

When faced with a challenge or when something goes wrong, it can be easy to start doubting yourself and your abilities. As such, you might begin to stop moving forward and instead you might want to curl up in a ball and hide away from the world. You might want to give up altogether and let the world pass you. However, Disney's motto teaches us that we can't do that. We can't give up, we can't hide and we can't let ourselves drown in self-pity. Instead, we must keep moving forward and try to make the best out of any situation. We must take responsibility for our actions and solve our problems.

Keep Moving Forward Regardless of Obstacles

At some point in your life, you might encounter a significant obstacle that prevents you from moving forward. You might have a health problem that prevents you from working as you usually do, or you might not be sure what you want to do with your life. As such, these obstacles can stop you from moving forward and be detrimental to your progress. When you encounter an obstacle in life, it's easy to give up and stop moving forward – it's easy to feel like you don't have the strength to keep going. However, Disney's motto teaches us that we can't let a problem stop us from moving forward because the pain will never disappear until we deal with it.

Take Care of Yourself and Celebrate Every Victory

Disney's motto encourages us to keep moving forward but also reminds us that we must take care of ourselves along the way. You can't just keep moving forward without ever stopping for a break or without ever celebrating your victories. When you achieve a goal or something goes well for you, you should take the time to celebrate and appreciate yourself for what you've accomplished. You can keep moving forward much longer when you take care of yourself. You don't risk burning out so quickly if you always make time to celebrate your small victories and your more significant achievements.

Conclusion

The Disney company has another famous motto to guide their business practices. It's also known as the 'big red shoe' principle, referring to the bright red shoes worn by Mickey Mouse in his first film appearance. This principle is used by all businesses under the Walt Disney Company umbrella, including ESPN, ABC and Marvel Studios. There are many mottos that we see every day, but few of them have the staying power of the one that we can find on almost any piece of merchandise from any Disney Park:

> Above all else, keep your friends close and your enemies closer.
>
> – Opus

Disney's motto is a great philosophy to live by. It's an optimistic philosophy that helps you stay focused on your dreams while ensuring that you don't forget to take care of yourself. We can apply Disney's motto to all aspects of life. Whether you're trying to make better decisions, solve problems or stay positive, Disney's motto can help you make the most out of every day and achieve your wildest dreams.

Chapter 20

HIGH-VALUE MAN

Kevin Samuels, a famous Black online image consultant, is reported to have coined the phrase high-value man, which today refers to a man of means and influence. A high-value man epitomises masculinity, charm, leadership and sophistication. Such a man is a man of means and power, loved by women, revered by men and moves gallantly through life's challenges with courage and pride.

High-value men are perceived to be more attractive and have more personality traits that make them desirable. They typically have excellent social skills, good body language and charisma that can benefit them in many ways. While these men may not necessarily be rich or powerful, they usually are more attractive. They have more access to resources than average men, which can translate into several benefits for the high-value man, such as an easier time finding romantic partners, a higher likelihood of being hired for a position and more opportunities to advance within an organisation. However, it is essential to note that there is no one way to become a high-value man. There is some variation in exactly what makes someone a high-value man. It may be down to physical appearance or personality traits rather than money or power.

A high-value man is not needy. He is detached and does not seek validation or approval. Instead, he wants to lead by example, be a source of inspiration and demonstrate his value through his actions rather than relying on words. He doesn't need anyone else's approval because he knows he is enough. High-value men are genuinely independent and are not afraid to be their authentic selves to attract the right woman.

From our childhood, we depend on external validation to enable us to find out if we are doing well in life. Whenever we accomplish something or do some excellent job, we tend to look to our parents to congratulate us and pat us on our back. We also expect them to praise us when sharing our creations and grades in school. All this in a way may be necessary because it helps us to work with others and collaborate when we enter adulthood. However, it becomes a problem when we count solely on external validation as a measure of success and stop listening to our inner voice to decide how we are doing.

When we depend exclusively on external validation, we stop ourselves from doing many things. We may stop ourselves from expressing our authentic selves, fearing what others may think of us. We may also alter our thoughts or beliefs based on others' feelings rather than what we believe. Most importantly, we might stop ourselves from creating in a way that feels true to our identity. We live in an age of technology, causing social isolation and intensifying our need for external validation. Social media especially gives one an instant dopamine hit when someone likes the post, and destroys one's confidence and mood if one gets trolled or doesn't get likes.

The more we lean on external validation in our lives, the more it can lead to a feeling of disconnection from ourselves that can leave us aggrieved and disappointed. Depending on others' approval can leave us feeling depressed and cut short our potential. Turning to others constantly to feel good is harmful and unhealthful. We could self-validate better by turning inwards instead of seeking approval from the outside or reframing our negative thoughts.

When we aren't sure we are enough, we seek external validation. We hunger for others to tell us that what we are doing is good or that we are accepted. We must work on our relationship with ourselves to enhance and love ourselves. We often criticise ourselves. If we peek within with kindness and understanding, we start to improve our relationship with ourselves. We will stop looking outside to determine how we are doing.

We must reflect on our past achievements often for our well-being. We tend to focus on the future and lack in our lives, which makes us feel more disenchanted with ourselves, the antidote for which is to stop in order to take note of all the small achievements we have had so far. When we stop and take note of all the small accomplishments, we realise that we are doing better than what our mind leads us to believe. We see how far we have come. We remind ourselves of all that we have learned and, in the process, catch a glimpse of how much we have grown.

Most of us tend to seek validation, and the need exists in almost every one of us. In the process we abandon our rights, endure abuse and are forced to seek compromise with others to keep the peace. When we win a prize, get a dream job, obtain a promotion or earn a medal, we can't wait to share it with those we love. We want to validate our wins and celebrate them with those close to us.

People become people-pleasers, because they seek validation from the outer world. Nice guys are nice to the world predominantly because they want to be liked and accepted. The more they put their power energy in the outer world, the more they lose it. A high-value man has high value because he is completely himself. What do I mean by that? When he talks to a girl, he is not thinking of getting rejected because he doesn't need her. He is looking for a good time to enjoy her company, not to impress her head. She holds little to no power over him. Remember, we lose our value when we give our power to the outer world. Therefore it is we who are giving the outer world any bribing power or manipulation opportunity. If we refuse to get sold, they can't bite you no matter how much they have. A high-value man is simply a man's ability to fulfil himself without needing anything external. A modest amount of value is completely mental. It is a person's energy and self-image that gives others a signal as to how to treat them. So in simple terms, it is detachment. This is the predominant ingredient in a high-value man's energy.

He's detached from outcomes because he knows there is an unlimited supply of everything in this world – enough women, money opportunities to go around, enough friends to not need to bend the knee to one person or job. He values his freedom above all else because *freedom* is detachment from all sorts of bondages in this world. And the paradox is when a man has himself detached, his chances of failure also diminish. The more he is detached, the more he seems to get it. The more open he is to losing a woman, the more open he can love her; and the closer she is to him, the more carefree he is about money and the more money and wealth he seems to make. That is the greatest paradox to our human mind, but not to the divine mind. The divine mind gives you more focus, so when you desperately try to get someone to love you, you are focused on them not loving you. Hence the divine mind looks at your energy of lack and gives more of what you're focused on. This is why the better it gets, the better it gets. A man who has a woman can easily get more attention from other women. A rich man gets bigger and better opportunities to amass even more wealth. Why? Because they are not lacking. A man who has a woman has no lack of women friends. And a man who is rich gets more money. Simply because the man who has more of something does not have the energy of lack so he is automatically detached from the outcome.

Detachment is akin to an abundance mindset. You can only detach from outcomes if you have a mindset that there are infinite outcomes. So I will get what I want one way or another Because these external things only help you express the innate value you have within all along. Just stop trading your value with lack. That's all, the opposite of lack will automatically manifest so long as you remove your attention from any lack. And then, the paradox comes into play. The more you let go of things, the more they come to you and the more carefree to become in your interactions. The more you detach from trying to make money desperately, the more your mind presents you with easy ideas for making money. Remember, lack is what gives the other world buying power to buy your value in return for bread crumbs. If you don't feel the desperate need to have something, you don't need to buy it. And you can only operate this way when you let go of any lack and become detached; then we're talking amendments all that you want. Remember, I am not saying that you stop desiring things, but the opposite of desiring things with detachment means that is coming from a place of abundance and devoid of lack. You can desire to have a beautiful girl in your life, but know that there are billions and billions of them; you can attract one without the desperate need for her to complete you or raise your value that nothing outside of you will because we're the source, the outer world is a reflection. Your energy is what brings people, circumstances and opportunities into your life. You feel insecure about people who come into your life to validate; you feel poor circumstances will happen in your life to validate this feeling. If you feel whole, the world will ensure you have everything that reflects wholeness. You see the paradox, the more you hold yourself, the more it's added to you, the more you feel and complete yourself, and the more it's taken from you. And this is why nice guys finish last. And high-value men seem to have such a huge polarity between the haves and have-nots. So to express your high value, start detaching yourself from outcomes and enjoy the process. Start enjoying the process of talking to a girl when you are not trying to get her. She comes to you by her elbow. When you desperately try to get her, she feels repelled. When you desperately try to be liked, you try hard and you become creepy. But you will seem charming when you're just yourself without any insecurities in the background. That is all there is to it when you value yourself rather than deriving your value from the outer world. You express the energy of the high-value man.

A high-value man's world revolves around his axis. He doesn't look for someone's permission to do things in life. His drive and his world come from inside him. He has his worldview and sticks to it by disregarding all the chaos of the outer world. He stays focused on one thing till that one thing gets done. Elon Musk may help you paint a better picture in your mind of what it means to disregard the chaos of the world and stick to the so-called insanity. A man of low value looks for others' opinions and advice on what he is trying to do. Hence he fails even when he is highly ambitious. His own family may not stand with him. A high-value man does not seek validation for his ideas. That is why low-value men can never come up with something exciting. The people discussing their ideas are most likely the naysayers who do not see the possibilities and therefore get discouraged and get their ideas shot down. But high-value men know how to capture and steward their ship with firmness and passion. If they fail, they try again. They drive themselves by educating themselves. They learn from the winners by reading their books and by following the leaders who have made it and gaining all sorts of knowledge regarding their passion by never looking back.

And once they are on course, the right people will join them to push them. They develop their drive and lead from within to detach from the masses. A high-value man does not identify himself with the groups. He gets deeply immersed in his world, and he sees the world through his lens. His lens could appear broken to the masses, so it is only natural for him not to identify with the mentality of the mass. Thus he seeks answers and follows his curiosity. You can guess such a man will end up in totally different circumstances than the masses, perhaps quite wealthy. So the first thing you need to become a high-value man is to divorce conformity. Stop trying to fit in with the folks who want to complain and blame the world. When you break this lens, you see your true worth and what you are capable of. And a high-value man has high value for the very reason that what he has to offer is rare. And if you're like everybody else, then you will be valued like everybody else. All the traits that make you look like you need something outside of yourself to make you feel valued rob a person of his value. A high-value man is honest with himself and has eliminated the weeds hindering his growth. Because, by the very definition of value, a person's value declines when he feels not enough and looks outside of himself to feel content. He is not to be mistaken as a loner, antisocial, high-value or lousy boy because these individuals also try to cope with their inner inadequacies by acting out a certain way. A high-value man revolves around his axis, and others revolve around him, like planets revolving around the sun, generating their gravitational pull. He becomes attractive, not a chaser, as he magnetises everything towards him.

Not to say that he becomes arrogant and does not even listen to others but always values others' advice. A high-value man is attractive because he is not chasing money and fame. It is all just a by-product. A high-value man who is driven and works continuously on himself cannot get shaken by the outside world. A man like that doesn't have to brag by showing his Ferrari, Gucci or Jimmy Choo to ladies. His whole being screams of high value and dependability. And like the moth drawn to the flame, the entire world will get attracted to revolve around his axis. Just be cautious of all the low-value behaviours we have adopted and detach from them. When you become conscious, the low-value behaviour will start losing its power. Stand tall and put your chest out. You're going to have everything inside to become a high-value man.

A high-value man does not need you to validate him because he is already highly valued. A high-value man is not needy. He is detached and does value himself. He doesn't require you to tell him that he's excellent. He knows it, and so do others. No minor roles exist in a high-value man's personality because his character gets set in stone. He figures out what he wants and how to get it. When he sets his mind to it, he has the confidence and self-esteem to know he can attract women. He can also be open to others and accept them for who they are without judging them or trying to change them. A high-value man will not make you feel small because he appreciates your uniqueness and personality. There are many ways to become a high-value man. First, you must learn to set boundaries, which means you must know when to say no. You must also know when to let go of unhealthy relationships and toxic people who bring you down. Lastly, it would help if you surround yourself with positive people who inspire and support you. To attract a high-value woman into your life, becoming a high-value man is essential.

Chapter 21

HIGH-VALUE WOMAN

Getting to be a high-value woman is possible, but it is important to have the right traits. Basically, a high-value woman is one who understands her worth. She knows that she is special, that her feelings matter and that she deserves to be happy. In addition, she knows how to treat herself with care and love. She knows that she is capable of taking on the challenges that will come her way.

A high-value woman does not play games or try. to impress men with her looks. Instead, she focuses on her own journey and puts herself first. She knows that making herself happy will make others happy. This allows her to forgive those who hurt her. A high-value woman also knows that her feelings matter, and that she can learn from the things that hurt her. She knows how to express herself in a way that is truthful.

What Makes a High-Value Woman

Unlike many women, a high-value woman doesn't operate from a place of neediness or a need to prove herself. Rather, she knows that her needs are essential to her happiness and that she can achieve happiness and love on her own terms.

High-value women are full of sexuality and femininity. They value expressing feelings, thoughts and opinions, and they know how to express themselves. They know how to care for themselves physically, emotionally and spiritually. They value the power of compassion in the world and know how to make others feel good.

A high-value woman has a heart of gold. She knows it is impossible to make others happy without making herself happy first. She knows she will not be able to find true love unless she first finds happiness in herself. Rather than getting wrapped up in a romantic relationship, she finds joy in her everyday life.

A high-value woman isn't afraid of getting rejected. She takes risks to achieve intimacy. She knows that her worth is based on her own self-respect and her ability to be vulnerable. She knows no one should be treated poorly and that she should set boundaries in her relationship. She doesn't allow others to make her feel bad. She knows she can hold her own in a relationship even if it doesn't go the way she wants it to go.

A high-value woman knows that she is worth the effort she puts into making herself happy. She knows that if she does the best she can, she will succeed in any situation.

Traits of a High-Value Woman

Having high value in your life means being strong, confident and emotionally fearless. It means being able to hold your own despite the actions of others. It means you are not afraid to speak your mind.

A high-value woman knows her worth is beyond physical appearance. She knows she is worthy of love and compassion. Moreover, she is aware that ignorance is a disease. Ultimately, she knows she can hold her own in any situation.

When confronted by others, a high-value woman doesn't shy away from saying what she thinks. She speaks from her heart and from authenticity. She also listens to others with compassion and empathy.

She doesn't play games or manipulate others to get what she wants. A high-value woman has no problem with setting healthy boundaries.

Habits of a High-Value Woman

Having a growth mindset means that a woman enjoys learning and is willing to improve herself. This is a powerful attribute that will lead to a positive attitude. Developing these traits can help you become a high-value woman.

High-value women have a strong self-awareness and are aware of their shortcomings. They are self-reliant and take care of themselves. They know how to handle their emotions and how to validate their feelings. They also know what their priorities are and how to fulfil them. These traits make them attractive to men.

High-value women also take their time to get to know a person. They have a positive attitude and don't engage in drama. They are also good communicators. They know how to initiate quality conversations and maintain them.

Low-Value vs. High-Value Woman

Often men find themselves paired with low-value women. These women are typically intimidated by ambitious men and do not have a lot of financial resources to help them live a life of luxury.

Women who value themselves are responsible and take care of themselves. They take time to exercise, eat healthy food and take care of their appearance. They are self-aware and work on repairing any wounds in their past.

While the term 'high-value woman' is used in reference to a woman who is independent, self-reliant and strong, there are many qualities of high-value women that are not associated with this description.

One of the most important traits of a high-value woman is her ability to recognise when love is just not right. A high-value woman is not afraid to walk away from a toxic relationship, and she isn't afraid to express her feelings.

Conclusion

Choosing a high-value woman will not only bolster your ego, it will also enhance your overall well-being. These women aren't narcissists, but rather self-aware and receptive to your best interests. They have an understanding of the male–female dynamics, and they will appreciate the homage paid to their masculine counterparts. The best part is they're not in need of a man to be their personal sex doctor.

It is a well-known fact that males and females have a natural balance of testosterone, and a high-value woman is a perfect complement to this dynamic. A high-value woman will also be a great source of novelty for males who may be looking for a second fiddle, and she may even be a natural magnet for a good man.

Chapter 22

THE LAW OF ASSUMPTION

The law of assumption stems from the idea that we constantly make assumptions about other people's motives, attitudes and beliefs. We assume that people think, feel and act a certain way and make those assumptions based on their past experiences. It's important to remember that everyone has unique values, goals and beliefs. We must therefore be careful not to jump to conclusions when interacting with others. Instead of assuming that someone is acting in a self-serving manner when they behave differently than you expect, it's best to take the time to get to know them better before drawing any conclusions. Doing so will enable you to gauge their true motives more accurately.

The law of assumption is also the idea that we assume what we observe. We assume that other people are like us because we see them acting in similar ways, and they see us working similarly. We assume that things happen for a reason or that they will turn out well. There are two key things to remember about the law of assumption. Firstly, it's an automatic human tendency. You see someone act a certain way and automatically assume they're like you. Secondly, you must be aware of your assumptions and how they might affect your life. Trying to take back control by being aware of your assumptions can help you make better decisions and take better care of yourself.

The law of assumption, which I will be mainly focusing here, is a philosophy put forth by Neville Goddard. Goddard, born on 15 February 1905 in Barbados, was a metaphysical teacher. He taught the law of attraction through speeches on television, radio, books and live seminars. He asserted that what we assume to be true we call into our reality. The law of assumption uses imagination as a trigger for realising our dreams and aspirations. It declares that what we can imagine we can create.

The law of assumption is a means of manifesting wishes by holding a state of mind and the feeling that those desires, wishes and aspirations have already been fulfilled. Goddard clarified that achieving a desired goal has everything to do with one's state of mind rather than mere action.

According to the law of assumption, your life manifests your persistent assumptions. For example, if you deep down believe you don't deserve large sums of money and don't feel worthy of a lavish income, your life will make you toil for money. You will have to work hard for a minuscule amount in return. Construction workers and agricultural labourers work hard for daily wages that are just enough to cover their daily expenses. It is very difficult for them to assume a life of wealth and luxury, so they are stuck in such a life.

Similarly, if we do not love ourselves and assume we are unlovable, the law of assumption will keep one away from genuine love and relationships. Goddard taught the essence of the law of assumption almost a century ago, but this keeps happening naturally in our lives because our assumptions get out pictured. Without realising this truth behind our manifestations, we tend to give credit to myriad other reasons or to a series of events that brought about the manifestation, making us oblivious to the real cause of the phenomenon, which is our assumption. A man who many women love will appear a certain way to others. People will attribute his looks, money or charm to the cause of his success with ladies. The same is the case for a rich man. No one will believe the cause of his success is his assumptions.

If you successfully apply this law in your life, it will completely change you. Still, sometimes we forget or become ignorant of the real cause and give credit to outward circumstances instead of our assumptions and thoughts. We don't realise that we cannot stop using this law as this law is the law of life itself. Hence, the quality of your assumptions and thoughts will shape the days to come. That is why the more worse a life of a man seems, the more worse it gets for him simply because of his state of mind; he is probably assuming the worst and expecting the worst to come into his life. And so it is if you begin to assume the good and accept all your desires. If you feel worthy of it and encourage them in your mind, you will have them. This law cannot be put on hold or stopped. You cannot avoid the law of assumption so long as you're thinking, so why not use it properly since you cannot stop using it?

Sometimes, people unconsciously apply the law and get the girl of their dreams or manifest their dream job. Oftentimes, when someone manifests a victorious life through assumption, most people point towards the person's incredible luck. They may also declare that it would have happened anyway. Or they would point to the series of events for their success. But the person who assumes and manifests will most often become aware that they are the ones who caused it because a creator knows his creation. Sometimes change or success may come about in such a natural way that the person who made his assumption consciously or unconsciously may not realise it and believe it would have happened anyway. But it doesn't. You change your assumptions about life, and then life reflects on you. Of course, a man who has a lot of money versus a man who doesn't are completely different people. So for the law to make you wealthy, it will have to change you drastically. In your changing, you will naturally reflect the prosperity consciousness within onto your reality as the accumulation of wealth. So we should be vigilant because we can quickly get back to our old thinking habits, abuse the law and manifest terrible things in our life. We cannot stop using this law. So we may use it well.

Here are some practical steps for applying the law to find what you want. You must be very clear about what you want. If you are confused, then you manifest confusion. So define what you want clearly. Then put yourself into a relaxed passive state called the alpha state – a sleeping meditative state in scientific terms. Sit or lay down. Be as relaxed as you can be. Now imagine a scene that implies fulfilling your desire, a short 10–20-second clip in first-person view. Imagine someone dear to you congratulating you on your wonderful wealthy life, your mother or a best friend hugging you or being genuinely happy for you. Feel yourself right into that scene. Make the scene as real as possible in your mind, as though it is happening right now. The passive state will help you feel it real in and out. Now repeat the scene over and over again till you feel as though it is happening right now. And as you feel the satisfaction of it, fall asleep in that state. It is best to practise this 30 minutes before bedtime to easily fall asleep with your wish fulfilled if you successfully impress your subconscious mind with this method. You will wake up the following day completely fulfilled, as though you have manifested your desire fully.

If you wish, you can repeat it as many times as you want, or you can let it be after feeling satisfied. And then, a series of events will unfold that will lead you to fulfil your desire. The change you experience will depend on how massive the desire or dream was. If you want millions, you will have them, but not in the current version of you; you will have to switch your identity to become the person to whom it is natural to have millions or be worthy of it. That is how this law works. You could affirm your new assumption each night or whenever you feel like it.

Joe Vitale, a star in the movie *Secret*, repeatedly affirmed by repeating this – I am earning a lavish, steady, dependable income doing something I love with ease. As a result, his revenue increased tenfold. Shankar, a businessman, affirmed that the girl by name Radhika whom he loved wouldn't be able to live without him. His affirmation came true. So techniques do not matter. You can use whatever method you like or no method at all. Just be aware of your assumptions, change them to how you want them and stick with them. Persist in the new assumptions; as I warned you earlier, you will suddenly change your reality. So be careful about what you assume. As this law can bring good or bad. It has no preference.

If you want something and persist, it will happen, and you will change. That is, why don't just say you want millions. Say you want a great income doing something you love because you might get millions but hate your work. And it might make your life miserable. The law will get you what you want, and you might not like how it will do it. So be careful. Imagine what is excellent and beautiful and look away from all the negative things, and don't give any attention to the useless news and drama of others. It all influences your assumptions, and you will manifest them in your life. Again, you cannot stop applying this law. You might as well use it to get what you want and have a great life. So do it intentionally and choose positively.

Chapter 23

THE POWER OF 'OM' CHANTING

I never thought much of chanting 'Om' until I decided to give it a try. I soon realised that chanting 'Om' could be a powerful way to bring peace to life. Every time I chant Om, I experience a sense of spiritual joy that fills my body and mind with positive vibrations. Chanting 'Om' has also helped to reduce my stress and anxiety, as the vibrations of the chant help to relax my body, mind and soul. I now make it a daily practice to chant 'Om', and I'm so glad I did. It's been a game-changer for me, and I highly recommend it to anyone looking to bring more peace and harmony into their life. Whether you recite a mantra or chant 'Om', its vibrations will bring you peace and tranquillity.

The vibration created by the chant brings spiritual joy like no other. As I chant, I feel a sense of peace washing over me, and my worries seem to fade away. The chant has also helped me to become more mindful and aware of my thoughts and feelings, allowing me to make healthier choices. The energy of the chant is like a balm to my soul, and I am grateful for its calming presence in my life. So, take a few moments out of your day to chant 'Om' and see how it can transform your life. Chanting 'Om' is a spiritual practice that can bring immense physical and mental benefits. So, if you're feeling overwhelmed or stressed, why not try it? You never know what kind of transformation it might bring.

If you're a seasoned 'Om' practitioner or someone who's just started chanting the mantra, you would most likely be aware of the benefits it can bring upon you. But if you are not, you are probably wondering how to chant 'Om' the right way and also wanting to know of its benefits. You will find all that discussed briefly here to help you reap the benefits of chanting 'Om'.

Meaning of 'Om'

'Om', a word derived from Sanskrit, means 'to hear'. It is one of the most powerful sounds in the universe. Using 'Om' can help nudge your spiritual growth. It can also improve your body posture, eyesight and spinal strength. 'Om' is a seed mantra, meaning that it is the first sound that emerged from the emptiness of the universe during its creation and is the highest level of vibration. It is a sacred syllable used by many spiritualists around the world. Using 'Om' can help change your negative behaviours. 'Om' represents God in everything. It is also the seed of all creation. It is said to symbolise the beginning, the middle and the end. The symbol itself has three curves. The upper curve represents the subconscious mind, the middle the present and the bottom the dream state.

Power of 'Aum'

During an 'Aum' chant, the chanter could touch the cosmic vibration of the Supreme Sound. That to me sounds like a miracle, especially when it comes to healing. The 'Aum' or 'Om' mantra has the magical power to make your mind, heart and body feel good. Plus, the ability to bring clarity and peace. And it can even help increase metabolism and decrease blood pressure. Chanting the 'Aum' is believed to enhance neuroplasticity, which allows your brain to change and adapt to new conditions. It can also help regulate hormonal imbalances, improve mood and reduce stress. A study published in 2011 investigated the effects of 'Aum' sound on the vagus nerve, a part of the autonomic nervous system. It showed that chanting the 'Aum' syllable can increase the supply of cosmic energy into the body, which also helps in treating depression. There is a belief that chanting the 'Aum' syllable would lead to a more profound spiritual experience and chanting the 'Aum' mantra with other people can produce positive vibrations.

The Correct Way of Chanting 'Om'

Whether you are chanting a word or a complete phrase, you should know some crucial rules. 'Om' chanting should be done comfortably, and you should not be in a hurry. It is also important to relax your jaw muscles and breathing. To chant 'Om', you need to sit in a comfortable position. It would help if you are cross-legged, with your feet firmly on the floor. You should also be in a position where you can feel the vibration of the sound in your body. It would help if you do not think about what you are chanting but stay focused on the feeling of the sound. It would help if you chant 'Om' silently, but you can also chant it mentally. Elders say that silent chanting is the highest form of chanting. Using the same position you would for regular meditation, you should inhale and exhale the sound.

Benefits of Chanting 'Om'

'Om' can help you meditate, strengthen your body and increase concentration. It is also helpful for individuals suffering from chronic stress, depression and anxiety. It also helps pregnant women to have a calm foetus. The word 'Om' stimulates the vagus nerve, which controls heart rate and stomach acidity. It also increases digestion and improves visual scanning and psychomotor speed. Chanting also stimulates the supramarginal gyrus and middle frontal cortex. 'Om' chanting has the power to help you connect with your inner self. 'Om' also cleanses negativity from your mind. It also reduces stress, confusion and imbalance. It also improves the immune system. The 'Om' syllable creates a sacred vibration that cleanses the aura and nourishes every cell in your body. 'Om' also helps you sleep better. It induces a deep state of meditation. It also creates a calming effect on the brain and central nervous system. It also improves memory and concentration. It is also helpful for individuals suffering from sinus problems.

Scientific Evidence of the Power of 'Om'

'Om' chanting is a way to reduce stress, anxiety, depression and negative affective states. However, there is not yet a solid scientific base for this claim. Despite this, scientists are investigating the effects of 'Om' chanting. Shirley Telles, a neurophysiologist at the Patanjali Research Foundation in Haridwar, conducted a study to investigate the effect of 'Om' chanting on the processing of negative images. The researchers used a two-way repeated-measures ANOVA to analyse the data. They compared participants' resting EEG signals and measured their heart rate and respiration. They also evaluated participants' weight, blood pressure, peak expiratory flow and stress levels. The participants were then divided into two groups. The study group was given 'Om' chanting instructions. They were required to hold their breath for a period of 64 seconds. They also had to chant the mantra silently. Afterwards, questionnaires were given. The researchers analysed the time–frequency data to identify regular spacing and harmony. In addition, they observed an irregular waveform, which they attributed to unsteadiness in mind.

'Om' for Good Health and Peace

'Om' chanting has many benefits for both the mind and body. It may also help reduce anxiety and improve concentration. 'Om' chanting also promotes a healthy lifestyle. It helps reduce stress and improves blood circulation, which will help your body fight off diseases. We can do 'Om' chanting at any time of the day. A study done by Macquarie University found that chanting 'Om' has some health benefits. It increases alpha waves in the brain, which are associated with relaxation. It also improved theta waves associated with concentration and deep sleep. 'Om' chanting can also create internal vibrations, which help balance hormones, heart rate and blood pressure. The 'Om' syllable also helps with pain relief. 'Om' is said to be in harmony with the universe's vibrations because of which it activates all the senses as the sound is linked to the crown and third eye chakras.

Vibratory Nature of 'Om' and Impact on Chakras

'Om' chanting is a powerful practice that can positively impact your chakras and your health. It is a simple way to clear your mind of negative thoughts and cleanse your body of toxins. It also has long-term benefits for your body and mind. The best part about 'Om' chanting is that it is not just a ritual but also a powerful tool for improving your health. One of the best things about 'Om' chanting is that it helps you to connect with the divine. The sound of 'Om' invokes all that is on the deepest level; hence, chanting the sound will help one raise their energy levels.

How Many Times to Chant 'Om' Daily

'Om' is a divine word, a universal syllable that binds human beings with God at the soul level. The term represents the infinite power that created the universe.

The word 'Om' has an uplifting effect on our brain. It increases alpha waves in the brain, which is associated with relaxation. When you chant 'Om', you can experience an immediate calming effect in your mind and body. It clears your airways, clears your sinuses and strengthens your vocal cords. There is proof that it can increase concentration and boost one's immune system. The mantra should be pronounced high in tone and with great devotion.

Conclusion

Chanting the sacred syllable of 'Om' (Aum) has been a game-changer in my life. Whenever I feel overwhelmed by stress or anxiety, I chant this ancient mantra for a few moments. The vibration of the syllable creates a deep, spiritual joy that helps to bring peace into my life. It's like a magical reset button for my mind and soul. I've also noticed that chanting 'Om' has positively affected my relationships. It helped me to stay centred and focused, making communicating with the people around me more accessible. I'm more patient and understanding and can better connect with those around me. Chanting 'Om' has been a blessing in my life, and I would recommend it to anyone looking for an easy way to bring peace and joy into their life. If you're feeling overwhelmed, take a few moments to chant 'Om' and let the vibration wash away your worries. You won't regret it!

Chapter 24

THE POWER OF SILENCE

As someone constantly surrounded by noise, the power of silence was an alien concept to me – until I discovered its transformative power recently. It all started with a simple practice of sitting in silence for 10 minutes each day. At first, I found it hard to stay focused and be still, but eventually, I could feel my inner stillness flooding me with peace unknown. Then I began to understand the value of silence and how it can bring us closer to bliss. I learnt that it's not about the absence of sound but about the presence of peace because I can listen to my thoughts, find clarity in my emotions and connect with the world around me without words. I began to uncover my true self and discovered a newfound fondness for the power of silence. Now I value moments of stillness and resort to them to nourish my soul. Silence has transformed my life, and I'm so glad it has become a part of my daily routine.

Working for the police department, I used to think that being busy and productive was the way to success and fulfilment. But when I started cultivating the power of silence, I was amazed at what it could do to my life. By taking time out of my day to be still, I found an inner stillness and peace that I hadn't felt before. The inner rejuvenation and bliss that I experienced were incredible. I felt more energised and motivated and was more present and mindful of my thoughts and actions. I discovered I could use my newfound inner stillness to make better decisions, gain clarity and insight into my goals and develop deeper relationships with others. Silence had not only transformed my life but also enabled me to reach success and joy never imagined before. I realised that the power of silence could help anyone live in peace, harmony and joy. So, whether you are trying to find a quiet place in a noisy world or need to find some solitude and focus, silence is the most potent tool you can use. Silence is also a powerful way to communicate with God.

What Is the Power of Silence?

Practising silence is valuable, but most people have misconceptions about its power. There is an essential distinction between silence that is imprisoning and silence that is liberating. Silence can be a very effective tool to use in communicating with others. It provides time to think and gives your mind room to process information. In addition, silence helps to calm the body. When your body is calm, natural biological processes can heal it. Silence also allows you to relax, which is crucial to making rational decisions. In addition, silence can help you deal with anger.

When you are tumultuous, finding a place of quiet is not always easy. It takes planning and support to find the calm you need. There are many places to find quiet, from monasteries to hills and flotation tanks. One of the best ways to find quiet is to walk in nature. You may even want to spend some time in a garden or sit in a sensory deprivation tank. In addition to being a powerful tool, silence can also be a gift. It can help you speak up for yourself and let others know how you feel. You can also practise silence as a mindful meditation practice.

Why Is Silence the Most Potent Tool?

Silence is one of the most powerful communication tools you have. It benefits both mental and physical health. The right amount of silence can help reduce stress and improve focus. It can also help you to think about the situation in a more thoughtful way.

Silence is a form of communication that we overlook. But it's a powerful tool we can use in various social situations. If you are in a leadership position, you can use silence to motivate others. If you are a salesperson, silence can help you communicate your knowledge and understanding of the product or service you are selling.

In addition to being a great sales tool, we can use silence in various ways. Using a pause to command an audience's attention can be an effective strategy, mainly when using a phone. Silence is also a great way to defuse anchors. Silence can often defuse situations when a client or prospect is threatening or aggressive. We can use silence as a way to convey confidence without revealing the actual reason for being confident. A good salesperson knows how to use silence to get more information from a customer. They can also use this technique to show that they are considerate of their customer's needs.

Why Is Silence More Powerful Than Words?

Using silence to communicate may sound counterproductive, but it can be very beneficial in certain situations. Silence allows you to think through your feelings and improve your overall well-being. Silence can also be a sign of respect in some cultures. Silence is also an excellent way to avoid confrontation. When angry, they tend to say things they wouldn't usually say. By staying silent, you may save a relationship. An excellent example of using silence is using appropriate body language, which includes eye contact, which is crucial because it shows that you give the other person your full attention.

Another example of using silence to communicate is an ad hoc method, which may include text messaging, e-mail or even telephone conversations. While these may be more convenient, speaking when you are truly ready is the best strategy to save you from saying something you will regret later. Another example of using silence to communicate would be to use it as a filter. Silence may sound counterproductive, but it can be beneficial when dealing with anger or grief.

The Power of Silence in a Relationship

Using silence to communicate in a relationship can be helpful. It can help you to clear your mind and focus on yourself. It also allows you to learn more about your partner's feelings. In addition, it can help you to avoid conflicts. While some might think that being silent is a sign of weakness or a lack of confidence, it is not. It can be a sign that you care.

If you are having problems with your partner, you may feel like you don't have the power to fix things. However, being silent can signify your willingness to let your partner work on themselves. If your partner isn't ready to change, it may be difficult for you to get the relationship back on track.

Sometimes, you might need to be more assertive with your partner. If this is the case, you may want to practise being more proactive. By communicating your feelings, you can ensure your partner knows that you understand. However, if you are still unsure what to say, you can try finding out your partner's feelings by allowing yourself to begin a conversation. Acknowledging your partner's feelings will validate them and open the door to a larger conversation.

Silence Is Needed to Drown Out the Noise of the World

Whether you're trying to nap or blaze the trails, noise can be a big deal. And while it may be easy to dismiss a room full of yelling brats as an assault on the senses, there are ways to keep the peace. Fortunately, more than a few people dedicate themselves to keeping the peace. One such individual is the Norwegian explorer Erling Kagge. In 1993, Kagge made history by becoming the first person to cross Antarctica alone for 50 days, and during his trek, he learnt a lot about the power of silence and the importance of making time for it in our noisy, hectic lives.

Another worthy contender is an all-rounder of a yeoman named George Michelsen Foy. Foy was known for his penchant for nihilism, but he was also on the hunt for the best and brightest. When Foy got worried about all of the toxic noise in his life, he set on a quest for absolute silence. Fortunately, he had the misfortune of meeting several notable luminaries along the way. Among Foy's group of friends, one, in particular, is the explorer mentioned above, and it's no secret that they bonded over the good old days of yore.

Silence Is the Language of God

Quite simply, silence is the language of God. Unlike words, silence is a way to bring you closer to the divine and is a necessary component of any serious academic or intellectual pursuit. Silence is a compelling medium and is the perfect solution for many problems. Aside from the apparent reason for being heavenly, it also serves as a conduit for intellectual formation, communication with other people and a robust network. It can also be a companion in the oneness of all things. The best way to get the most out of silence is to take it in for 15–30 minutes daily. You can do this by settling into a quiet corner and closing your eyes. Becoming aware of your breathing and exhaling is also a good idea. These practices will help you develop a more self-aware, conscious mind. Aside from its apparent benefits, silence can also be a boon to spiritual formation. By observing the art of breathing and exhaling, you will gain insight into your mind and learn to be more present in the here and now.

Conclusion

Sometimes the cacophony of everyday life – the honking traffic, screeching trains, shouting passersby and other detestable sounds punctuating our daily routines – makes us feel that we should somehow escape all the toxic noise which we hear even in the dead of night. Author Michelson came to think of the city as having this monster breath. When all the noise started to get on my nerves and began to freak me out, I got myself forced into the sanctuary of silence. I never knew the power of silence until I tried this myself. After being in a rut for months, I decided to try it and see if it could help me find some inner stillness. At first, it wasn't easy to stay quiet. I was used to the hustle and bustle of my daily life, and suddenly being alone with my thoughts was overwhelming. But I stuck with it, and soon enough I was able to find a sense of inner rejuvenation. As I stayed quiet, I found myself letting go of my worries and stresses and feeling a sense of bliss. I was able to better focus my energy on things that mattered to me and develop a deeper connection to my inner self. Silence can be a powerful tool, which has undoubtedly changed my life.

Chapter 25

THE SOUL IS STRONGER THAN ITS SURROUNDINGS

The soul is stronger than its surroundings. William James' words hold true not just in the case of our physical body but it is also true for our spiritual body. Our souls are more robust than anything that can come against them. The more we walk in love, the more we can rise above whatever comes our way. When we fill our minds with hate or anger, it takes a toll on our bodies and our spirits. It destroys us from within. Forgiveness is one of the most powerful tools in dealing with pain and suffering. If we can forgive others and ourselves, we can move forward, no matter what happens in life. By forgiving others and ourselves, we begin to heal. This process can take time, but it is worth every moment of effort.

The soul is the essence of who we are. It is what gives us our personality, our sense of self and our emotions. The soul comprises many parts, including our personality, values, beliefs and emotions. These parts all work together to help us express who we are and make the right decisions for us. One way to keep the soul healthy is to care for your body and mind. Eat a healthy diet and get enough rest. Exercise helps to keep your body strong and can improve mood and sleep quality. Taking care of your brain can also help keep your soul strong. There are also things you can do to support your soul at work. These include respecting others, doing your best and caring for yourself.

The soul is more robust than its surroundings. This is a sentence we can interpret in many different ways, but there are two key things to remember here. First, the word 'soul' can refer to a person's consciousness or true self. In other words, it can refer to your true identity and the part of you that exists on a level beyond your physical body. It can also refer to something more profound, like your essence or true nature. Second, the statement is saying that your soul is more potent than everything else around you. When you compare yourself to other people, circumstances and even the world around you, you will find that your soul is always stronger than anything else. As a result, you will be able to overcome any obstacle and achieve success in life.

Chapter 26

WHEN YOU BLAME OTHERS

Are you more likely to own up to your mistakes or play the blame game when something goes wrong? Most of us are sharp to point fingers and play the blame game. It's much more comfortable to blame others or circumstances than to take full responsibility for our actions. It's also easier to blame others for our actions rather than take a deeper look at why we made the blunder and face possible consequences, at work or in personal relationships. Blame shifting takes less work and is less emotionally taxing – at least in the moment.

'Blame is a defence mechanism', as it helps us preserve our sense of esteem or pride by evading awareness of our issues. It protects us from criticism, negative consequences, attention and whatever we are afraid of or helps us stay in denial that we are in fact the ones who are making mistakes. We usually use this as a weapon when we are in attack mode. Sometimes deep-rooted negative experiences from our childhood predispose us to act that way.

Blaming others feels good, which is the hidden payoff of the victim mentality. I used to blame everybody but myself. And it felt good. It relieved me of responsibility and put all the fault onto the world. But that's not what happens. The baggage of blame does not leave us. We never indeed will be able to leave it. Unless we take responsibility, that baggage will remain on our chests forever. That is what happens with most of the coping mechanisms of the ego. They feel relatable and comfortable at the moment. They make us feel familiar. And the price we pay for it is that we never change. We will never be fully able to let go of the baggage of the past and the burden of blame. When I realised my happiness was in my hands, I dropped the luggage of guilt.

The victim mentality cannot survive in the light of self-love because you will not allow yourself to feel bad because of things that happened years ago. You will prioritise your peace over what has happened or what will happen. It will make you feel satisfied with yourself. Victim mentality is rooted in the lack of the world that's not giving you what you want. The universe is against you, and so on. We already know that what we focus on stays in your reality. So whatever you feel yourself to be a victim of continues to make you its victim unless you drop this baggage. Become uninterested in the narrative of that victim. Inside you tell it that I don't care about what happened, what is happening and what will happen. Because what no longer serves me is no longer a topic of interest to me. You refuse that narrative, and you will feel liberated. It will make you insanely free. You will feel as though nothing can truly bring you down because you're bulletproof, simply because you have taken the responsibility of making yourself happy. So the external world slowly fades away into the background.

You start to look at things differently. You begin to choose the best for you and others. And trust me, it is the best feeling in the world. In the past, I used to blame God for all my misfortunes because of the teaching that God is the most merciful and benevolent, but real-world experience has made me realise that this is not quite how it all works. Terrible things will happen under the umbrella of the most loving and kind God, which is why I started looking for answers about how reality works and God works. And guess what? It made sense because infinite will precisely give us whatever we focus on. Words don't matter. If you pray for more money while you are focused on lack, you will get more lack.

Infinite responds to your feeling or state of being, not your words. So we got what we were focusing on, which is lack. So there is no one to blame but ourselves, but let's change the word 'blame' to 'change'. There is no one to change but the self. It is knowing from application and experience. You can run around and try to change people and circumstances, and you will get nowhere. Nothing really will change unless you change yourself. Then you become dangerously free, almost imperturbable. Because once you have the cheat code to this life, you can have anything, experience anything and be anyone by simply changing your inner world. That gives you complete dominion over your life. So you're truly the expression of the infinite in the state of being because this is the whole point of this existence.

But blame separates us from our true selves. We become little human beings with no control whatsoever, which is a sad state to be in. I have been there, and it almost crushed me. You can't seem to find any way out. Because how can you if the infinite is against you? So it plays out exactly that way in your reality, and there is no way out. The only way out is again to change yourself. Try to encourage the thoughts of freedom in your mind. It is the antidote to a victim mentality. Freedom is our most innate desire. We want freedom above all else, and we seek freedom from the victim mentality as well. We cannot see it in that state of being in lack, but when we take responsibility for our life, things begin to work. You start getting the things you always wanted. And those things aren't even that important to you anymore because the freedom you feel inside you and your body and mind is the best manifestation of this mindset shift.

Now, how do we deal with blamers? When someone starts blaming us for everything, we should critically scrutinise the thought that we are being blamed for everything. Write down various ways in which you are being blamed and how it is affecting your life. Weigh the pros and cons of dissociating from that person or making the other person aware of it. Instead of bottling up the hostile feelings rising inside us, we should seek out a trusted confidant to help us sort out our thoughts and feelings and consider ways to avoid such toxic relationships in the future. Further, one should take time for introspection and look out for patterns which are attracting hostile behaviour from others. After identifying the patterns if we change our prejudices or judgements about them, we will find that their behaviour will change to match our assumption about them.

Blaming others makes people around us start resenting us or even walk away from us. Another outcome of blaming could be a loss of communication or trust. People who get accused may avoid communicating to prevent having to experience getting blamed. When you point a finger, five fingers point at you, leading to a loss of self-esteem, feelings of worthlessness and even permanent emotional damage. Depending on your situation, you might end up losing friendships, relationships or jobs. Blaming could also lead to loneliness and abandonment as the people you blame could leave and never return.

Finally, believing we are victims will take us nowhere and prove harmful to our growth. If all we do is believe we are a victim, we will have nothing to change or improve. In other words, we will believe that we are perfect the way we are and will not change. The circumstances or the people we blame have neither any clue that we are blaming them, nor do they care. We turn out to be prisoners of our loathing and grow into resentful old individuals. It may be convenient to blame others for our unhappiness because it delivers us some instant gratification. Still, by repudiating our faults, we are in the long run stopping ourselves from achieving our true potential.

Part II

HEALTH AND NUTRITION

Chapter 27

A DIRTY SECRET TO A HEALTHY SKIN

Vidyanka religiously exercised every day. She was a teetotaller and never smoked cigarettes. Being married to an influential bureaucrat, she took good care of herself. She always began her day with green juice, ate clean and led a stress-free life. But her skin experienced frequent breakouts; it always appeared to look dull, blemished, red and dry. A close look at her skin revealed clogged pores with junk waiting in there to get squeezed out. Vidyanka tried expensive cleansers, creams, sanitisers and special treatments like pore strips, face masks and facials to treat her skin woes. Her skin stayed the same. As lifestyle changes did not help her, she felt bored and frustrated with life. Looking to bring back some excitement in her life, she joined her friends on a trekking expedition. The following day into the trek, she discovered that she had left her toilet kit behind with expensive cleansers and soaps. Fast forward to the end of the hike, which came about two weeks later, it felt terrific for Vidyanka to notice that her skin condition had considerably improved and had gained a certain glow. After initially attributing it to salubrious conditions in the hills, she subsequently realised that the soap- and cleanser-free days were the real magic behind it. At the end of a soap-free year, as Vidyanka scanned her flawless complexion, her mind began to ruminate on the torment the deep dark red spots, the painful bumps and the frequent cysts had caused her. A year had rolled by for her without 'I can't leave the house today' blues creeping on her.

The skin of an average human adult covers an area of about 2 sqm or 22 sqft. It is the largest organ in the body. There are over 1 trillion microbes on an individual's skin. Our ancestors developed this symbiotic relationship with the microbes, which continues to this day and has become part of the human skin ecosystem. Our physiology has evolved intimately adapted to the microbial exposures that hold sway since the hunter-gatherer days, contrary to today's clean-living conditions. Human body odour is potent, but our hunter ancestors probably used water, natural herbs and scents beneficial to the human microflora to stay clean and odour-free. Unfortunately, modern hygienic living, sanitisers, environmental pollutants, other skincare products, chemicals and antibiotics are throwing our skin microbiomes out of balance. When we throw our skin's ecosystem off-balance, pathogens appear to take command, wreak havoc and cause many skin conditions.

In cities and towns, there's been a growing prevalence of allergies in the last couple of decades, and experts affirm that it is on account of an obsession with cleanliness. The hygiene hypothesis suggests that the increased prevalence of allergy disorders and many chronic inflammatory disorders, including those of skin, correspond to a changed pattern of exposure to microbes, owing to economic development and changing lifestyles. In 1873, Charles Harrison Blackley noticed that hay fever, which pollens cause, was uncommon among farmers who had frequent exposure to pollen. The skin is not just a physical barrier to the outside world; it is intelligent. There is increasing evidence that lack of exposure to germs that were part of our evolutionary history has led to an unfavourable upregulation of our immune system, contributing to chronic inflammatory conditions. Studies at the Medical College of Georgia have found that babies in households with multiple pets have fewer allergies at age six or seven not just to animals but also to ragweed, wild plants, ticks and mites.

Our skin is a window to our overall health. Like our ancestors, we should not be afraid to get dirty. During the central part of human history, we have worked in natural environments and interacted with the outdoor world by contacting soil regularly. We are deficient as we have lost touch with Mother Earth. Therefore, we should spend enough time outdoors doing activities like gardening and camping to get natural exposure to a variety of soil-based microorganisms. Sitting in a park, hiking and camping can also help our skins to come in contact with soil microbes. Learning to harness things that make our hands and feet dirty will help us radiate a healthy, beautiful glow. A Swedish study has found that in families that wash their dishes by hand, allergic disease in children was less common than that of families who used a dishwasher.

Further, wearing clothes made of natural fibres seems to hold a natural balance of bacteria, while clothes made of synthetic fibres cause imbalances in skin's microbial ecosystem. Washing clothes in a washing machine may only help the pathogens and not kill the harmful bacteria.

Studies further reveal that washing and drying clothes in the sun is good for the skin.

During my childhood, I loved playing in the mud. I have fond memories of playing in the rain and rolling in the puddles to the extent of being reprimanded and punished by my parents. Scientists have now confirmed that playing in mud is healthy. Today's sanitised world contributes to increased levels of childhood allergies and asthma. Exposure to dirt and germs work to fuel a child's immune system. Therefore, kids and adults reap enormous benefits from muddy, messy play. Recent research has shown that dirt contains *Mycobacterium vaccae*, a bacterium that is known to bolster the immune system and increase the levels of the neurotransmitter serotonin in our brain, which soothes, calms and helps us relax. Scientists say regular exposure to dirt may help reduce a kid's susceptibility to depression. Playing in mud makes one happier! Playing in the soil also induces children to appreciate the environment and connect with nature. A bacterium called *Nitrosomonas eutropha* found in dirt and untreated water can live on the skin, but we wash it away with soap and shampoo. This bacterium serves as a built-in cleanser, deodorant and immune booster by feeding on the ammonia in our sweat and converting it into nitrite and nitric oxide.

I recently experimented to see how my skin felt if I stopped using soap for three weeks. Over the years, I've spent thousands of rupees on cleansers, scrubs, moisturisers and so on, only to discover that water is all I need to keep me as clean as a whistle! Monsoons are not a good time to go soapless as the heat and humidity make a perfect breeding ground for pathogens to generate odour. Having plunged into the experiment, I showered with no soap or shampoo. I found it extremely challenging, especially when I came home after a long run soaked in grime and sweat. I later learnt that sweating contributes to healthy skin bacteria. A week later, I noticed a significant difference in my skin from not using soap. When I had to attend a wedding function during the weekend, insecurity set in. I worried if I would stink. It turned out that bathing with water sufficed for removing body odours. Although I didn't smell like a bouquet of fresh flowers, neither did I smell like a goat, nor did I wear a stench. In just one week, my skin felt transformed from a patchy, scaly dry skin to a certain softness. I thought I was the only one doing this experiment for a moment. When I checked it out on the web, I found that thousands of people had already gone soapless. I found some of them had gone soap-free for more than a decade. When I discovered that several companies abroad, such as Mother Dirt, Tula and so on, had launched microbe-nurturing and live bacterial culture-containing skincare and haircare products to populate our skin with beneficial microbes, it amazed me to no end.

There are several natural alternatives or holistic methods for cleansing skin without harming the microbial balance. As recently as 50 years ago, in India, people used green gram and red gram flour mixtures as cleansers. The classic cleaner that kept Cleopatra looking so beautiful was milk. A trip to the kitchen will reveal several natural cleansers hiding in your pantry. Oatmeal, soap nut, lemons, sugar, honey, besan (chickpeas), turmeric, yoghurt, tomatoes, orange peel, cucumber, papaya, aloe vera, Fuller's earth, baking soda, almond oil, olive oil, coconut oil, eggs and so on are some of them. Shikakai is an excellent hair cleanser, and coconut fibre is an excellent scrubber for the skin. Most natural cleaners also provide vitamins, minerals and enzymes. The bacteria seem to love them. These soap substitutes are inexpensive, time-tested and have proven to clean and improve the skin's overall texture and appearance naturally without disrupting the fragile ecosystem of the skin.

Today, an average consumer in cities spends approximately two hundred and fifty rupees on skincare daily while using 515 synthetic chemicals daily to eradicate dermatological concerns. Why are we in such a germ-phobic culture? Why can't we take care of the bacteria on our skin and keep them happy and harmonious? Why are we ravaging our skin microbiome by applying various lotions and cosmetics to cover our skin blemishes to get that glow? The concomitant microbial rage to our insane skin disruptions gets manifested as flares, breakouts, psoriasis, rosacea, eczema and random bouts of insensitivity. The power of the gut, skin and brain axis and its role in skin health is mind-blowing. The skin thinks and interfaces with the bacteria and the brain. It's a two-way street, and our skin is a repository of cells equivalent to 16 human brains. The soul of any radiant and healthy skin depends on creating a beneficial symbiosis between the secret world of microscopic bugs and the human skin. Learning to love the bugs in our bodies and protecting our microbial comrades to harness their full potential is the best skincare recipe ever. Our ancestors knew this secret. Vidyanka accidentally stumbled on this dirty secret. Given a choice, would you go for the soap-free lifestyle of our ancestral hunter-gatherers, or opt for the modern-day skincare recipe containing a cosmetic cocktail of toxic chemicals? What would be your choice?

Chapter 28

WEIGHT LOSS PLAN WITHOUT EXERCISE DURING A LOCKDOWN (PANDEMIC)

It's a pandemic time. Lockdowns are in place in several countries. Binging during the pandemic is not just about Netflix. People are ploughing through the pandemic with portions and portions of food, as stress-eating and boredom are propelling them through their lockdown provisions and making people crazy worried about weight gain.

But, people wanting to lose weight during this pandemic have no access to the gyms and playgrounds as all gyms were closed due to social distancing restrictions. Although working out or incorporating exercise into one's life improves health and prolongs life, pandemic or no pandemic, one need not have to go to a gym to lose weight. People are under the misconception that the only effective way to lose weight is to hit the gym or clock miles with their running shoes. Most of us fall prey to this myth, and during regular times, we get that covetous gym membership that makes us proud! More often than not, the gym becomes one of those new toys that the infant enjoys – rattled, played, slept on and so on, only to eventually lose interest a week later! Some become the epicentre of family jokes when those gym shoes gathering dust inside the closet are spotted! Phew! Why this sigh!

The very thought of working out makes people lazy. The mind always wants quick-fix solutions. With pandemic stress already weighing heavy in our minds today, our senses tango between slouching or slogging our way to fitness! More often than not, the former wins and the latter remains compromised. It's not that people don't want a fit self – they yearn for it, but just that the challenging route makes them tired even before they get started!

Don't lose heart. You can have the cake and eat it too! What if I told you that you could shed pounds without having to enrol yourself into any gym or working out at home?! With an effective plan made of ten easy steps, anyone can lose up to 10 kg during the lockdown without hitting the gym or having to slog away at home. Yes, you have read it right, without having to hit the gym or any form of workout.

Don't believe me? This plan has had many predecessors, so you aren't my guinea pig! I have patrons who have enjoyed a visible and incredible transformation within seven days. This plan is different from any other weight loss regime because it is a sustainable option. One that allows you to follow the regime long term. Seeing the changes will motivate you to keep sticking to the regime for one more day and then another. Be it a wedding, a photoshoot or the upcoming summer season, with this plan you can make a visible impact that will tell your story!

I have put this in a simple follow-through pattern – a ten-step process. To make things easier for you and help keep track of how much effort you are putting in, I have allotted specific reward points to each step. You award the corresponding reward points to yourself with every step you accomplish. The goal is to earn approximately 60 to 70 reward points each day. A minimum of 60 points equates to 1800 points per month! If one day = 60 reward points, then one month = 60×30 = 1800 reward points and earning 1800 reward points translates to 5 kg weight loss.

Remember, this chart is a goal. It is a motivation and driving force to achieve an end. It is not a Rubicon that one has to cross. Go slow, take one step a day and build your velocity with time. An organised mind is an efficient mind. Let me kickstart your weight loss journey with the first two stages in this first part.

LOSE WEIGHT DURING A LOCKDOWN WITHOUT EXERCISE: PART 1

The first step is to chew a morsel 25 to 30 times, which will entitle you to 15 reward points. Most mothers tell children not to 'gobble' their food but eat more slowly. And there is so much truth to the old saying that chewing your food 32 times will make you lose weight. Most of us believe that we are chewing our food adequately. Sadly, the truth is an average human chews just six times before gulping down a morsel. Research has proven a direct correlation between chewing and weight gain. When we binge on food or eat too fast, the brain does not have the time to realise the radiation of hunger. That makes us eat more than required, hence the weight gain. When you eat slowly and chew properly, you eat only the amounts needed by the body as the brain gets sufficient time to register the signals of contentment from the stomach.

Horace Fletcher, 'The Great Masticator' and an American health guru, followed the mantra 'nature will castigate those who don't masticate'. His advice was to use every tooth to chew a mouthful, i.e. 32 times per morsel. The man himself chewed 100 times a minute. Fletcher, the legend known for his Yale Gymnasium experiments, touted that this mastication method could open the door to hidden strengths.

Not convinced enough? Think this then. When you chew 30 times, you give proper attention to each food particle. You break it down into smaller pieces. These tiny particles are more comfortable to digest when they reach the stomach. Why? Because the more time a morsel spends inside your mouth, the more saliva is released. Saliva is the secret ingredient that breaks down food. The more you chew, the better the digestive process and the less weight gain. Processed foods cause weight gain because they require least amount of chewing. Think apple slices instead of applesauce. Follow the great Mahatma's counsel: 'Chew your drink and drink your food'.

The second step is using a smaller plate for meals, entitling you to 10 reward points each day. Everyone prefers a dish filled with food, not one with a smaller and, most probably, sufficient portion. At mealtimes, people often tend to pile up their plates with food, irrespective of the level of hunger they experience. Such a phenomenon is all too common! According to a recent study in the *Journal of Applied Experimental Psychology*, most people feel satisfied only when filling 70 per cent of their plates with food. Why do we do this? It is because we subconsciously anchor the serving size to the scale of the plate and not to our desire. Thus, people end up eating a lot more than what they need to sustain themselves! When it comes to eating less, experimenters have long understood that a simple way to cut calories is to use a smaller plate. Presuming that an average dinner is 800 calories, this easy modification would result in an approximate weight loss of more than 5 kg in a short time.

Therefore, the second step of the diet plan circumvents weight gain by employing smaller plates, like half or quarter plates. As long as they are not full-sized plates, you are good to go. Imagine the difference between food that takes 70 per cent on a full plate with the 70 per cent quantity of food that will fill a half/quarter plate!

If you are sceptical and speculate that a smaller plate means second or more servings, then rest easy. The first serving will be more than enough to satiate the hunger for most people. There might be a few who might crave a second or third serving, but if they wait for two minutes before they go for it, they find that the craving has vanished. The study I quoted above also details an experiment conducted on over 200 households in Syracuse for four months. The results proved that the members of families that got smaller plates had lost at least three pounds more than those that used larger dishes. You can drop 9 kg in a year just by changing plates, according to the 'Small Plate Movement'. To achieve this, you may start with a dish between 9 and 10 inches in diameter. I will outline the other eight steps in the pages to follow.

We have a mindset rampant today that is obsessed with weight. While I believe it is great to concentrate on your body's health and well-being, there is an obsessive nature to weight loss that is highly prevalent in the society that powers this – 'You are not good enough' notion that gets thrust on us. Loving our bodies and knowing that we are perfect enough is the absolute remedy for any weight loss hardships we are facing. In this regard, activities like meditation can help us love our bodies and get in touch with that infinite, eternal stream of energy that pulsates inside all of us.

When we love ourselves and align ourselves emotionally and spiritually, we will automatically eat the right foods in the right amounts and stop eating when we are full. All we need to do is listen to our body and eat things that make us feel good, vibrant and alive. When we love ourselves inside out, we will automatically reach for foods that are in alignment with our spiritual and emotional self, which in turn will make us feel so right and light that we will never have to go on a diet ever again.

LOSE WEIGHT DURING A LOCKDOWN WITHOUT EXERCISE: PART 2

Welcome back to the second instalment of the diet plan. In the first part of the diet plan, I outlined the first two steps out of ten steps where I challenged your body to shed those extra pounds that's always sagging around without setting foot inside a gym! Let me do a quick recap before we continue to lose all that accumulated fat and get fit. This diet plan that I have designed to help one lose weight during the current lockdown without ever stepping into a gym envisages ten steps. In the forgoing part, I detailed two steps that would earn you 25 points if you implemented them, and in this instalment, you are being exposed to three more, which could make you an additional 18 reward points if executed each day. As pointed out earlier, each of the ten steps has a certain weightage or reward points. To achieve the weight loss goal of 5 kg per month, one would have to earn 1800 reward points in 30 days, which would require one to score a minimum of 60 reward points daily. After having skimmed through the first part, you now know why it is critical to eat from a small plate, chew your food 25–30 times before swallowing and take small breaks between servings. Now, let's dive forth and propel this incredible quest onward.

The third step in this diet plan helps you earn 5 reward points if you open a 'Food Journal' and make entries of all that you are devouring during the day, every day till the day you achieve your weight loss goal. Pandemics are stressful times. Staying cooped up at home during stressful moments may mean raiding the refrigerator frequently as the body craves high-calorie and high-sugar snacks and junk food. These items provide bursts of energy and solace during stressful times. We can easily fall into the trap of overeating during such times unless one consciously tracks what one is eating in a journal to make one mindful of what and how much to eat. We don't realise that it's often the tiny in-between snacks, a small nibble here and a little bite of chocolate there that's potentially keeping us away from losing weight. When we write every snack we nibble on and every juice or soda we gulp down, we become more accountable for consuming. Food journals also help us uncover the unhealthy habits that keep us from losing weight. When we become mindful of our eating patterns, we realise how and where we are going wrong and eventually control uncontrolled binging. Research reveals that people who journal what they eat lose twice the weight as those who don't believe in the journal's power. We also get spurred to eat by distinct triggers, which we may not know. Food journals help us recognise such triggers. For instance, some unconsciously reach for food when they watch TV or while driving or feel angry, bored, sad, happy or nervous. Journals help us identify such triggers and make us aware that we unconsciously reach for food. They hold us back from indulging in mindless eating habits at the nick of time. Journals can also help us know whether we eat adequately from each food group and get good fibre, minerals and vitamins from fruits and vegetables.

The fourth step, which can help melt all those unwanted fat, is intermittent fasting. Implementing intermittent fasting each day will earn you 10 reward points. This strategy could prove game-changing if religiously followed not only for weight loss but also for boosting immunity. Intermittent fasting was a way of life for our ancestors for about 2 million years. They ate when they had food; when left with nothing, they go out of caves looking for food. Our bodies have evolved on a sporadic diet, allowing human bodies to burn fat and build immunity.

Strengthening one's immune system is critical during a pandemic. Fasting is one of the best ways to boost immunity and achieve weight loss simultaneously. As pandemics are stressful times, fasting could cause cortisol levels to rise, but the protocol I am proposing here is the mildest version of intermittent fasting. It's a version that is easy to follow with the slightest discomfort. Intermittent fasting can improve immunity because fasting effectively regulates the immune system by diminishing the number of inflammatory cytokines stimulating an inflammatory response in the body. Fasting also stimulates autophagy, which inhibits viral infections and the replication of intracellular parasites. The body therefore could probably elicit a similar reaction to the COVID-19 virus. The process of autophagy is part of the innate immune system that utilises pattern recognition receptors to identify viral cell invaders. Catabolism during fasting also helps the body get rid of intracellular pathogens.

As already mentioned, the intermittent fasting protocol I am advocating is straightforward, putting the slightest or almost no stress on the body. We fast after our dinner until we partake in our breakfast the following day. The intermittent fasting I am recommending does not constrain your food choices, nor does it limit the quantity of the food you can consume. All it requires is that you advance your time of dinner to either 18:00 or 19:00 hours and delay your breakfast the next day a bit to either 08:00 or 09:00 hours so you are on a fast for 14 hours, and your eating window gets limited to 10 hours in which you can eat with no restrictions. However, eating nutrient-dense foods like fruits and vegetables and shying away from sugary calorie-rich snacks and sodas can boost your results. For best results, limit carbs to dinner and stay hydrated with plenty of water throughout the day. It's that simple. But if religiously followed, the effects and benefits are mind-boggling. After adapting to a 14-hour fast, try a 16-hour fast with an eight-hour eating window to get even more out of intermittent fasting. Just this tiny and straightforward tweak goes to bring about a host of benefits besides weight loss and improved immunity, such as decreased fat mass, reduced blood pressure, improved insulin sensitivity to fight diabetes, improved brain health, reduced oxidative damage to cells and DNA and higher autophagy for cells to repair themselves.

The reason why intermittent fasting works is that it accesses stored fat energy in our body. Some food we eat is more than our immediate energy needs and therefore gets stored as fat for later use. Insulin rises and converts the excess energy into glycogen that is stored in the liver or muscles. Our bodies however have limited capacity to store glycogen. Once the entire storage gets used up, the liver converts excess glucose to fat by a process called de novo lipogenesis. Some gets stored in the liver, and the surplus gets stored in various body fat parts. We therefore have two energy systems. The glycogen system is easily accessible but has only limited storage space, and the other is the body fat, which has unlimited storage space but is remarkably inaccessible.

When we are intermittently fasting, we exist in two states. During the eating window, we are in a fed state, which is a high insulin state, and during the fasting period, we are in a low-insulin fasted state. If we eat the moment we wake up and do not stop eating until we go to bed, we will gain weight because we are always in a fed state, and we have not permitted our bodies to access stored body fat by being in a fasted state. Being in a fasting window during intermittent fasting allows our bodies a certain amount of time to burn stored energy. That in essence is what intermittent fasting is all about and why it is proving to be a game-changer for losing weight and gaining lean mass.

Having looked at the first four steps, we have now arrived at the fifth step. The fifth step is a straightforward but effective step, which helps you reduce the quantity of food you require to feel satiated. It will make you feel full with much less food. Following this step each day will earn you 3 reward points. This step requires ingesting a tablespoon of psyllium husk before every meal. Psyllium husk, colloquially known as *isabgol* or *ispaghula*, comes in two varieties: tablet and powder. While the pill is more comfortable to ingest, the powder form is more popular. Thirty minutes before every meal, mix a spoon of psyllium husk in 300 ml water and gulp it down. Assuming you have two main meals a day, the total comes to 600 ml water and two tablespoons of husk.

Once ingested, psyllium husk expands inside our bodies and makes us feel full, decreasing the feeling of hunger. When we sit down to eat, we take smaller portions, resulting in weight reduction. I suggest you have the psyllium husk with water half an hour before a meal because research has shown that drinking water around mealtime could hamper digestion. Small sips of water do not affect us, but drinking more than a glass can lower our digestive powers. Studies recommend drinking water either 2 hours after having a meal or 30 mins before one. The more water you drink during a meal, the lesser the quantity of gastric enzymes secreted. Over and above, by taking the husk before a meal, you give it time to absorb the water and expand further in the stomach.

Finally, every dominant religion from Christianity to Buddhism to Hinduism held the practice of fasting. For our forefathers, intermittent fasting was a way of life. They spent their waking hours hunting, gathering and trekking, and there was often only one big meal eaten when food was available. Seven thousand years ago may seem like forever, but it's a small bleep in time when it comes to human evolution. It transpires that our ancestors understood what they were doing, both spiritually and scientifically speaking. It's time for us to remember who we are and from where we have come. The act of fasting will help us quiet our minds so that our souls can speak more clearly to us. It could also awaken us and give us more natural energy, flexibility, clarity of mind and overall lightness of being.

LOSE WEIGHT DURING A LOCKDOWN WITHOUT EXERCISE: PART 3

Welcome back to the third edition of the ten-step diet plan. In the first two editions of the plan, I had outlined five steps. The first five steps, if fully implemented, would earn 43 points. This edition lists the sixth, seventh and eighth steps, which helps one score 20 points. Let me do a quick recap before we dive into the new steps. This diet plan envisages ten steps with a certain weightage or reward points. To achieve the weight loss goal of 5 kg per month, one would have to earn 1800 reward points in 30 days, which would require one to score a minimum of 60 reward points daily.

To start with, self-hypnosis is the sixth step of this diet plan. Implementing this daily for ten minutes would earn one 5 reward points. Self-hypnosis is an excellent tool for eating healthy, staying healthy and losing weight as it untangles the underlying biological or metabolic causes of weight gain. It may appear like a wacky approach to weight loss, but self-hypnosis may help us end self-sabotage, turn off cravings and emotional eating and put us on the road to our weight loss goals. Several studies show that subjects who used hypnosis lost more than twice as much weight as those who didn't. And a 2014 study found that women who used hypnosis improved their weight, body mass index (BMI), eating behaviour and even some aspects of body image.

Hypnosis is an excellent way of resolving underlying psychological problems which cause one to experience intense cravings, driving one to eat mindlessly or binge crazily at night. We keep overeating or choosing unhealthy foods because we have these automatic behaviours stored in our subconscious minds. These behaviours we cannot access consciously and change as our conditioning has imprinted this into our subconscious.

We may want to lose the flab at the conscious plane and get back in shape. Consciously we may determine ourselves to eat healthily and get back in form. We may try every trendy diet only to become hopelessly discouraged, sad and depressed in the end. We may try to change our eating habits using our willpower, but we can do so only for a short period depending on the amount of conscious effort we put into it. Despite all the effort we put into it, we will revert to the default settings.

Self-hypnosis gets to the root of your problem, whether it be overeating, craving the wrong foods or emotional eating, by overwriting the default settings in our subconscious mind and helping us transition to weight loss and healthy eating a lot easier. As our subconscious mind protects us from losing anything, it will go to any length to protect us from losing weight, but when we use self-hypnosis for weight loss, we can reprogramme our subconscious minds to allow our body to release the extra weight. As a result, our brain automatically adjusts our appetite, metabolic rate and physical energy by controlling the secretion of various endocrine glands. By giving our brain suggestions, we can change the entrenched programmes and automatically change our relationship with food to the extent that we stop feeling hunger pangs and stop binging on unhealthy foods.

A quarter of people can't get hypnotised as some brains don't work that way. For such people, meditation or visualisation can be a good substitute as it can deliver similar or equivalent results. It's impossible to visit a hypnotherapist during a pandemic for therapeutic hypnosis treatments. Still you can use apps and self-hypnosis-guided sessions or meditations available on the internet. However, the efficacy of self-hypnosis will depend on the authenticity of the trainer and the downloaded audio.

My daughter, an architect in Mumbai, wanted to know if she could have a coffee while on an intermittent fast. Drinking black coffee is perfectly all right because, as a thumb rule, the body will continue being in a fasted state when we consume less than 50 calories. One cup (240 ml) of black coffee contains about three calories and minimal amounts of protein, fat and trace minerals. Drinking coffee won't significantly disrupt our intermittent fast if we keep it black, with no added ingredients. I advise you to drink plenty of water during the fast as water helps stimulate your metabolism, rinses your body of waste and acts as an appetite suppressant. Also, drinking more water helps your body to stop retaining water, leading you to drop those extra pounds of water weight. Drinking water on an empty stomach first thing in the morning will flush out toxins and increase the body's efficiency to fight against infections. It will also help in preventing kidney stones and bladder infections.

In intermittent fasting, we planned to break the overnight fast either at eight or nine in the morning. Now let's embark on the sixth step of our diet plan. We aim at extending our intermittent fast longer metabolically but not technically by consuming a cup of coffee with a tablespoon of ghee or pasture-fed butter mixed in it. This step will earn you 5 reward points. The combination may sound unappealing, but it doesn't taste bad! Believe me. Instead of breaking your fast with breakfast every morning, have one cup of coffee mixed with either one tablespoon of ghee or pasture-fed butter. You will save time on breakfast and have a high-energy meal substitute that keeps the hunger pangs at bay till it is time for lunch. The amalgamation of coffee and ghee gives the body an injection of fat instead of carbohydrates. When the body does not have carbs on hand, it uses up the stored fat to create the energy needed. It's an ideal partner to intermittent fasting because fats in the coffee will give you a good energy boost and keep you feeling full for another two or three hours, as it will take one into ketosis. Ketosis uses fat as fuel, and many low-carb diet regimens, like Atkins, are based on it. When the body burns fat, it strips the extra calories, leading to weight loss. I have borrowed this idea from bestselling author and creator of Bulletproof Coffee, Mr Dave Asprey. A carb-filled breakfast, for most of us, is a moment on the lips, forever on the hips. It also comes hand in hand with hypoglycaemia. Hypoglycaemia or low blood sugar causes lethargy and sleepiness, which is why we feel so sluggish after a substantial carb breakfast!

It's 10 or 11 a.m., just two hours after ghee-laced coffee, when those hunger pangs begin to crop up. What do you do? Instead of binging on unhealthy chips and processed food, we can opt for a nutrient-rich green smoothie, which is the eighth step. This step will earn you 10 points.

Green smoothies are a great way to get your daily recommended serving of fruits and veggies. Green smoothies with plenty of green leafy vegetables and fruits deliver us with a powerful upswing of vitamins, minerals, antioxidants and other nutrients without bogging down our digestive system. Since we consume natural, whole foods in the most optimum form for digestion and nutrient absorption, we will have more energy to get things done and enjoy our day. A perfect smoothie should have a balanced combination of proteins, good healthy fats, complex carbohydrates, vitamins and nutrients. We may mix 20–30 grams of whey/vegan protein powder to get that extra dose of energy or two to three eggs. These smoothies make for perfect low-calorie food items while filled to the brim with healthy ingredients. They will keep us feeling full long after mealtime, making them the most excellent tool to achieve weight loss. When we make a smoothie, we have absolute control over the ingredients. We can pick and choose the nutrients we need, all the while keeping those dreaded calories out of the picture.

An even better smoothie will include components that promote weight loss by increasing the metabolic rate. Think about it; a single drink that is not only nutrient-rich and provides kick-ass energy but also enhances weight loss! So, what are these miraculous ingredients that help lose weight? Let me list them down for you.

1. Chia seeds – Full of protein, fibre, calcium, antioxidants and the wondrous omega-3 fatty acid, chia seeds will absorb all those unhealthy toxins from your digestive tract.
2. Cayenne pepper – Add just a pinch of cayenne pepper to your smoothie, and you will feel less hungry throughout the day due to capsaicin, a compound that reduces our appetite for fat and carbs!
3. Avocado – Everybody craves fat. It is a universal truth. Avocado is full of healthy fat. Consuming it sustains the craving while giving the body vitamins and minerals too.
4. Greek yoghurt – It has the highest level of proteins compared to other yoghurts that keep you full for longer! Avoid flavoured versions because they are full of sugar, not an ingredient you want.

5. Coconut oil – Any MCT (medium-chain triglycerides) oil is a superfood. It has a high ratio of healthy fats that the body readily uses as fuel for energy, which keeps the body fit and enhances weight loss.

Besides these, berries like raspberry and strawberry are good options for smoothies. They are fibre-rich and boost the levels of antioxidants in the body. For flavour, add a hint of cinnamon to the smoothie. It will keep blood sugar at an optimal level. And stop glucose from being stored as fat in the body. Cinnamon is a must for those who want to get rid of abdominal fat. Fruits and leafy green vegetables are excellent ingredients for smoothies.

Last but not least, switch to stevia. If you feel your smoothie is not sweet enough, add stevia instead of sugar. This plant-based sweetener is a natural alternative and has zero calories.

We are now almost at the end of the ten-step plan to weight loss. Getting slimmer is like a leaky faucet; it requires constant maintenance. If you follow the eight steps outlined so far every day, you can be sure you are on the right path. Besides, following the eight steps outlined so far can earn you 63 points. Switch between the steps every week or five days to keep things lively. It will keep boredom at bay. Don't forget to watch out for the last edition of this series. Be sure to hit the bull's eye for all the diet plan steps.

Finally, just as how self-hypnosis helps us break out of old habits and patterns, we can solve the mystery of life by connecting to the desires and intentions of our soul and finding the purpose of our life through spiritual hypnosis. Using techniques like soul speak and past life regression, we can explore and experience profound transformation and deep meaning at the level of our soul. Spiritual hypnosis is a vehicle through which we can navigate the unmanifest realm of existence and the nature of reality. It will help us connect to the soul and live from purpose during our time on this planet earth.

LOSE WEIGHT DURING A LOCKDOWN WITHOUT EXERCISE: PART 4

We have now reached the fourth and the final edition of the diet plan that details an easy-to-implement ten-step plan that helps one shed weight during a lockdown without having to step into a gym. To those who have followed the previous steps scrupulously, pat yourself on the back! You have done incredibly well! As you will soon reach the end of the incredible journey of saying sayonara to those extra, unwanted 5 kg.

Before we dive deep into the final instalment of the diet plan, let me give you a gist of this effective weight loss regimen. This easy-to-implement diet plan envisages a ten-step process to shed 5 kg during a month. Each step has corresponding points. Your goal is to achieve at least 60 points per day, i.e. 1800 points in a month. This equates to one losing 5 kg in 30 days! The cherry on the top of the cake? No tiresome exercises, no stressful workouts and no costly gym membership!

Here we go! To begin with, we think we are human beings, but in the real sense, we are more of microbial beings because we are host to about 100 trillion bacterial cells, so we comprise ten times more microbial cells than human cells. With 2 million genes in 300–500 different kinds of bacteria in our gut, the microbiome contains ten times the amount of genes that we have in our human genome.

The microbes in our gut play a key role in digesting the food and synthesising nutrients from our diet. The microbiome in our gut gets influenced by our diets, by our lifestyle and the microbiome we inherit from our parents, which in turn affects our mood, immune system and metabolism.

Some people despite following a diet don't seem to lose weight because gut bacteria may determine how easy or how hard it is for one to lose weight. The gut bacteria can affect how one's food is digested, how the fat gets stored and whether one feels hungry or full. Thus, healthy gut bacteria may be essential for maintaining a healthy weight.

Research in mice has revealed how gut microflora may play an important role in obesity. The relative abundance of two dominant types of bacteria – Bacteroidetes and Firmicutes – determine whether mice will be obese or thin. The authors also found that colonising microbiota from lean mice into obese mice made the obese mice thin, and vice versa. The gut microbiome plays a vital role in weight loss, insulin resistance and fat deposition. In another experiment, colonising mice gut with bacteria called Clostridium made them leaner by blocking the intestine's ability to absorb fat. The importance of faecal transplants and probiotics is now being widely investigated as ways to restore a healthy microbiota.

There also seems to be a link between the gut microbiome and the immune system. The gut bacteria probably produce many biochemicals which boost the immune system. If one immediately controls the health of the trillions of microbes living in our gut, we will not only strengthen our immune system against the COVID-19 virus but also lose weight quickly with little effort. The declining microbial diversity in our gut is a leading cause for our susceptibility to coronavirus and other pathogens.

So, a healthy microbiome can prevent potentially dangerous immune overreactions that damage lungs and other vital organs. One reason immunity decreases is because microbial diversity in our gut decreases as we age.

Besides, gut microbes are happy to provide weight loss and other health-promoting services in return for plant-based foods and healthy fats. Getting 30 grams of fibre from plant sources of different colours helps diversify our microbiota, which contributes to our overall health. The gut microbiome of overweight individuals shows dysbiosis associated with inflammation and lowered immune function. This is because of an increased extraction of energy from food.

Hence, eating a wide range of plant-based foods; use of healthy fats like high-quality extra virgin olive oil, lean meat or fish; avoiding alcohol, sugary drinks and artificial sweeteners or other additives can improve the composition of the gut microbiome.

There is ample evidence to show that dietary fibre and microbial diversity complement each other for weight loss and different positive health outcomes in humans. The plant foods consumed by us which have resisted digestion by human enzymes in the stomach are devoured by the bacteria when they arrive in the gut. That is the reason why I had suggested consuming psyllium husk in one of the previous steps of this diet plan. Microorganisms in the gut extract the nutrients, vitamins and energy from the fibres to produce various biocompounds and short-chain fatty acids which are being linked to improved immune function, weight loss and decreased inflammation.

We can also support our microbiome by regularly eating natural yoghurt and cheeses, which contain live microbes (probiotics). Traditional fermented foods made from whole grains, like idlis, dosas and fermented rice, is another option. Antibiotics have a damaging effect on our microbiome diversity. The gut bacteria also produce neurotransmitters, including serotonin, dopamine, and GABA, which regulate our mood. Researchers have discovered a second nervous system in the gut which communicates with the brain. The wellness of both our body and our mind therefore largely depends on our gut health.

Keeping in mind the clout the microflora in our gut has on our health, let us now embark on the ninth step of the diet plan in which we try to leverage the human microbiome for weight loss. Every time an individual implements this step, he or she will earn 10 reward points. This step envisages having two handfuls or 75 grams of raw, fresh vegetable salad along with every main meal. Fresh and raw vegetables are not only full of minerals and vitamins but also have a meagre calorie count. Salads add volume to one's meal along with the vital fibre that helps in digestion. When one adds quantity to a meal with such nutritional powerhouses, they will consume less high-calorie foods. The high water content in fresh vegetables will further fill up one's stomach. As a result, one will eat smaller portions of the main course. A *sine qua non* to making the salad enjoyable is to make the salad both visually appealing and tasty by garnishing it with spices and good salad dressing which tingles your taste buds.

The main meal accompanying the salad should be plant-based with minimum animal products and processed items. A 'plant-based diet' includes vegetables, fruits, whole grains, legumes and nuts as the main items, but it does not stop one from including small amounts of eggs, poultry, seafood, meat or dairy. The focus here is on eating more of the right plants, avoiding the wrong kind, eliminating unhealthy foods and moderating one's intake of healthier animal products.

During pandemics, one may always think about food because of boredom, fear and anxiety. There may be an unquenchable desire to binge on the tastiest snack at two in the night? We can put to an end to such unhealthy eating habits by adding lots of proteins and fat to one's meal. Proteins not only increase your metabolism but can also reduce your calorie intake by 400 calories per day! This diet plan also envisages combining the benefits of a plant-based diet with that of a keto diet by adding liberal amounts of fats from avocados, olives, oils, nuts, seeds, coconut, pasture-raised eggs and ghee. This diet eliminates problems of conventional keto diets where consumption of large amounts of meat, high-fat dairy and things like butter coffee can wreak havoc on your microbiome. Hence, the penultimate step in the journey to being slimmer is to load every meal with a potent mix of plant-based proteins, fats and low carbohydrates. The basic idea is to lower insulin to help the body burn more fat. Furthermore, with a lower level of insulin, the kidneys work to remove excess water and sodium from the body. This means no more bloating and that hideous water weight!

Thus, in this diet plan, I recommend 40 per cent calories from carbohydrates, 30 per cent from proteins and 30 per cent from fat with a focus on whole, unrefined carbohydrate sources and whole-food fats. For vegans, protein sources could be soy protein tofu, legumes like chickpeas, green peas, lentils and so on, peanut butter, almond butter and hemp protein. There is no dearth of proteins for nonvegetarians. However, only minimal use of animal proteins gets allowed on this diet plan. The bulk of the meal may, however, comprise whole grains and low-carb vegetables such as broccoli, cauliflower, spinach and all green leafy vegetables, Brussels sprouts, lettuce, cucumber, celery and so on. For cooking the meal, coconut oil is the best as it has MCT. Oils containing MCT fats help satiate more than other oils, plus they boost the metabolic rate, besides helping one to get into ketosis and fat-burning mode.

The last and final step in the diet plan which will fetch one 2 reward points is the practice of drinking little hot water after each meal to which we have added a twist of lemon after the hot water has been simmered with a few ginger slices, one teaspoon of cinnamon and a pinch of turmeric. The secret of fat loss is not to have your sugar levels rise after your meal. Cinnamon prevents blood sugar from spiking. One should drink this immediately after eating this meal. At this point, you may be probably shaking the head and furrowing those eyebrows. It may be because, in one of my previous steps, I had mentioned that one should avoid drinking water until 2 hours after a meal. Read through this step once again. A little cup of water is fine. Only when we drink more than a glass or two that digestive issues can arise. You might wonder at the efficacy of taking warm water after meals to lose weight. *Au contraire mon ami* – warm water spurs on weight loss as per research and studies. This is because hot water increases the speed of metabolism by increasing the body temperature. Additionally, it washes down any food particles that may get stuck in the food pipe after we have had our fill of gastronomic pleasures. The spices we have added to the cup of water will help remove any toxins from our system. They even decrease bloating, a common issue with people living in warm countries.

We have now come to the end of the ten-step diet plan. During normal times, going to the gym is cumbersome and expensive for most of us, besides it requires too much effort. My diet plan takes a hard pass on both these issues. I have based every step of this weight loss journey on scientific research and practical results. Make sure to achieve the grand total of 1800 points by the end of a month. Grab that goal and work towards your dream physique! Once there, you will be amazed to see the results. Get ready to garner admiration from all quarters! One last tip before I say adios: consistency is the key. Be consistent, try scoring a minimum of 60 points out of 75 points in the ten steps. You might in the end get blown away after seeing the incredible results.

Chapter 29

MIND-BLOWING BENEFITS OF TREE-HUGGING

Forests and wooded areas are my soul place. I was always incredibly drawn to them, even as a child, and that feeling has only amplified over the years. Every visit to a dense forest is an emotionally moving experience for me. Something about the trees is so mesmerising and touching. The silence in the depths of the forests feels like the pin-drop silence in a church before the commencement of a sermon. Answers to my problems emerge in the quiet and murmurs of a forest. When I go into a forest, my turbulent mind clears out, like the muddy, turbid water which becomes transparent once the dirt settles down. My first foray into a wooded area happened after I failed to qualify for a medical seat, which disturbed me deeply. And a strange force overtook me and sucked me into a forest near my house in Hyderabad.

Prior to this, the farthest I had ventured was to the fringes of this forest, where my buddies and I occasionally went hunting with our catapults, or discuss stories of recent movies we saw while sitting on large rocks that abounded there. But on that day the forest tugged me in. I felt no fear or apprehension whatsoever as I felt led by some strange benevolent spirit that seemed to wish everything best for me. The deeper I ventured into the forest, the more mystical and spellbound it became to me. The thick and lush canopies of the towering trees shielding the forest floor from the sun created an eeriness that would have scared me otherwise. I found dried fallen leaves embellishing the soil in magnificent greens and cheerful yellows. The woody incense from broken branches rotting and composting silently on the jungle floor rose like a vapour and filled my nostrils. The expanse of glorious trees that reached out and towered into the skies appeared to outdo one another in the demonstration of their devotion to the Sun God, who in turn, pleased by their love, seemed to shine the benevolence of golden glow on them, making the leaves of the tree glimmer and shimmer in his luminance. Then the wind blew, and the trees and leaves swayed to their tune and rhythm.

Inside the woods the soul of creation was boisterous. As if the choir composed of flora and fauna were singing the melody of creation. The crickets and sudden gusts of wind occasionally pierced the eerie silence of the woods. At one point, a troupe of shambling squirrels traversed the winding trail in front of me probably to forage. They seemed startled to see me. Then out of nowhere, a solitary songbird decided to express its joy with its unique melody, as other beaked counterparts joined in creating a symphony. The haunting melody which filled the forest air seemed like an elixir for my soul.

Suddenly, I heard some rustling noises of scuttling animals emerge from the depths of the woods, followed by the clicking of bats, the yelping of frogs and the buzzing of insects amidst the swishing of the cunningly woven webs of leaves. Instinctually, simultaneously enraptured by the sheer beauty and fear, under a fight-or-flight response, I hid behind the trunk of a massive tree and embraced it like a frightened child embracing its mother. As I held on, I felt a deep sense of peace, stillness and a sense of safety invade and anchor me to the moment's beauty. And the overpowering silence inside the forest soothed my troubled mind and gave me the answers and a perspective on life with such profound clarity that when I walked out of the forest I was convinced that God had better plans for me. Looking back and connecting the dots, I feel grateful and indebted to the forest for providing my life with a better direction and a future than I was aspiring to at that time. Had I wallowed in self-pity and disappointment, and had I made wrong choices under the prevailing mood, I can't imagine how misled my life would have been. I can't thank the forest enough for donning the role of a spiritual guide and mentor during such trying times.

Hugging a tree is a meditative experience, for when we come in contact with a tree, the life energy ebbing within us gets a taste of the life force pulsating through the tree. The trees vibrate at a higher frequency than we do. The life force of a tree is uncontaminated and not coloured with base desires, unlike that of a human. A tree, unlike a human mind, is not occupied with doing, nor is it busy hankering after possessions or restless over something or the other. A tree is always in a state of meditation and perpetual bliss. Unlike the human mind, there is no guilt, taint, anger or resentment. So when humans embrace a tree, their minds and spirits osmotically imbibe the deep serenity abiding inside a tree and leave feeling refreshed and rejuvenated.

When we hug a tree, our awareness is greatly enhanced. Our entire body is involved in this experience. Our senses awaken, positive hormones are released and our heart rate and breathing quiet down. The level of oxytocin, a hormone responsible for feeling calm and emotional bonding, increases when we hug a tree. Embracing a tree also increases serotonin and dopamine neurotransmitters, making you feel serene and happy. Holistic healing happens when we spend time in forests, a spontaneous gift of nature. All these positive changes help us feel emotionally and physically better. Trees are like humans in many ways, and we can liken their tree rings to our fingerprints. They use water like us and sweat (transpire) like us. Like humans, they too have roots, and new research reveals that trees live in communities like us. Finally, hugging a tree builds appreciation and gratitude for this outstanding aspect of nature. While we may enjoy a tree's shade, fruit or even a swing hanging from it, embracing the tree helps us connect to it more directly. Having a direct connection with the tree may also encourage us to work hard to protect trees.

Everyone loves trees. They are beautiful, natural and straightforward. And they probably have more benefits than we think. Tree-hugging is becoming popular with people who try to reconnect with nature and understand their environment better. But what is this weird thing called 'tree-hugging' anyway? Tree-hugging is also known as arboreal therapy or tree-climbing therapy. It is a type of active meditation in which you climb a tree every day to achieve a different state of mind and gain many benefits. Tree-hugging is common for anyone seeking to reconnect with nature. People from all walks of life have taken to the new craze, which has proven benefits and consequences. Climbing trees is a beneficial exercise and can help you get closer to nature, reduce stress and do much more.

It is common knowledge that embracing the outdoors and spending time with nature can bring significant benefits. Another well-known practice is standing or kneeling beside a tree with one's arms wrapped around it. This practice too has many positive benefits for your physical, mental and spiritual health. A form of yoga called arboreal yoga involves climbing trees and posing in unusual positions to complement the strength, flexibility and balance gained from holding poses on the ground. While it might sound absurd initially, there are many benefits to arboreal yoga that you won't find in other forms of yoga. And what's more – you don't need any special equipment or clothing to practise it!

Did you know that hugging a tree can also boost your immune system, lower stress and even reduce pain? There are also many mental health benefits associated with tree-hugging. Tree-hugging can help people feel more connected to nature and can bring people joy and happiness. It can also reduce stress, anxiety, depression and other psychiatric illnesses. Additionally, tree-hugging can help people with social pressure feel more comfortable around others. There is evidence that tree-hugging can promote mindfulness.

India has its historical version of tree-hugging. The Chipko movement of the 1970s, which gained traction as a way of resisting the destruction of forests, was all about embracing trees. *Chipko*, meaning 'to hug' in Hindi, reflected the movement's primary tactic of clinging to trees to prevent loggers from cutting them down. The Chipko movement got its inspiration from Mahatma Gandhi's philosophy of satyagraha. We can trace the provenance of the Chipko movement to Khejarli village – a village named after khejri trees (*Prosopis cineraria*) – in Rajasthan. The Bishnois who lived there worshipped and protected these trees because they believed the khejri trees are symbolic of purity, wealth and good fortune.

The Maharaja of Marwar, in 1730, decided to build a new palace in Khejarli village by chopping down khejri trees. Amrita Devi Bishnoi, a spunky protestor, wouldn't let that happen. She and her three daughters faced the king's soldiers by embracing the trees with their arms. The soldiers beheaded all four of them. The villagers were horrified by king's action and decided to punish his soldiers, but they also met with death punishment. The incident, later christened the Khejarli massacre, continues to inspire people and ecologists to safeguard our ecological bounty. So find a tree and cuddle it. You will feel better and be inspired to protect and conserve them.

Trees benefit humankind in myriad ways. They are an essential part of most ecosystems. They are necessary for water holding and help to filter toxic airborne particles. Trees provide shelter for birds and other animals and can help mitigate the effects of climate change by absorbing more carbon dioxide from the atmosphere. They also regulate the soil's pH level and can help prevent erosion and landslides. In addition, trees have many economic benefits, such as providing shelter, reducing air pollution, increasing property values and providing habitats for wildlife.

In addition, they can help reduce storm surges and flooding in coastal areas. In addition to their importance to ecosystems, trees are essential for cooling the air by reducing the amount of solar radiation that reaches the surface. They also provide a habitat for wildlife, and many birds use them as nesting sites. In addition, trees can reduce noise pollution by shading the ground below them and providing a windbreak in urban areas where trees can absorb some of the kinetic energy from winds that would otherwise get transmitted into people's homes. Trees are also important because they can store large amounts of carbon in their roots, which helps mitigate climate change by sequestering carbon dioxide. They also help to moderate the effects of climate change by slowing down the rate of global warming.

Nothing is better than seeing a beautiful tree in your backyard or the park next to your house. For all these reasons, taking care of the trees in your neighbourhood is essential. By planting a tree near your home or workplace, you can also help improve local biodiversity, which can positively impact wildlife and the environment.

Finally, tree-hugging can effectively make people more aware of environmental care. Tree-hugging also helps people reduce their carbon footprint by reducing energy use. Some concerns about tree-hugging are that it can be time-consuming, and not everyone has the time or resources to participate. Also, tree-huggers may come across as naive or idealistic. However, these concerns are addressable through education and awareness.

CHAPTER 30

HEALING POWERS OF GROUNDING

Getting grounded is a way to connect with the earth's natural energy field. Thousands of people all over the world have benefited from the miraculous healing powers of grounding. This simple concept involves putting your feet on the ground. This simple action allows your body to absorb earth's healing free electrons. These electrons prevent inflammation and are critical for our health. They neutralise free radicals, which is one of the main features of aging. They also prevent mitochondrial damage. When you are grounded, you feel calm and centred, strong and solid. It's a physical connection with the earth.

Getting your feet on the ground is also an easy way to increase your energy and focus. It's also beneficial for your sleep, which is essential for your body's healing processes. It promotes deeper, more restful sleep, which can help reduce stress. In addition, grounding promotes lucid dreaming and increases ESP abilities. Those who practise grounding believe that lack of contact with the earth's natural surface causes many health issues. They also believe that the grounding method reduces inflammation. They also claim that grounding improves blood circulation, which improves the delivery of oxygen and nutrients to the body.

During the past two decades, scientists have focused their attention on the human body's relationship with the earth. These scientists have published several studies on the effects of grounding on health. While most pilot studies involved a few subjects, these studies have opened up a new frontier for research on inflammation. Chronic inflammation can cause fatigue, brain fog and mood problems. It is thought to be caused by excessive reactive oxygen species. Studies have shown that direct physical contact with the earth can lead to rapid anti-inflammatory effects. The electrical potential of the earth is essential for a healthy body. Contact with the earth also improves respiratory efficiency and circulatory efficiency. It has also been shown to reduce blood pressure and blood viscosity.

Recent scientific research has also explored the benefits of grounding for mood, muscle damage and chronic pain. Some studies have shown that grounding can decrease pain and increase blood flow. Grounding the body strengthens its defences and helps restore the body's natural rhythm. Grounding also helps to restore the body's natural hormonal balance. Recent studies have shown that grounding can reduce stress and improve sleep.

Grounding can be accomplished by lying on a special conductive device, touching the earth or going barefoot outside. It is important to remember that while grounding techniques are effective, they can't replace medical advice. Rather, they can be used as a complementary treatment to what you are already doing. A good rule of thumb is to try to incorporate grounding activities into your daily routine. It can be as simple as lying in the grass outside your house. Another good way to ground yourself is to listen to music. You may even want to create a mental grounding toolkit with calming music, pictures of loved ones and herbal tea. You can also try a 'body scan' which involves playing with the direction and speed of your breath.

Several grounding devices are now available in the market. Using grounding devices can help in a lot of ways, including improving your health. Using grounding devices is a simple way to improve your mental health, and it can also help you to cure illnesses and heal wounds. It can also help to improve your circulation. In the electrical industry, grounding is an essential component of most electrical systems. It helps to ensure that power is properly distributed and that circuits are not overloaded. It also helps to prevent fires.

Using grounding devices can provide health benefits, including better sleep, less pain and better circulation. If you have any concerns about using grounding devices, you should read the product's instructions carefully. There is a small risk of an electrical shock, however. Electrical grounding is important because it keeps electrical currents out of your body. It can protect you from the harmful effects of EMF radiation. It can also reduce pain and stress and promote wound healing. Grounding devices come in different forms, including desk chairs, mattress pads, blankets and more. They may be used indoors or outside. Grounding can provide general health benefits, including reduced stress and pain, improved circulation and enhanced immune function. It can also reduce inflammation, which can affect brain function and mood.

Grounding is a practice that can be performed both indoors and outdoors. Indoors, you may need to use grounding mats, socks and equipment. Outdoors, you may want to walk barefoot on sand, grass or concrete. Grounding exercises can be used in your home to help rebalance your energy and increase circulation. They can also help you to reduce stress and fatigue. In fact, some grounding enthusiasts say that they sleep better, feel more energised and experience less pain. Grounding also improves mood. You may want to sing along to songs, recite passages and do other activities that ground you in the present moment. Cold exposure has been shown to increase immunity, elevate mood and reduce fat. It has also been shown to reduce depression and chronic fatigue.

The best way to practise grounding is to get into the present moment. This allows the body to regain its normal physiology. The body may feel better immediately, but it may take several sessions before you see a significant change. Another positive aspect of grounding is that it can be done on a regular basis. This means you can avoid the negative effects of chronic inflammation on the brain and nervous system.

Earth grounding also incorporates Eastern religious practices, including barefoot walking, swimming and meditation. It also incorporates the chakra, which is the energy centre of the human body. It has also been shown to improve circulation, which aids in the delivery of oxygen and nutrients to the body.

Six Important Benefits of Grounding

Circulation

Increasing evidence indicates that grounding can be beneficial to the circulatory system. The grounding method can help to reduce blood viscosity, which is a major risk factor for heart disease. The viscosity of the blood is largely controlled by the electrical charge in the bloodstream. The stronger the negative charge, the more likely cells are to repel. The less viscosity, the easier blood can flow through capillaries. Grounding also increases the surface charge of red blood cells, which helps reduce blood viscosity and improve blood flow. Another benefit of grounding due to better blood circulation, is reduced risk of blood clots. Grounding improves blood circulation and helps the body deliver oxygen and nutrients to cells. It also reduces stress and can help to relieve symptoms of inflammation. One study found that grounding reduces blood pressure and stress hormones. A second study found that grounding can help to reduce heartbeat gaps. Another study found that grounding improves the body's response to trauma. Grounding has also been shown to be beneficial for people with Lyme disease. Lyme disease is characterised by poor circulation and thick blood. Lyme also has a tendency to cause a Herxheimer reaction, an inflammatory response to the die-off of bacteria. In response to this, the immune system sends more neutrophils to the site of the pathogen. The neutrophils encapsulate the pathogen and release reactive oxygen molecules. The blood then clears the spirochetes from the body.

Immunity

Grounding helps to restore natural defences in the body, which is important for people with chronic pain and illness. It can help reduce stress hormone secretion and may increase the activity of the parasympathetic nervous system. Besides improving the immune system, it also improves eyesight. Another study found that grounding increases the number of neutrophils in the body. Neutrophils are immune cells that help protect the body against infection. The higher the number of neutrophils, the better the immune system. Studies have shown that grounding can improve the ability of the vagus nerve to function. This nerve is linked to the heart and digestive tract, and it is responsible for regulating the activity of the parasympathetic system. It's also been shown to boost immune function, normalise hormone and cellular rhythms and improve metabolism and circulation. It's also been shown to help people suffering from insomnia and anxiety.

Mental Health

Grounding is a great way to enhance your mental health. It involves a series of simple activities designed to increase your awareness of your surroundings. These activities can be done indoors or outdoors. The benefits of grounding on mental health can include improved sleep patterns, a heightened sense of self-awareness and even pain relief.

Grounding can help people with PTSD, traumatic memories and other intense emotions. Grounding also helps reduce the amount of stress hormones in the body. Stress is a common factor in many health conditions, including anxiety and depression. The stress reduction associated with grounding has been shown to decrease the symptoms of anxiety. It's also believed that grounding can help you release the past. When you're grounded, you feel strong and centred, and you also have less pain. Getting grounded can also help you release stress and fear, which can help you live a more stress-free life. It has also been shown to improve sleep, which can reduce the risk of depression. It also reduces oxidative damage, one of the main causes of aging. Grounding has also been shown to be beneficial for people with autism, PTSD and osteoporosis. It has also been shown to improve healing from trauma and reduce pain associated with autoimmune disorders.

Pain, Inflammation and Stress

Recent scientific research has looked at grounding for chronic pain and inflammation. Chronic inflammation can lead to a variety of health issues. Inflammation occurs when free radicals stress cells. The free radicals cause chronic pain and inflammation. These free radicals can feed the inflammation process, which leads to disease and aging. The benefits of grounding on diseases include a reduction of the chronic pain caused by inflammation. It has also been shown to reduce stress levels and to normalise the stress hormone cortisol. It also showed that grounding improves sleep, circulation, blood sugar levels, stress levels and thyroid function. It also reduces inflammation, which is linked to depression. Grounding normalises your autonomic nervous system, which is responsible for controlling your body's self-regulating systems. It also normalises your stress hormone, cortisol. It has also been shown to reduce chronic inflammation, which is associated with depression. Grounding also prevents the body's natural healing ability from being turned off. It can help people get their work done and take charge of their lives. It's a healthy and affordable way to improve your health. The grounding method has been shown to reduce inflammation, which helps to maintain normal brain function. In addition, it can reduce stress. Stress affects many health conditions and has been linked to cognitive impairment. Chronic inflammation has been linked to heart disease, fatigue, brain fog and mood disorders.

Sleep

Grounding has also been shown to reduce apnoea. In a study of 60 people who had chronic pain, those who were grounded reported less pain and improved sleep. They also reported reduced inflammation and improved circulation. It has also been shown to improve sleep, which can reduce the risk of depression. It also reduces oxidative damage, one of the main causes of aging. Grounding has also been shown to increase lucid dreaming, which can help you improve memory and concentration. In addition, it can help people release stress and fear, which can help them live a more stress-free life. It also reduces oxidative damage, which is one of the main causes of aging. In addition to improving blood circulation, grounding also helps to regulate the body's circadian rhythm. A person who is grounded feels strong and centred. This is because a grounded person has electrons flowing between the body and the earth. The electrons help to reduce free radicals and to redistribute energy from the head to the body.

Healthier Legs and Feet

Taking the time to walk barefoot on the earth or immerse in natural water has many benefits for your health. For example, you can reduce arthritis and joint problems.

In fact, studies have shown that walking barefoot improves circulation in the lower extremities. The benefits of grounding are gaining serious attention from scientists. There have been over 20 peer-reviewed studies on grounding's health benefits. One found that walking barefoot improved blood flow to the legs, which led to lower blood pressure. Another study found that grounding reduced inflammation in the body. Grounding also helps correct hormone imbalances. A study performed at the University of California, San Diego, in 2013 demonstrated that grounding the bare foot can improve the functionality of a variety of tendons, muscles and ligaments. As a bonus, grounding one's feet can improve blood circulation to the legs and feet, leading to healthier legs and feet. As a side benefit, it reduces the risk of varicose veins.

Conclusion

Using grounding to improve one's health has been around for centuries. In the past, people walked barefoot and wore leather shoes. Now, most people wear shoes with rubber soles. The scientific community is still debating whether grounding is an effective way to improve one's health. Although there is not yet a definitive answer, a few studies have shown that a few minutes of grounding each day may have some benefits.

The best way to know if grounding will help you is to try it out for yourself. You may not notice an immediate improvement, but after a few sessions you will start to feel the benefits. Grounding is a simple, natural approach that can improve your overall health and quality of life. It has been practised for centuries, and there is a growing body of scientific evidence to support its effectiveness. People who practise grounding tend to be more calm and centred. They are also strong. They have more energy, and they feel better.

In addition to providing physical benefits, grounding can provide an environment free of unwanted static and positive charges. Aside from providing a calming effect, grounding can stabilise the temperature of the body and improve cardiac health. Grounding provides public health benefits, including reduced stress and pain, improved circulation and enhanced immune function. It can also reduce inflammation, which can affect brain function and mood.

Chapter 31

WHY SPRINTING IS THE BEST ANTI-AGEING EXERCISE

Using sprinting as an anti-ageing exercise can help you maintain a healthy body, reduce fat and lose weight. It can also improve your mood and make you feel younger.

What Is the Running Speed That Qualifies as Sprint

Depending on the individual, the speed of running may vary. It may be as low as 4.5 miles per hour or as high as 12.2 miles per hour. It is also dependent on the person's experience and fitness level.

There are two main types of running: jogging and sprinting. The former is the slowest of the two and the latter is the fastest. The most common definition of jogging is to run at a slow pace, while the latter is to run at a fast rate. Both are related exercises, but the latter has the advantage of being able to be done in short bursts, while the former can only be done in a continuous fashion.

The best form of sprinting is to perform a series of short, high-speed sprints. The best performers can achieve an average of 40 kilometres or about 25 miles per hour. This is not as fast as running at a normal pace, but it is still very impressive. It is also very difficult to master, as the body has to be prepared to deal with the speed bumps that are part of every jogger's life.

Sprinting is not limited to a certain time and place, although it's a popular exercise in many countries. In fact, it's the most popular sport in the world and has been featured in the Olympics since the seventh century. In the early twentieth century, it was a men's only sport. The modern era paved the way for women to compete on the same track as men.

Sprinting Boosts Metabolism

Amongst the many benefits of sprinting, it can boost metabolism, increase your muscle mass and burn fat. Besides that, it can also improve blood cholesterol levels and help control high blood pressure. It can also protect your balance and help ward off osteoporosis. When sprinting, your body burns calories to recover from exercise and build muscles. This is called the afterburn effect, or EPOC. The amount of calories you burn is dependent on your pace and weight.

Studies have found that athletes who perform speed workouts tend to have a lower body fat percentage than those who do slow-paced running. They also tend to have better bone density, which helps reduce the risk of coronary artery disease.

While sprinting does not burn as many calories as long-duration physical activity, it does produce feel-good endorphins that can boost your confidence and relieve stress. It can also increase lung power, which can be a major factor in improving cardiovascular health.

A recent study published in *Osteoporosis International* revealed that older sprinters have higher bone density than their younger counterparts. It also showed that sprinting increases lean muscle mass. It is a good idea to use high-intensity interval training in your sprint workouts, as this is known to jump-start your metabolic functioning. In addition, high-intensity workouts are much more time efficient than steady-state cardio.

Sprinting Makes Muscle

Using a sprinting routine is an effective anti-ageing exercise. This type of exercise can increase muscle mass and build muscle. It also burns fat. This can help reduce the risk of heart disease and osteoporosis. It is considered a low-impact exercise and doesn't require any special equipment. It also increases a runner's overall endurance. Besides improving cardiovascular health, sprinting may help to control high blood pressure. It may also lower cholesterol levels.

It has been shown that aging is accompanied by loss of fast-twitch muscle fibres. These fibres are responsible for power generation.

However, the selective atrophy of these fibres can be reversed by resistive training.

In a sprint, the leg muscles work twice as fast as they do during a traditional jog. This forces the skeleton to become stronger. It also tones the upper body muscles.

The speed at which a runner can perform a sprint depends on many factors, including genetics and external conditions. A person can only sustain a sprint for 30 seconds. This means that if you want to improve your speed, you should do repetitions at the highest intensity you can handle.

It is also important to note that sprinting is an anaerobic exercise. This means that the body needs to burn more calories during the workout and after the workout to recover. This makes sprinting an excellent way to burn fat.

Sprinting Improves Mental and Emotional Health

Besides improving heart and skeletal health, sprinting also has a positive effect on mental and emotional well-being. According to researchers, the body responds to exercise with the release of serotonin and dopamine, which are known to ease stress. In addition, exercise triggers the release of endorphins, which provide an athlete with relief and optimism.

Another benefit of sprinting is its ability to reduce insulin resistance, a condition that can develop into type 2 diabetes. This is because westerners have less sensitivity to insulin, which shuttles sugar into the cells. When the cells become resistant, they build up a dangerous amount of glucose in the blood.

In a study on young adults, aerobic exercise was found to improve their mental well-being. However, the exact reason for the improvement is unknown. Aside from self-efficacy, possible causes include unclear neurobiological mechanisms and hormonal responses.

The same study found that moderate-intensity running increases blood flow to the prefrontal cortex, a part of the brain responsible for executive functions. The prefrontal cortex is involved in regulating mood.

While there is no direct correlation between physical activity and the release of serotonin or dopamine, the effects of both are often referred to as the 'runner's high'. Studies show that regular exercise is associated with lower rates of depression.

Sprinting Is Good for Fat and Weight Loss

Whether you are looking to lose weight or simply increase your muscle mass, sprinting is a great way to get fit. It has many benefits and can also help boost your confidence. It can accelerate fat loss.

Sprinting boosts your metabolism and helps you burn calories after your workout. It is an anaerobic exercise, which means it is an intense form of working out. Sprinting is also a good way to increase bone density. This is because it uses your fast-twitch fibres, which improves your muscle strength. In addition, sprinting increases the production of human growth hormone, which is an anti-aging aid. Another benefit of sprinting is its ability to reduce blood pressure. It also improves heart function. When your heart pumps harder, it increases blood circulation. This is important because it makes it more likely you will not get cardiovascular disease.

It is important to know how to do a proper sprinting workout. You should always start with a warm-up. This should include some light jogging, speed walking and dynamic stretches. This will prepare your body for the intense intensity of sprinting.

If you are a beginner, you should give yourself time to adapt. You should also allow your body some time to rest after your workout. Depending on your level of fitness, you should plan on a recovery period of 60–120 seconds.

Sprinting Boosts Mitochondria and Hormones

Among the most effective anti-aging exercises is sprinting. The reason is that sprinting boosts mitochondria and hormones. It also helps to reduce body fat. It is important to incorporate sprinting into your life to maximise its benefits.

Sprinting works to increase the production of human growth hormone, which is the fountain of youth. This hormone helps the body to develop efficient musculature, improve cognition and enhance overall health.

During a sprint, a muscle is able to produce more ATP than it can use, thus improving the ability to replenish its phosphocreatine store. More ATP means more energy. Sprinting also stimulates a growth hormone that promotes lean muscle development. This hormone is known as dihydrotestosterone. Increasing levels of this hormone are found in young men. It increases muscle strength, improves lean muscle mass and decreases the number of fat cells.

Another hormone called MOTS-c, which is encoded in the mitochondria, plays a role in stress responses. It instructs proteins to interact with the nuclear genome. This gene is also involved in the process of mitochondrial biogenesis.

Research shows that a proper sprint workout can help to reduce the amount of fat in the body by up to 75 per cent. However, this type of workout should be done in a controlled fashion. In addition, sprinting should be followed by an extended recovery period. This is because sprinting is a high-stress activity.

Sprinting Erases Age and Restores Youth

During a sprint workout, the body releases growth hormones. This release promotes efficient musculature and helps to restore youth. This activity also increases circulation and improves heart health. It improves muscle strength, balance, coordination and bone density. In addition to increasing your strength, it also optimises your endurance

There are two types of exercise: aerobic and resistance. Both are beneficial, but aerobic exercise is more effective at restoring youth. It's best to start exercising at an early age, because it will help to build muscle and increase bone density. It's also important to perform the activity against natural gravity, which forces the body to perform against its own weight. This can be dangerous, however, because it can strain the bones and muscles.

Another anti-aging activity is squats. Squats strengthen your core and improve bone density. It works on the entire body, including the midsection and lats. The calf raise is a great way to develop muscle mass, and it will also boost the size of your calves. Squats will also improve coordination and balance. It's a good way to start a sprint workout, as it helps to combine both muscle and cardio training.

While it's easy to find products that will make you look younger, the only way to truly reverse aging is to do some type of sustained exercises. The earlier you begin, the more likely you will be able to replicate the younger you.

Chapter 32

ARE EXOGENOUS KETONES BENEFICIAL FOR ENDURANCE RUNNERS?

There are three sources of calories, namely carbohydrates, fat and protein. Carbohydrates are the primary fuel for most runners, but our bodies can't store adequate amounts of carb fuel. That's why bonking or hitting the wall happens for some during marathons and ultramarathons. There is a way out of this problem as a fourth source of energy exists called ketones. We have all heard of a diet called the ketogenic diet, which requires the consumption of vast amounts of fats upwards of 90 per cent. But can ketones help runners as efficiently as glucose?

Our human bodies do not produce ketones under normal circumstances. We make ketones while fasting or consuming empty diets or ultra-low-carb diets. During such times, the body has to rely on stored fats. When the body starts burning fats for energy, ketones get produced. The body can use such ketones for energy. Ketone is a good fuel for the brain and helps runners perform better. Many ultramarathoners have adopted ketogenic diets and have improved their performance due to decreased production of ketones. All this may be fine, but adhering to ketogenic diets is challenging and cumbersome, although some who have cultivated it have stuck to it for years and have lost a tonne of weight. There is a way out for those who find it difficult to follow a ketogenic diet in the form of exogenous ketones. We can buy such exogenous ketones as a supplement from stores. Such supplements boost the level of ketones in the blood, just like on a ketogenic diet. Surprisingly, a study has shown that such supplements could produce ketones in the body even when taken alongside a sugary drink. However, several other studies have revealed no impact or decline in performance due to consuming exogenous ketones. Studies witnessed diverse outcomes because some researchers conducted studies for races as short as 800 metres.

For athletes to reap the benefits of ketones, they must take exogenous ketone supplements half an hour before the race or event, along with water or any sports drink. The stomachs of many athletes cannot handle ketone drinks, so they must check whether it agrees with their system a few days before the race or take it over a while till their system gets adapted to it. For now, the apparent benefits of ketones appear to be less glycogen use and better lactate levels.

Further, ketone esters were used in some studies, while in others, ketone salts got used. Another interesting finding is that ketone supplementation improves post-race recovery by enhancing the activity of mTORC1, which signals mTORC1 leading to muscular growth and healing.

Research on the use of exogenous ketones for athletes is still ongoing. Some studies have shown that exogenous ketones can improve performance, while others have shown no or even a negative effect. More research is needed to determine the optimal dosage and timing of exogenous ketones for athletes.

One of the benefits of ketones is that they can help athletes to use less glycogen. Glycogen is a type of carbohydrate that gets stored in the muscles and liver. It is the body's primary source of energy for short-term exercise. When athletes use exogenous ketones, they can conserve their glycogen stores later in the race, which can be especially beneficial for endurance athletes competing in long-distance events.

Another benefit of ketones is that they can help improve lactate clearance. Lactate is a byproduct of exercise that can build up in the muscles and make it difficult to continue exercising. Exogenous ketones can help improve lactate clearance, which can help athletes to maintain their performance for longer.

Finally, studies have shown that ketones improved recovery after exercise. Ketones can help reduce inflammation and promote muscle repair and allow athletes to recover more quickly from training and competition.

Drawbacks of Ketones

There are a few drawbacks in using exogenous ketones. One drawback is that they can be expensive. Another disadvantage is that they can cause side effects, such as nausea, vomiting, and diarrhoea. In addition, some people may be unable to tolerate exogenous ketones, especially those with a sensitive stomach.

Conclusion

Research on exogenous ketones for athletes is still ongoing. However, available evidence suggests that exogenous ketones may be beneficial for some athletes, especially those who are undergoing training for long-distance events. If you are considering using exogenous ketones, talk to your doctor or a sports nutritionist to see if they suit you.

Here are some additional things to keep in mind when using exogenous ketones:

* Start with a low dose and gradually increase it. Some people may experience side effects, such as nausea or vomiting when they first start using exogenous ketones.
* Taking exogenous ketones with food or water will help prevent stomach upset.
* Listen to your body. If you experience any adverse side effects, stop using exogenous ketones and consult your doctor.

Exogenous ketones are a relatively new supplement, and more research is needed to determine their long-term safety and efficacy. However, available evidence suggests they may be a safe and effective way to improve performance for some endurance runners.

Chapter 33

WHICH IS THE BEST FUEL FOR RUNNING? SUGAR OR KETONES?

Running is a sport which burns a lot of calories. When you subtract the calories your body uses to breathe and do other essential functions, you will end with the number of calories that your body burns. Running burns more calories than walking and even more than mild activities like walking or gardening. The rate at which your body burns calories depends on your metabolism. If you have a high level of metabolism, you burn calories faster. If you have a slower metabolism, you burn fewer calories at a given speed. Accelerating your metabolism consists in working out and eating the right foods. When you run, you accelerate your metabolism by requiring your body to work harder than before. A slower metabolism means it takes longer for your body to burn calories. As a result, you burn fewer calories in the long run. The best way to speed up your metabolism is to increase the intensity of your activity. That is why sprinting consumes more energy than jogging.

When it comes to running, we all have our personal preferences. Some like to go at a slow and steady pace, while some prefer to go at a higher rate of speed. Others prefer to run during the night while others prefer to do it during the day. It is essential to understand that running is tough on our bodies. We are constantly putting strain on our joints, tendons, ligaments and muscles. But, if we go faster, running becomes much more intensive on your body, so runners will tell you to keep it slow and steady, although some prefer sprinting.

Running is an excellent way to stay fit and maintain a healthy lifestyle. It is a great cardiovascular workout that strengthens your heart and lungs. If you run long distances, running can also be challenging. To keep pace and prevent fatigue, you might need to refuel. For runners, nothing feels more frustrating than running out of fuel. Whether planning your next long run or training for a race, you always have to consider how many calories you'll need. If you don't refuel properly, your performance may start to suffer. Even if you're running on empty, your body may not sense it that way. That's because your running will begin to feel uninspired and flat. The runners can refuel on two fuel types, either glucose or ketones. Some runners swear by one, and others swear by the other. Which is the best fuel to sustain running? Which works best at keeping you going? Or is there another option?

When it comes to burning fat and losing weight, an old saying goes: what you eat affects how much you burn. What you burn affects how much you eat. What you eat and how you burn that food directly impact your appetite and how much you burn when it comes to your metabolism. What you eat also has a direct impact on your metabolism. However, its effect on your metabolism differs depending on whether you're eating on the ketogenic or carbohydrate metabolism model. When you eat on the ketogenic model, you take in a lot of fat and low-carb foods. Your body converts these foods into ketones which provide it with energy. Your organs and tissues then use these ketones to generate energy. The net result is that you burn fat and lose weight instead of carbohydrates. When you eat on the carbohydrate metabolism model, you take in carbohydrates and other foods and break them down into glucose. Glucose becomes the body's primary source of energy. The net result is that you burn carbohydrates and gain weight instead of fat if the amount of calories consumed far exceeds the energy expended by the body.

Typically, our body runs on glucose or blood sugar. The sugars found in sports drinks and gels provide a quick burst of energy, which can be especially handy for long-distance runners. The downsides are that these products can be expensive and don't always taste so great. Our cells will only use glucose for energy, but if glycogen stores get depleted and glucose is in short supply, our bodies commence using stored fat by converting stored fat in the liver into ketones. Similarly, during fasting, our body depletes its stored glycogen sources, primarily carbohydrates and fats. The body, to maintain blood sugar levels during a fast, starts breaking fats into ketones which gain entry into our tissues and organs and generate energy to sustain our bodies during a fast.

The ketones, or ketone bodies, are acidic and therefore can be used by cells in the usual way. Instead, the liver converts into a substance called β-hydroxybutyrate, or BHB, which can generate energy like a glucose molecule would produce energy which is why ketosis is also known as the "housekeeping" and "detox" phase of the ketogenic diet. When the body starts to use fats instead of glucose to produce energy until it has run out of stored fat.

Two common types of fuel for runners are sugar and ketones. Ketones are probably the best fuel for running. Running is a big commitment, so runners know the importance of fuelling their bodies before and during workouts. Ketones work best for runners because they provide more sustained energy than sugar. The *Journal of Physiology* found that ketones give more energy to muscles by enhancing glucose uptake and reducing lactic acid accumulation. Research has also shown that ketones cause less fatigue, leading to improved performance in prolonged exercise such as running. Additionally, ketones can help reduce inflammation while increasing insulin sensitivity – two benefits which can help delay muscle fatigue during running. Ketogenic diets are high-fat, low-carb diets that help your body produce ketones naturally – perfect for athletes hoping to run longer distances!

But don't forget about sugar as a source of fuel too! Sugar is just as important because it helps keep your brain alert and ready to go when needed!

Some people don't even feel like they're getting enough energy from eating a high-fat diet (e.g. if they're vegetarian), so they may opt for sugar-fuelled gels or sports drinks instead. Sugars provide instant energy, an easy absorption rate into the bloodstream and a quick recovery time afterwards. However, decreasing dependence on glucose or using glucose sparingly is better because glucose can have adverse side effects on your health, such as weight gain or increased blood pressure levels.

Finally, sugar or ketones may be the question of the day for runners. Sugar provides an instant boost of energy that can help you maintain your pace. But when you're on the run, it also causes insulin to spike as your body tries to process it. If you don't drink enough water, this can lead to dehydration or even hyponatraemia. Ketones is another option. They have a slower release than sugar and take longer to digest before they enter the bloodstream; they can help you sustain your running without the risk of dehydration or hyponatraemia. Ketones is also a cleaner source than sugar, which might be better for some people who want their bodies to rely on fat rather than carbohydrates for energy. In conclusion, both sources might work well for different people in different situations. The choice ultimately depends on your personal preference and what fits your lifestyle best!

Chapter 34

CORONAVIRUS GENETIC VACCINE IS A MEDICAL MIRACLE

Contagion, a 2011 film directed by Steven Soderbergh, witnessed a massive revival in popularity because of its stunning similarities with the current pandemic's onset. The film depicts an outbreak of a deadly virus and medical researchers worldwide attempting to contain it. The movie mirrored the existing corona pandemic eerily well. One of the two things in the film, which viewers deemed inaccurate, was developing the vaccine in a short time. The viewers felt the development of a vaccine portrayed by the director in the movie to be unrealistic.

Further, as the film unfolds, CDC inadvertently stumbles on a weakened virus strain in a monkey. Scientist Hextail (Jennifer Ehle), using an attenuated virus, inoculates herself with it to circumvent the 'informed consent test subject process' and visits her infected father to check if she has developed an immunity. As she fails to contract the virus from her father, they proclaim the vaccine a success, and the vaccine miraculously zooms into mass production.

Vaccines had easily staved off hundreds of millions of demises since 1796 when Edward Jenner inoculated a boy with cowpox to prevent smallpox. Outside Hollywood, vaccine development is a long, complicated process, costing up to $500 million and often lasting 10–15 years, encompassing several years of testing and some more for obtaining authorisation from the health authorities for its delivery as a viable vaccine. But science has proved itself to be stranger than fiction. Even before the pandemic could complete a year of its existence, COVID-19 vaccines have arrived at unimaginable breakneck speed due to the scientists' stupendous efforts. The UK, EU, the US and a few other nations have commenced administering COVID-19 vaccines within a year of coronavirus unleashing a devastating pandemic.

All vaccines strive to expose the body to an antigen that won't cause disease and provoke an immune response that can block or kill the virus when a person becomes infected. Scientists have employed at least eight types of vaccines against the coronavirus, most important being attenuated viruses, DNA or RNA vaccines and viral protein-based vaccines. More than 50 teams are working on formulating vaccines against coronavirus worldwide, adopting either one or more approaches listed above.

Of them, mRNA is the recent unusual approach to vaccines. Cells make use of mRNA to make proteins. mRNA vaccines have strands of genetic material called mRNA inside a special coating. That coating protects the mRNA from enzymes in the body that would otherwise break it down. It also helps the mRNA enter the dendritic cells and macrophages in the lymph node near the vaccination site. mRNA contains the code to make a portion of the 'spike protein' unique to SARS-CoV-2. The mRNA vaccine does not cause any harm to the person vaccinated as only a part of the antigenic protein is made. After the spike protein assembles, the cell disassembles the mRNA strand and digests it using enzymes in the cell. The significance of this process is that the mRNA never enters the nucleus. Hence, it disproves the validity of anti-vaccination activists' claim that mRNA vaccines can modify genetic material. Once expressed on the cell surface, the protein or the antigen stimulates the immune system to begin generating antibodies and activating T-cells to fight off the SARS-CoV-2 virus, which indicates that the immune system is all set to protect against future infections.

Researchers have experimented with mRNA vaccines for decades; however, there have been no licensed mRNA vaccines thus far. Some early-stage clinical trials using mRNA vaccines for influenza, Zika, rabies and cytomegalovirus failed to yield much success due to free RNA instability in the body. Along with Karikó and Weissman, Pardi overcame the shortcomings by developing a technique of encasing mRNA in tiny bubbles of fat known as lipid nanoparticles (LNPs), which protected and enhanced its delivery into cells.

The first approved COVID-19 vaccines globally with demonstrable efficacy, developed by Pfizer-BioNTech and Moderna, are based on mRNA technology. Pfizer-BioNTech was granted an Emergency Use Authorisation on 11 December 2020, and Moderna on 17 December 2020. The clinical trial data for the Pfizer and Moderna vaccines indicate that they are about 95 per cent effective in preventing illness when doctors administer both shots of the dual-injection immunisation, three weeks to a month apart. The main difference between the two vaccines is that we can store Moderna's vaccine for 30 days in a typical household refrigerator. There is no need for it to be refrigerated to –70° C (–94 F) during transport, as is the case with the vaccine from BioNTech-Pfizer. At Imperial College in London, Robin Shattock's team is working on a 'self-amplifying RNA' vaccine that will be far cheaper than the BioNTech/Pfizer vaccine ($39 for two shots) or the Moderna jab ($74 for two jabs) and require as little as one-hundredth of the amount of vaccine. The mRNA technique means we can halt future pandemics more swiftly as the carrier is already available and waiting to carry the next vaccine.

India's first mRNA vaccine, HGCO19, developed by the Pune-based Gennova, has received approval from Indian Drug Regulators to initiate phase 1 and phase 2 clinical trials. COVID-19 vaccine trials in India are progressing well. Two of the five vaccines undergoing human clinical trials in India have reached the phase 3 stage. Bharat Biotech claims that the inactivated vaccines it is developing for COVID-19 called Covaxin are the safest, with lesser adverse effects when compared to mRNA vaccines. The Serum Institute of India is testing the other Oxford-AstraZeneca vaccine, CShield. Covidshield is one of the three coronavirus vaccines under consideration for emergency use authorisation in India after Pfizer's BNT162b2 and Bharat Biotech's Covaxin. India has recorded more than 10 million COVID-19 cases and over 145,000 deaths from the disease. India is planning to begin vaccinating people against COVID-19 in January this year. The vaccination programme aims to reach 300 million people by early August.

In *I Am legend*, a 2007 film starring Will Smith adapted from the novel of the identical name, Smith stars as Robert Neville, a US Army virologist who lives in New York City after a virus has wholly wiped out humanity. In the movie, the virus, which they reckon will cure cancer, instead of doing so, on the contrary, turns everyone infected into mutant vampire-like beings. Anti-vaccine activists worldwide are conjuring up similar scenarios over the safety of the mRNA vaccines, which the researchers are trying for the first time in the history of humanity.

Anti-vaccination activists claim that mRNA vaccines represent genetic manipulation as it intervenes directly with the inoculated person's genes. They contend that any damage caused by mRNA vaccination will be irreversible. Patients will have to live with consequences like Down syndrome, Klinefelter syndrome, Turner syndrome and so on because the genetic defect would be forever. Hence, they consider mRNA vaccines a crime against humanity that has been perpetrated in such a big way in history despite scientists dispelling such uncorroborated fears to be untrue convincingly.

At the moment, the greatest miracle and the most significant medical advance in the last 100 years appear to be the mRNA vaccines. We will remember 2020 as the most unprecedented year for the medical world to make a quantum leap from traditional vaccines to genetic vaccines. This modern miracle is a testament to human ingenuity.

Finally, just as we need a vaccine to overcome the pandemic, we desperately need a spiritual vaccine to immunise ourselves against the mindset of hate and sectarianism. We can all endogenously generate spiritual vaccines against hate and dissolve all hatred by connecting with the divine within each one of us.

Chapter 35

A CONCISE GUIDE TO A PLANT-BASED DIET

Plant-based diets are gaining popularity for a good reason. There are numerous Bollywood celebrities who have gone plant-based for several years now. Many celebs including Virat Kohli, John Abraham, Aamir Khan, Akshay Kumar, Alia Bhatt, Anushka Sharma, Jacqueline Fernandez, Richa Chadha, Shahid Kapoor, Shraddha Kapoor and Sonam Kapoor have become vegetarians. Many are enthusiastic animal lovers and asserted that as the primary purpose for abandoning nonvegetarian foods.

They're not only healthy, but they also help prevent certain diseases and even reverse them. Additionally, eating plant-based is beneficial for the environment and kinder to animals. A diet that's low in animal products has many benefits for your health and the planet as a whole. As a result of these benefits, more people are choosing plant-based foods over animal products.

If you want to improve your health, help the environment and aid in animal rights? A plant-based diet can do that. A plant-based diet involves eating primarily fruits, vegetables, nuts, seeds and grains. The diet mainly comprises plant parts or products derived from them which is why it is called a plant-based diet. In contrast, an animal-based diet includes lots of meat, such as chicken and red meat, and dairy products like eggs and cheese. While plant-based diets are generally healthy, it's still important to talk to your doctor before making any significant changes to your diet. It's essential to remember that there is not enough evidence to support these claims.

Why Go Plant-Based?

If you're like us, you're probably not considering a plant-based diet for one reason alone. Instead, you might think about it for a variety of reasons. Here are just some of the reasons why you might want to consider switching to a plant-based diet.

- A plant-based diet can help you to improve your health in many different ways. For example, a plant-based diet can help prevent and reverse diseases such as heart disease, diabetes and certain types of cancers by reducing the risk of chronic diseases.
- A plant-based diet can do wonders to help the environment. Not only does it help to reduce carbon emissions but also it helps to preserve water and soil.
- Furthermore, a plant-based diet can help reduce animals' suffering. It can eliminate the consumption of animal-based products.

Health Benefits of a Plant-Based Diet

A plant-based diet has many benefits, including increased cognitive and physical energy. Research has shown that eating a plant-based diet can help improve brain health, especially for people with Alzheimer's. It also can help improve blood sugar control in people with diabetes. A plant-based diet can also help reduce the risk of heart disease since it is low in saturated fat and cholesterol. Plant-based diets tend to be lower in calories and fat, which can help you maintain a healthy weight. A plant-based diet can also help you feel fuller longer after meals, which can help keep you from overeating and gaining weight.

Do you know that a plant-based diet can help reduce your risk of cancer, stroke and diabetes? It is also linked to lower blood pressure, reduced risk of developing hypertension or preeclampsia during pregnancy and a lower risk of contracting type 2 diabetes in later life.

Besides, if you're following a plant-based diet, you may see a reduction in inflammation throughout your body. A decrease in inflammation can assist in the prevention of diseases of heart, diabetes and certain types of cancers. Additionally, a plant-based diet can assist in the reduction of blood pressure. A plant-based diet can also help in weight loss and management due to its high fibre content. Furthermore, a plant-based diet can reduce the risk of digestive issues such as irritable bowel syndrome.

Research indicates that people who eat plant-based diets have a lower BMI and lower obesity, diabetes and heart disease rates than those who eat meat. Plant-based diets are high in fibre, complex carbohydrates and water content from fruit and vegetables.

Plant-Based Diet Improves Cognitive Health

A plant-based diet is healthy to eat low in saturated fat and cholesterol. It's also high in fibre, vitamins, minerals and antioxidants. This type of eating can help you feel more alert and focused, improving your cognitive performance and physical energy levels. And it can help you feel less hungry between meals. In addition to its mental benefits, a plant-based diet also improves mood by reducing inflammation in the body. Eating a healthy plant-based diet can make you feel better inside and out!

Environment Benefits of a Plant-Based Diet

If you choose to adopt a plant-based diet, you benefit the environment not only by reducing your carbon footprint but also by preserving water and soil. To illustrate, if you eat two pounds of beef, it will take about 2500 gallons of water to produce that much meat. Moreover, a plant-based diet uses soil nutrients more efficiently. By contrast, the growing of animals for food uses much more soil nutrients. Plants like legumes, grains and seeds are excellent ways to replenish the soil.

Animal products like meat, dairy, eggs and fish – are more responsible for climate change, sea level rise, ocean acidification and global extinction rates than all automobiles, aeroplanes and ships on the planet combined. It will have a massive impact if people lessen their meat and dairy consumption by half. We could save a third of the water and land we use and feed more people because half the food humans grow is used to feed animals. Eating a plant-based diet requires significantly less land, water and energy

Animal Rights Benefits of a Plant-Based Diet

More plant-based meals lower the demand for meat, dairy and eggs, dramatically reducing animal suffering on factory farms worldwide. Substituting beef, dairy and eggs with plant-based proteins even weekly once can enhance energy and prevent diseases.

A plant-based diet can reduce animal suffering if you're an animal rights activist by eliminating the consumption of animals. We're not saying that everyone following a plant-based diet is an animal rights activist. Instead, we're saying that a plant-based diet is a way to reduce the suffering of animals.

Tips to Transition to a Plant-Based Diet

If you're interested in transitioning to a plant-based diet, there are a few things that you can do to make the transition process more manageable. First off, start small. Start by eating one plant-based meal per day. Perhaps you start with an apple for breakfast, a salad for lunch and veggies and rice for dinner. Follow this up by setting goals for yourself. For example, you might want to aim to eat 100 per cent plant-based by a specific date, or you might want to reduce the amount of meat you consume. Finally, you'll want to prepare your meals ahead of time will make it easier to transition to a plant-based diet and will allow you to avoid the all too common unhealthy 'quick fix' meals like getting fast food or eating something harmful.

Here are some tips: start small – build healthy eating habits – avoid food fad diets – prepare your meals ahead of time – get support – be patient.

Be Patient

While a plant-based diet can do wonders for your health, it will take time for you to notice the benefits. It can take two to six weeks for your body to adjust to a new diet fully. If you follow the tips we have shared in this article, you will likely notice benefits after a few weeks. However, it is essential to be patient as your body starts to change.

Conclusion

Finally, we hope this article has inspired you to consider adopting a plant-based diet. A plant-based diet can do wonders to improve your health, help the environment and aid in animal rights. Furthermore, a plant-based diet is effortless to follow because you can eat almost anything that grows out of the ground.

Chapter 36

BERBERINE: A SUPPLEMENT WITH MULTIPLE BENEFITS

Berberine is a natural compound found in various plants and herbs, including goldenseal, barberry, Oregon grape and Chinese club moss. It is often used as a natural dietary supplement to combat many health conditions. Research reveals berberine to have various properties that may help support overall health, such as a healthy digestive function and metabolism, and proper immune function and inflammation control. Berberine also helps manage diabetes, obesity and other metabolic disorders by supporting healthy blood sugar levels, lowering heart disease risk and proper digestion. It helps in keeping a healthy metabolism by regulating insulin and increasing the expression of several genes involved in fat breakdown.

Research touts berberine as a potential therapy for many conditions. Its ability to improve blood circulation and reduce inflammation is well known. Berberine may also help treat autoimmune diseases such as rheumatoid arthritis and psoriasis. It may also help reduce inflammation associated with diabetes and Crohn's disease. Furthermore, berberine may reduce inflammation in the body by inhibiting nuclear factor kappa B (NF-kB), an inflammatory molecule that plays a role in many diseases.

Berberine also appears to have antidepressant effects. In one study on mice given a high-fat diet, berberine helped improve anxiety-like behaviour by increasing brain chemicals called neurotransmitters such as serotonin and dopamine. Another study showed that berberine reduced depressive-like behaviour in mice with chronic mild stress (CMS). There are currently no human studies looking at the effects of berberine on depression or other mental health conditions. However, we know that it may benefit those with type 2 diabetes due to its ability to lower blood glucose levels.

There is adequate documentation of berberine's anticancer properties. In particular, Berberine has shown promise as an effective treatment for liver cancer. A few clinical studies had shown promising results in combination with other therapies. For example, a 2014 study on mice found that berberine could effectively induce apoptosis (programmed cell death) in liver cancer cells. Berberine may also be able to target other types of cancer, including colon cancer and pancreatic cancer. Other studies have suggested that berberine may help prevent cancer by reducing the amount of DNA damage caused by oxidative stress. Berberine appears to have the ability to prevent certain cancers by inhibiting tumour growth at the cellular level, which may explain why it has historically been used in Chinese medicine to treat cancers. As a natural compound, however, we need more research before confirming the benefits of berberine in humans with certain cancers.

Mechanism of Action of Berberine

Metformin activates the AMPK pathway leading to increased metabolic rate, reduced appetite and improved insulin sensitivity. Berberine also activates the AMPK pathway, but differently than metformin.

Berberine increases the levels of adenosine in the body. It also inhibits the enzymes responsible for breaking down adenosine in the body, thereby increasing adenosine levels. Increased adenosine levels lead to increased blood flow, improved blood sugar control and high fat burning, among other benefits. Berberine also blocks specific receptors in the body responsible for increasing fat storage and decreasing metabolism, thus helping one lose weight.

Berberine increases the activity of genes, which increases the production of enzymes that metabolise fat and glucose, increasing the fat-burning capacity, reducing fat absorption and lowering cholesterol and blood sugar levels. It decreases blood lipid levels by increasing the secretion of bile acids from the liver and reduces cholesterol levels by increasing the expression of LDL receptors in the liver.

Research reveals that the berberine administration increases the levels of GLP-1, a hormone that helps control blood sugar, by about 40 per cent and the levels of blood sugar by about 10 per cent. It also reduces the level of insulin, reduces the absorption of fats from the intestine, reduces the fatty acids in the liver, increases glucose uptake by muscles, increases the conversion of excess blood sugar to fat, prevents fat storage in the liver, prevents fat storage in other organs like muscles, and prevents the conversion of sugar to fat

Berberine for Fatty Liver Disease

Fatty liver is a condition where your liver has too much fat stored in it, leading to a range of health issues. Thanks to its cholesterol-lowering properties, berberine has been shown to combat fatty liver. In one study, researchers found berberine significantly reduces cholesterol levels in patients with type 2 diabetes, which may help prevent fatty liver. As you may know, high cholesterol levels are associated with an increased risk of developing fatty liver. Doctors often advise people with high cholesterol to consider regular monitoring for signs of fatty liver, especially if they also have type 2 diabetes.

High blood sugar and high blood fat levels usually cause fatty liver. It is best to avoid high-sugar and high-fat foods. However, if you have fatty liver and high blood sugar, you may want to consider a blood sugar lowering medication. Or you may consider following a low fat diet and exercise if you have high blood fats.

It is very potent in reducing the fat content in the liver and prevents the risk of developing non-alcoholic fatty liver disease. It improves the lipid profile and decreases the level of fats in the blood by increasing the metabolic rate. Moreover, it inhibits the formation of fat in the liver by increasing the production of an enzyme that breaks down fat. It also lowers the amount of sugar in the blood by decreasing the absorption of food. It is a potent herb to prevent and treat fatty liver.

Anti-ageing Effects of Berberine

Berberine helps to reduce the signs of ageing, such as wrinkles, by increasing collagen production in the skin. Collagen is the protein that keeps our skin firm and supple. As we age, the production of collagen declines, and we start to see wrinkles and saggy skin. There is proof that berberine increases collagen production, slowing ageing and giving you a younger, firmer complexion. Berberine is also helpful for your hair, making it shinier and more robust.

It helps to reduce the signs of ageing, like wrinkles and saggy skin, by increasing the production of elastin and collagen in your skin. It also helps to fight free radicals that cause damage to your skin and make you look older.

Effects of Berberine Administration on Human Microbiome

Researchers have shown that berberine has a beneficial effect on the human microbiome by increasing beneficial bacteria. Studies have shown that it might help prevent and treat certain diseases by affecting the gut microbiota. One study from 2017 enrolled 60 patients with type 2 diabetes who gave either berberine or metformin for 12 weeks. The researchers found that both groups had similar blood sugar levels and fat metabolism decreases, but berberine reduced blood sugar significantly more than metformin. The researchers hypothesised that this might be due to its effect on the gut microbiota, as there was an increase in the number of beneficial bacteria, such as bifidobacteria, and a decrease in the number of pathogenic bacteria.

Another study published in *PLOS ONE* in 2017 investigated the impact of a berberine-rich diet on the gut bacteria of Chinese adults with metabolic risk factors. Researchers found that the berberine-rich diet significantly decreased the Firmicutes/Bacteroidetes ratio in the gut microbiota, which may indicate a beneficial metabolic influence. Additionally, the berberine-rich diet significantly increased the abundance of bacteria from the genera Allobaculum, Bulleidia and Oscillibacter compared with the control diet. Furthermore, the berberine-rich diet significantly decreased the number of bacteria from Desulfovibrio, Prevotella and Selenomonas compared with the control diet. The results of this study suggest that a berberine-rich diet may improve metabolic health by modifying the gut microbiota.

Sleep-Boosting Benefits of Berberine

In a study on the effect of berberine on sleep in humans, healthy individuals were given 500 mg berberine three times a day for three days. Researchers told the individuals to report their sleep quality, anxiety and stress levels before and after taking berberine. Results showed that berberine improved the sleep quality of individuals. There was also a stress reduction and anxiety levels, which is also helpful for better sleep.

Researchers have demonstrated the possible sleep-boosting benefits of berberine in animal studies, but there is also research on how it affects human sleep. In a study published in the *Journal of Medicinal Food* in 2014, healthy adults who took 500 mg berberine daily for five days reported improved ease of falling asleep and a more restful sleep than those in the placebo group. Researchers believe that the herb's active compounds, especially berberine, might help to improve sleep and reduce insomnia risk by increasing melatonin production, lowering stress hormone secretion and reducing anxiety.

Effect of Berberine on Exercise

The anti-inflammatory properties of berberine make it an excellent option for athletes. The supplement reduces the risk of exercise-related injuries, improves athletic performance and helps the body heal faster after physical activity. It can also reduce the likelihood of stress on the cardiovascular system.

The benefits of berberine for exercise go beyond reducing inflammation. The supplement helps increase endurance and stamina and reduces muscle fatigue. It also improves blood flow to muscles and improves physical performance.

Berberine supplementation may improve several aspects of exercise performance in healthy and diseased populations by increasing endurance in healthy and unhealthy people. It has also increased muscle strength and endurance in healthy populations.

Running too fast or too far can cause a variety of health problems. These issues can include muscle injury, cardiovascular system stress and even blood sugar control problems. Research shows that berberine might help prevent these problems by decreasing oxidative stress, improving blood sugar control and reducing inflammation.

Administration of berberine increases the activity of AMPK, an enzyme responsible for controlling the body's metabolism, and mediates many of the benefits of exercise. AMPK also plays a role in increasing cellular resistance to stress and repairing cellular damage from stress. When cellular stress levels are high, AMPK activity is low. By increasing cellular AMPK levels, cellular stress gets reduced, and cellular health is improved.

Does Berberine Blunt the Effects of Exercise Like Metformin?

Metformin has been shown to blunt exercise in specific scenarios, though this is not something that happens in every system. There are instances when metformin has been shown to improve exercise performance, particularly in people with type 2 diabetes.

The same is true of berberine. There is evidence that it can improve exercise performance, particularly in people who are overweight or obese. It also seems to benefit exercise in people with type 2 diabetes, though not to the extent of metformin.

There are multiple ways in which berberine appears to improve exercise, including increasing the rate at which fat is used as fuel and decreasing the amount of glucose as fuel. It also enhances muscle sensitivity to insulin, an essential consideration for people who exercise.

It seems to improve athletic performance because berberine stimulates the production of adenosine, a naturally produced compound in the body that increases blood flow to muscles, improves muscle efficiency and decreases perceptions of effort during exercise. In other words, adenosine makes exercise feel easier.

Adenosine is also an essential compound for muscle repair and recovery. Therefore, athletes and people who engage in intense or frequent exercise may benefit from berberine even more than people who exercise for health.

Theoretically, as metformin is an insulin sensitiser, there is a chance that it could blunt the desired effects of exercise. However, there is currently no evidence to suggest that this is true. Research reveals that berberine can improve insulin sensitivity even during exercise. Therefore, we can assume that berberine will significantly affect exercise results more than metformin.

To date, there is no evidence that berberine can blunt the benefits of exercise. However, there is some evidence that it could be beneficial for people who are obese or have a high body fat percentage and people who have type 2 diabetes. For example, a study published in the *International Journal of Endocrinology* found that berberine significantly reduced the amount of fat in the abdominal region compared to a placebo.

Effect of Berberine on Sexual Health

Berberine is a natural product used as a metabolic regulator and anti-inflammatory agent. It may exhibit aphrodisiac properties and beneficial effects on male and female sexual health. It has been shown to increase the production of sex hormones, including testosterone, and decrease the conversion of testosterone into oestrogen. Additionally, berberine may improve sexual desire and quality of erection in men and sexual desire in women. Berberine benefits sexual desire and function in men and women by improving blood flow to the reproductive organs and testosterone levels in men and increasing oestrogen levels in women. It also relieves stress and improves mood, which can further improve libido.

Berberine has potent anti-inflammatory properties as well as being a powerful AMP-activating compound. When activated, AMPs can increase nitric oxide production. Nitric oxide is critical for healthy sexual function, and one of the ways it helps is by relaxing blood vessels.

Libido is significant in sexual health, but unfortunately, it is often underdiscussed. Many people suffer from a lack of libido; unfortunately, most never seek treatment for their problems. Berberine may have beneficial effects on libido in both men and women. The compound may significantly increase the volume of ejaculatory fluid in men and increase sexual desire in both sexes. Additionally, research demonstrates that berberine can reduce the expression of specific genes involved in the proliferation of blood vessels, which is essential for penile erection and overall sexual function.

Conclusion

One can take berberine in many forms, including supplements and teas. Some people take it in capsule form, whereas others eat fresh or dried berries or use extracts from herbs such as goldenseal or Oregon grape root. For others, it's best to start with a small amount and work up to larger quantities over time. The recommended dosage varies based on a person's health needs and goals. Please pay attention to how much you're taking (in terms of the type and dose) and when you take it (i.e. before or after meals) to obtain the most benefit. Berberine shows fewer adverse effects when taken within recommended doses. The recommended dose of berberine is 500 mg three times a day, one each half-hour before breakfast, lunch and dinner. Unlike pharmaceuticals, it does not carry any known drug interactions.

Part III

TECHNOLOGY AND SOCIAL MEDIA

CHAPTER 37

HOW 5G TECH CAN ENHANCE THE BANDWIDTH OF POLICING IN FUTURE

Every few years, we see a significant revolution in telecommunications. In the 1990s, it was all about the internet. Nowadays, we are moving towards a 5G future, with immense implications for law enforcement. 5G is the next generation of mobile internet technology. Cellular telephone companies began deploying 5G broadband cellular networks worldwide in 2019, and it is the successor to 4G networks that give connectivity to most current cell phones. The first 5G networks were able to provide speeds up to 20 gigabits per second and will upwardly scale that number in the future. According to the GSM Association, 5G networks are expected to have 1.7 billion subscribers by 2025. As with previous generations, 5G cellular networks divide their service areas into small geographical areas called cells. All 5G wireless devices in a given cell are connected to the internet and telephone network via radio waves via a local antenna.

The new 5G networks have higher bandwidths, up to 10 gigabits per second, than current networks and can connect a more significant number of devices, improving the internet service quality. As a result of its increased bandwidth, 5G allows improvement of internet services in crowded areas. Due to the boosted bandwidth, the 5G networks will increasingly be used as general internet service providers (ISPs) for laptops and desktops, contending with existing ISPs such as cable internet. They will make feasible new applications in IoT and machine-to-machine areas. Cell phones with 4G capability will not be able to use the new networks, which require 5G-enabled wireless devices.

5G can revolutionise policing because it has a plethora of uses. The new standard will help the police detect crime, but it will also give them an advantage like never before with increased data transfer rates. The first and foremost benefit of 5G is that it will provide bandwidth to the police force that they have never had before, which means they can scan more CCTV footage in real time and use more cameras at once without being limited by how much information they can process at once which is just one use case of how 5G would make policing easier.

5G has already been tested in different areas. In contrast to 4G, which is suitable for data-intensive tasks such as videos and gaming, 5G will offer significantly higher data rates for video transmission and VR services. With 5G's speed capabilities, law enforcement can use it with many different applications, such as drones to transmit live video from ground-based officers' patrol cars or AR technology during investigations.

5G due to much faster speeds will help law enforcement in highly congested areas. It can also help deter criminal activity if used proactively for intelligence gathering. 5G networks can help law enforcement by assisting them in combating crime by being able to transmit data at faster rates and with lower latency. The fifth-generation wireless technology will ensure that every officer or agent on the ground has access to all the information they require at any given time.

In the future, several police gadgets such as the following will use 5G:

1. Smart body cameras – 5G will enhance video coverage, live video streaming and better quality.
2. IoT device management – when a 5G connection is unavailable, it will be possible to manage these devices through an IP or 4G network.
3. Wearable tech – police officers using 5G will be able to connect and get accurate time updates on traffic conditions and so on.
4. Self-driving cars – police officers will be able to communicate with other vehicles on the road to avoid accidents or make driving smoother.
5. Robots in the field – robots using 5G will be able to do factual crime scene investigations, collect evidence at a crime scene and even conduct interviews with victims.

The next generation of mobile tech, 5G, will also revolutionise how law enforcement agencies operate. First, it will enable agencies to improve their response times substantially. That's because it will allow them to transmit data over shorter distances and at higher speeds. That will allow police cars to receive collision alerts from other vehicles swiftly and will enable them to arrive early on the scene. It will also allow police officers to receive video feeds from body cameras and security cameras. Second, it will allow agencies to track crimes in progress more accurately. Third, it will allow agencies to share data more quickly and securely. And finally, it will allow law enforcement agencies to use drones more safely and effectively.

Law enforcement agencies can use this tech for many purposes, such as patrol cars, drones, VR, AR and face recognition technologies. And to identify, track and monitor individuals. The ACLU has released a new policy paper, 'Protecting Privacy in the Age of Surveillance Technology', that calls on governments and companies to take the lead in regulating surveillance technology. The paper argues that government agencies should establish privacy policies for their use of technology and implement surveillance protocols before allowing law enforcement advancements will improve their performance in terms of speed and usability and make policing much more effective than ever before.

With 5G technology, law enforcement agencies can expect to create a more efficient and less stressful environment for their officers and an improved level of transparency and accountability. 5G technology will enable faster, more reliable connectivity, no matter where the officers are, allowing them to access more data more quickly and more reliably. Consequently, enabling better communication between officers, including seeing each other's locations. Besides, 5G will allow officers to access real-time data from surveillance cameras that will enable them to make better decisions while on the job. Additionally, 5G technology will enable officers to focus on more critical tasks, such as building relationships with the community they serve. 5G technology allows real-time video streaming between officers, which will help create a more positive relationship with the community they serve.

5G is a major technological trend for the coming decade, but it has its challenges. One of the biggest challenges that 5G has is integrating it into existing telecommunications networks. It will also depend on how many countries get on board with this new technology as it slowly rolls out within their borders and how many people get 5G-enabled devices. A significant benefit of 5G is that it will relieve some of the pressure on 4G networks; faster speeds mean less lag time and better access to data. The real-world impact is still unknown, but likely, 5G will positively impact many aspects of our lives. This new network will be fast, more reliable and more secure while at the same time creating more work for network technicians.

Law enforcement agencies will use 5G to improve the efficiency of their crime-fighting efforts. As we have seen, the new wave of mobile technology that 5G brings will allow agencies to become more responsive to emergency calls, more accurate in identifying crime scenes and better able to track suspects. By using 5G, agencies would be able to save a significant amount of money. 5G is still in its infancy, but it should be much less than the cost of 4G or even 3G networks. The prices for different service providers will vary. But, as the 5G networks expand, there's no doubt that they will bring substantial savings. Additionally, 5G is much more secure than 4G or 3G, which means law enforcement agencies can count on it more. And with 5G, law enforcement agencies can further enhance their operations by leveraging its many functions. For example, it will enable officers to move around and interact with people in real time and securely share sensitive data. It will also allow them to use remote sensors and robots and conduct more efficient and safer operations. In the future, the use of 5G will be widespread. And while it will take the police some time to fully implement it in their operations, it will be worth the wait.

Chapter 38

AI CAN REVOLUTIONISE TRAFFIC MANAGEMENT IN INDIAN CITIES

As urbanisation expands and the percentage of the world's population living in urban areas continues to increase, the demand for effective and efficient urban transportation solutions is rising. Traffic management solutions in Indian cities have failed to meet the people's expectations as it has been unable to keep pace with the high-density urbanisation and the rapid adoption of new mobility solutions. AI could revolutionise traffic management in Indian cities in the next few years by improving operational efficiency, increasing safety and making transportation safer and more affordable. AI has already made its presence felt in various industries and fields, including healthcare, education and the military. AI is slowly entering the transportation sector and is bound to transform traffic management in Indian cities.

Deploying AI in the transport sector can improve operational efficiency. First, authorities can use AI to optimise routes, instead of each traffic operator manually calculating the best possible path. A computer programme can perform the function using real-time traffic data, saving time and money, especially during rush hour. Similarly, we can also use AI to manage vehicle flow, which would reduce delays caused by 'idling' in traffic or the practice of drivers keeping their vehicles stationary in a congested area to avoid being late. Finally, police can deploy AI to increase transparency which can prove valuable both to citizens and authorities as it can help reduce the incidence of traffic violations. Further, the use of AI in transportation in different countries is helping to identify traffic hazards, ease traffic congestion, reduce emissions, design and manage transport and analyse travel demand and pedestrian behaviour

In Bengaluru, an AI-based monitoring system developed by Siemens Mobility is under operation to collect data with intelligent cameras, adjust traffic lights in real time and thus facilitate traffic flow. In Pittsburgh, USA, a similar solution, called SurTrac, created by Rapid Flow Technologies, resulted in a 25 per cent reduction in travel times and a 20 per cent reduction in emissions which is a perfect example of how AI may represent a critical factor in achieving sustainable transportation.

AI algorithms are accurately tracking and counting freeway traffic and analysing traffic density in urban settings, which is helping towns and cities to design more efficient traffic management systems while at the same time improving road safety. CCTV cameras can spot dangerous events and other anomalies and provide insights into peak hours, chokepoints and bottlenecks. It can also quantify and track changes over a period to measure traffic congestion. As a result, town planners can significantly reduce urban traffic congestion.

With the increasing number of vehicles on Indian roads, managing traffic has become a Herculean task for city authorities. India is among the countries with the highest concentration of traffic congestion. To make matters worse, the number of vehicles keeps increasing, which presents a double whammy for city authorities: not only do they have to deal with existing congestion but also plan for the increasing number of vehicles on the road in the coming years. Traffic management solutions can help reduce congestion and ensure that roads are kept safe and accessible for all – but they need to be used intelligently. Fortunately, AI can help city authorities take the next step in traffic management.

In several countries, sensors and cameras embedded on the roads collect and transmit enormous traffic data to the cloud, which is analysing the data using big data analytics and an AI-powered system to provide an accurate picture of traffic in a given city. Such insights are valuable for predicting and managing traffic effectively. By sharing essential details like traffic predictions, accidents or road blockages and notifying them about the shortest route to their destination, AI can help commuters travel without traffic hassles. This way, AI can reduce unwanted traffic, improve road safety, and reduce wait times.

Traffic congestion costs Indian cities $21 billion a year. With more than 1.2 billion people travelling through its cities every year, India is one of the most congested countries globally; this has led to an average speed of fewer than five kilometres per hour in some of its largest cities. Worse, the country experiences traffic jams that last for hours every day. Traffic jams are so common in India that people from other cultures often ask, 'why don't Indians drive like Europeans?' In context, the total economic cost of traffic congestion in Indian cities was $21 billion in 2017, equivalent to 0.8 per cent of the country's GDP that year.

Traffic flow on the roads will invariably cause traffic incidents and hold-ups. AI systems help traffic flow with the least disruption during such traffic incidents. AI systems using computers and sensors can constantly monitor the entire network of CCTV cameras and look at incidents, queues and unusual traffic conditions and provide a constant flow of data. Whenever the AI-driven systems detect traffic incidents or anomalies, they alert the control centres. An AI system called Clearway can spot an incident within the first ten seconds after its occurrence and can function under any lighting and weather conditions. Not just on open roads, it works in the tunnels also. The AI system can detect debris, animals, stationary vehicles, fast- and slow-moving vehicles and vehicles travelling in the wrong direction.

India reports about 500,000 road accidents annually, with over 150,000 deaths. These statistics are one of the highest across the world. Human error due to driver fatigue is one of the main reasons for road accidents. We cannot eliminate human error by instructing drivers to drive more carefully. Fitting car cabins with computer vision will ensure better, safer driver monitoring. Such technology can stave off thousands of crashes and deaths every year by looking out for drowsiness and emotional recognition of those behind the wheels. Many drivers don't admit that fatigue or feeling a bit exhausted will impact their ability to drive. AI-driven tech can alert a driver whenever their driving is taking a significant hit due to fatigue and advise them to pull over and rest, ensuring the safety of the driver, the passenger and other road users. Another area in which technology can be valuable is driver distraction. If a driver is distracted – for example, by their mobile device – the tech can alert them immediately to stay focused on the road. Other distractions might include chatting to a back seat passenger, which could impair the concentration without the driver realising it.

AI systems can enhance road safety in several ways. First, AI, by analysing data collected by the roadside units of traffic police, which may include data about the weather, the driving behaviour of other motorists and the state of the road, can help the authorities issue accurate and reliable warnings about road conditions to the road users. Second, AI systems have proved useful in identifying dangerous driving behaviour, including excessive speeding, unsafe lane changes and failure to obey traffic signs. Third, AI is an excellent tool to identify risky drivers, which can help authorities issue warnings and, in extreme cases, even take proactive steps to prevent crashes, such as automatically blocking a driver's vehicle when the police suspect drunk driving.

The Minister of Road Transport and Highways, Nitin Gadkari, has announced his plans to use AI-based technology to improve transportation. The priority areas identified by the minister for AI applications include forensic post-crash investigations, the pattern of accidents due to black spots, fatigue indicators, sleep detectors and advanced vehicle collision avoidance systems. AI reduces the need for human interference in road safety systems, making them more efficient and effective.

The minister recently launched the AI-powered iRASTE Project for Road Safety for Nagpur Municipal Corporation's fleet of vehicles by equipping them with collision avoidance technology to reduce accidents and near misses by up to 60 per cent. The technology envisages the deployment of sensors to help map the dynamic risk of the entire road network, recommend engineering fixes for existing black spots and implement an AI-powered system for continuous monitoring of road infrastructure. Leveraging the power of AI – the project aims to achieve up to a 50 per cent decline in road accidents in Nagpur city and create a blueprint of Vision Zero for the country. For the first time in the country, a state-run bus corporation is probably using AI technology on a large scale to reduce accidents.

Further, the Karnataka State Road Transport Corporation (KSRTC), to limit road accidents and improve passenger safety in buses last June, has floated a tender for the implementation of an AI-powered collision warning system (CWS) and driver drowsiness system (DDS) for 1044 buses. CWS will provide forward-looking collision warnings (FLCW), lane departure warnings (LDW) and a virtual bumper. It will also generate real-time alerts. Last August, the Indian Institute of Technology in Mandi created an intelligent road monitoring system to prevent mishaps prompted by sharp or blind turns. The system functions through sensors that detect the speed, path, gradient of the slope and type of vehicle and alerts the driver about the oncoming turn.

In addition to making transportation cheaper, AI can also make travel more convenient. Thanks to several modern technologies in the airline, train and bus industries, this is possible. For example, airlines increasingly use 'smart' check-ins that allow passengers to check in online, print their boarding passes and track their bags' progress through the baggage handling system. Similarly, modern transport operators may no longer have to calculate the routes manually. Instead, they can use real-time journey planning software that uses live weather data to calculate the best possible route leading to reduced costs.

Smart cities are all the rage right now. They aim to take advantage of all of the digital disruption that is happening in the world today. These smart cities will be safer, less polluted and better connected. They will also be able to handle more people and more traffic by making better use of AI.

In the digital era, cities are facing unprecedented challenges to keep pace with the changing landscape. From rapid urbanisation to a changing climate, urban planners are exploring new ways to make city life easier, more efficient and more sustainable. To achieve this, they are turning to AI to drive better, more personalised city services and make urban areas more liveable. AI has the potential to transform city life by enhancing the way people move around and efficiently use resources. Cities can use AI to improve traffic management, identify and respond to emerging hazards and even plan for a growing population.

AI has therefore the potential to revolutionise traffic management in Indian cities by improving operational efficiency, increasing road safety and making transportation cheaper and more convenient for all. Deploying AI to improve road safety, identify and penalise traffic violators and enhance the accuracy of traffic signs and warnings is particularly important in densely populated cities where millions of people travel on poorly maintained roads every day.

Chapter 39

HACKING AS A SERVICE

It blew my friend away when an incredible marriage proposal came from Canada for his daughter. His joy knew no bounds. The prospective multimillionaire bridegroom was an investment banker who recently had reaped a windfall in the bullish crypto market. He boasted of a fleet of cars, including a Rolls Royce and a Lamborghini. My friend, who adored his daughter immensely, was delighted for her, but some intuitive gut feeling that sprung within him unawares agitated him and filled him with uneasiness. He approached the HaaS market to wipe his trepidations before handing over his daughter in marriage. From there, he hired a hacker from the comfort of his home. It was a hassle-free online process without any physical contact. Once he engaged the services of a HaaS team, the hackers, after remotely accessing the mobile phone of the Canadian groom, began feeding my friend with updates in real time. They let him peek at all the WhatsApp messages, call logs, text messages, Instagram, e-mails of the prospective groom while simultaneously furnishing him with the entire history of his online activities and transactions. The story that emerged from all the recent and deleted messages was entirely different from the given narrative. It turned out that the would-be groom was all the time taking them for a ride. My friend instantly cancelled the marriage and averted his daughter from becoming a sacrificial goat in the nick of time. The gut feeling experienced by my friend helped him save his daughter from the clutches of a big crook who had a history of luring girls.

Likewise, the homemaker wife of a prominent bureaucrat suspected her husband was having an affair with an employee in the office. And a wealthy business owner's son doubted his new girlfriend of two-timing him. They separately approached hackers and paid them upwards of $400 for accessing the WhatsApp chats and social media accounts, including their e-mail accounts. The clandestine jaunts, Rendezvous and retreats, romantic exploits and other cats were out of the bag in just four days. Eventually, the bureaucrat saved his marriage by abject surrender and a promise of total loyalty to his wife. The business owner's son, on the other hand, ditched his cheating fiancé after confronting her with the facts.

HaaS is the commercialisation or monetisation of hacking skills in which the hacker serves as a contractor. HaaS makes advanced code-breaking capabilities available to anyone with an internet browser and a credit card. The HaaS market is flourishing and continuing to expand new services. The services that HaaS provides includes Facebook hack, WhatsApp hack, Twitter hack, erasure of criminal record, upgradation of school results, database hack, android phone hack, ATM hack, blank credit card service to withdraw the amount of one's choice and myriad other benefits. Being a hacker may not be illegal; however, hacking into a computer or mobile phone without the permission of its owners is unlawful. The capacity of novice hackers to rapidly launch accelerated attacks has heightened the number of threats that several cybersecurity experts have to grapple with and stave off.

Besides, HaaS has now made it possible for any Tom, Dick and Harry with practically no hacking skills to launch attacks anywhere. HaaS is now a fast-growing business contributing to an exponential rise of cybercrime activities on the internet. As HaaS markets have supplied services of hackers to anyone willing to pay for the hacking services, even a non-hacker today can engage HaaS and become a cybercriminal. Although such hacking markets have existed on the dark web for a long time, only recently they have matured into fully developed marketplaces. As with any other marketplace, hackers compete intensely to outdo each other and provide their clients with the best services and bargains.

Furthermore, one can select the hackers based on the budget and the task and enter a contract. Some HaaS marketplaces offer a moneyback guarantee and get their services rated and ranked. Other services that one can outsource through hacking marketplaces include distributed denial of service (DDoS), phishing, breaking into social media accounts, hijacking telephone numbers, call blocking, disrupting communication networks, spreading malware and controlling the botnets. HaaS creates a pay-to-play environment that empowers amateurs and wannabe criminals to plan and launch attacks beyond their skills and capabilities, making the cybercrime landscape more sinister.

According to a report by Kaspersky Labs, the average HaaS price for a DDoS attack is $25 per hour. SecureWorks charges 1–5 per cent of the money drained from an online account to facilitate a client's entry into it. One can hire HaaS to commit an online bank heist for rates upwards of $40, and the price for illegal transfer of reward points is $10–$450. For getting unauthorised access into Instagram, Twitter, Snapchat or other social media platforms, SecureWorks has pegged the average hacker fee at $129. The cost of breaking into a cell phone is feasible at $21.60/month or more. The price for hijacking corporate e-mail is $500 and upwards. According to an FBI's *Internet Crime Report*, corporate e-mail hacking drained over $676 million from company coffers in 2017.

HaaS has rendered cyberspace more vulnerable and the cyberthreat terrain more precarious. Police are finding it incredibly challenging to deal with cybercriminals of the HaaS model. To combat these threats, cybersecurity professionals would have to hang around a lot and monitor the dark web to gather intelligence to help them identify and block attacks proactively. Identifying new phishing domains, watching them and proactively blocking them can help reduce hacker attacks. Social media monitoring, identifying and taking down fake company websites is another effective way to prevent unsuspecting customers from being phished. Hackers have also been breaking into police networks worldwide and leaking sensitive information. Engaging ethical hackers to plug the loopholes in police networks and maintaining sensitive information could go a long way in minimising damage from hacker attacks.

Chapter 40

CYBERCRIME AS A SERVICE

CCaaS depicts an organised business model where cybercriminals, malware developers and other threat actors sell their cybercrime services to potential customers. Virtually anyone can now embark on a cyberattack or participate in cybercrime because CCaaS makes it easy for them to access an expert cybercriminal's services, expertise or tools. The 'customer' does not need technical knowledge or coding skills because their CCaaS vendor does all the groundwork required to launch a successful cyberattack with minimal efforts quickly. Due to its shady and illegal nature, CCaaS primarily operates on the dark web.

CCaaS – or the sale of criminal services to the public – is a type of cybercrime that involves the use of remote access tools to conduct illegal activities on behalf of an individual or organisation. CCaaS is a severe threat because it enables cybercriminals to act with virtually no risk of getting caught or punished for their actions. CCaaS vendors or suppliers organise themselves like legitimate businesses with a clear hierarchy of personnel: engineers, leaders, developers, money mules and tech support representatives. The latter's services help customers work through the technical aspect of the attacks. They can walk customers through the process of using the 'product'.

Cybercriminal hacking operations are now so competent that nation-states are deploying CCaaS to carry out attacks on their behalf to keep their involvement hidden. A document by cybersecurity researchers at BlackBerry informs that the emergence of sophisticated CCaaS schemes implies that nation-states increasingly have the choice of working with groups that can carry out attacks for them.

The main goal of a CCaaS agency is to grow its business by selling its services. Suppliers hire engineers, developers and leaders to create and maintain websites, software applications and other technologies that enable them to commit crimes. Suppliers also hire money mules to receive customer payments and transfer the money to their accounts.

CCaaS uses software and online services as their primary tool to conduct their activities. CCaaS also uses social media to reach clients. The range of services offered by CCaaS vendors is extensive and diverse. They range from hacking into e-mail accounts to ransomware. CCaaS allows individuals to purchase the tools they need to commit crimes. For example, a cybercriminal may sell a software programme enabling a buyer to steal someone else's identity or credit card information. Tools such as these can be hazardous, especially if they fall into the hands of a malicious group or individual. CCaaS vendors provide benefits to anyone who wishes to hire them. They don't require clients to reveal their identities.

In most cases, CCaaS is a form of organised crime, with groups of malicious actors working together to commit cybercrime – much like traditional crime is conducted. Fewer malicious actors are involved in CCaaS, many of whom may be unaware that their activities are illegal. Cybercrime services are often advertised and sold online, usually on websites outside law enforcement's reach. For example, a site may allow one to hide his online presence and browse the web anonymously. While it is entirely legal, it is also something that the police would like to shut down. Cybercriminals can sell VPNs and proxies, which are illegal, for malicious activities. Some other sites and marketplaces allow individuals to hire hackers to break into someone's e-mail or social media account. Individuals can also buy a fake ID or driver's licence from these sites.

Some products offered in the CCaaS market help steal money from the bank accounts of unsuspecting people. Buyers can use other products on this market to steal personal information and then sell that information to other criminals. Some CCaaS vendors offer products and services to protect against these threats.

These services get marketed to the public via the internet, Dark Web or other media. Most cybercriminals however often prefer to sell their services through marketplaces that are accessible to anyone. You don't need any identification to purchase products through these websites. They don't have any verification process, which makes them very easy to access. The cybercriminals and developers of services may advertise them as lawful or may disguise them as legitimate services. CCaaS offerings may be sold directly by the supplier or contracted through a third party. Some vendors may accept payment in cryptocurrency to avoid tracing. CCaaS may also market their offerings as privacy software, data security, ransomware protection or other lawful services.

Some sell access to cybercrime tools, others offer consulting services to clients, and some others provide a mix of these two. The main commonality of all CCaaS suppliers is their organisation in a manner that will not allow them to be charged with criminal activity if law enforcement were to take action against them.

To date, there is very little research on CCaaS and its impact on law enforcement and society. The lack of information on CCaaS makes it challenging to understand the scale and scope of the threat. It's a big problem for police because it creates an opening for criminals to sell their services to the general public. They can do this through online marketplaces, websites and social media.

These sites are easily accessible and allow people to purchase products that will help them commit cybercrimes. They can buy malware, bulk SIM cards or proxy IPs. These products are widely available, and they are often very affordable. The availability of these products makes it much easier for people to commit cybercrimes. It also makes it much harder for law enforcement to catch criminals.

There are many types of CCaaS, ranging from malware delivery to information sharing. Malware delivery typically occurs through infected websites. Information sharing is the most common type of CCaaS. Threat actors share information to assist with the development of new malicious tools and techniques.

We have all heard of ransomware and other malware that holds a user's files hostage until they pay a certain amount. The buying, selling or leasing of malware is also a form of CCaaS. Cybercriminals may buy or lease exploits and then sell them to the highest bidder. There are many different types of CCaaS offerings. Some examples include remote access trojans, botnets, spyware, ransomware, data stealers and other malicious programmes and scripts.

The buying and selling of exploits is also a type of CCaaS. Exploits are programmes or scripts that take advantage of a computer, software bug or vulnerability to cause problems. Cybercriminals can buy these exploits from their original creators or developers and then sell them to other cybercriminals who may find them helpful. Advanced attackers may also offer DDoS services, e-mail spam services or exploit kits for sale to anyone interested in purchasing them.

Examples of CCaaS might be selling remote access to a malware-infected computer, selling access to a botnet or selling exploit kits. There are many benefits to selling your services through CCaaS, such as scaling your business as needed, choosing your customers and avoiding the risk of getting caught. To stay safe, you must ensure that you are following best practices for selling your services.

These services may range from data exfiltration to ransomware, DDoS attacks and other malicious activities. The main difference between CCaaS and different types of cloud hosting is that CaaS customers do not have legal rights to store data on the hosting platforms. CaaS providers typically lease virtual private servers (VPS) or physical servers that run decentralised software protocols like BitTorrent, open source software (OSS) or other open source network protocols to deliver custom content. It is important to note that since these servers do not have any rights to store data, they can be shut down anytime without warning.

As a result, CCaaS undermines law enforcement's ability to fight crime and protect citizens, making it harder for police to track down and prosecute criminals. Police are also more vulnerable to cyberattacks when they don't access secure networks. But there are ways that they can mitigate these risks. For example, they can buy their secure network, use encryption tools and train personnel to detect fraud signs.

Unfortunately, not all systems are secure. Most of them are likely to be vulnerable to some extent. What happens when a system is susceptible? Patching the system is imperative. Now, consider a situation where you have a system that many people actively use. What if that system is vulnerable and there is no patch available? In such a situation, wouldn't it be wise to leave the system vulnerable and let people know about the risk? What happens when someone chooses not to warn others about the risk of using a system? What happens when someone exploits that system without letting people know about the risk? What happens when someone sells that system for profit without letting people know about the risk. Such susceptibilities cannot always be patched or prevented.

Further, the number of crimes committed by CCaaS is not known, and the amount of money stolen has not been quantified. The FBI has acknowledged that CCaaS harms law enforcement because of the time spent entering data into the system instead of investigating cases. Quantifying the amount of money stolen by CCaaS is complicated because of several reported crimes.

CCaaS is offered on the internet at various prices for various services; for instance, it costs $1.50 for 15 minutes of chat with cybercrime law enforcement professionals. The CCaaS costs $7.00 for 100 e-mails to stop spam, it costs $27.00 for a one hour live chat focused on your computer, and it costs just $0.25 for a clone of your hard drive. The services are offered by cybercrime groups on the dark web. Besides the option to stop spam e-mails, it also offers other services like hacking computers and cloning hard drives.

CCaaS offers cyberweapons for rent by the hour, day or month. And they can be rented for a few dollars. For example, to rent a DDoS booter for a day, a client would only need to pay around $60. For around $400, customers can rent it for a week. Medium-level malware kits typically cost around $1000 and are designed for individual or domestic use. High-end malware kits are more expensive, costing between $10,000 and $100,000. These are used mainly by large-scale enterprises and governments.

However, if you want a high-end kit that can do things like bypassing antivirus software, you will have to spend thousands of dollars. Prices for renting a DDoS bot also vary, but you can expect to pay around $300 per month. As for hiring a hacker, the cost will depend on the person's skill set. You can expect to spend thousands of dollars on hiring a skilled hacker.

Those who want something more powerful can shell out tens of thousands of dollars for state-of-the-art software. What you pay for will depend on what you plan to do with it. The most basic malware kits are simple enough to use, even for those with no coding experience. However, they lack the power and flexibility of more advanced options.

Those looking to undertake more severe attacks can purchase more sophisticated malware kits for around $1000. Keep in mind that these prices do not include the cost of buying a remote server to host the malware.

However, these products are unreliable, and one can detect them with antivirus software. For more severe attacks, buyers will spend up to $50,000 on malware kits that are harder to see. The kits also come with support, so customers can ask the seller for help if they have any issues with the product.

It makes it easier for people to commit crimes and harder for police to catch criminals. Police must understand the technology and software used by cybercriminals to fight back and keep up with criminals. There are a few ways to detect CCaaS. You can use pattern recognition, analytical and AI software. AI has been used to help fight cybercrime for a few years, but it is now reaching a point where it can help police fight crime.

There are a few things that police officers can do to help the people they serve to protect themselves from the dangers of CCaaS. First, they can provide a solid working relationship with the community they serve. Policing is a job that requires a lot of trust and respect between officers and the public. One of the best ways to combat CCaaS is to have a strong relationship with the people of the police service and create awareness about cybercrime and the services which cybercriminals are providing so that they can guard themselves or at least take precautions from becoming victims of such cyberattacks.

The next crucial step is for law enforcement agencies to acknowledge and commit to combating the problem within the ranks. By increasing awareness and starting conversations about the issue, law enforcement agencies can help to mitigate the threat of CCaaS. Agencies can also train officers to deal with cybercriminals who either sell CCaaS discreetly or provide cybercrime service covertly for other reasons.

Lately, the rise of cybercrime has become a big problem for governments, businesses and ordinary people. Cybercrime using computers and networks such as hacking, identity theft and fraud are rising. While it is difficult to quantify the exact number of cybercrimes, various agencies monitor this problem. There are reports that the number of cybercrimes committed in 2016 was more than 10 million worldwide. In addition, the rising population of internet users combined with the easy access to malicious codes has created an environment conducive to cybercrime. As a result, more and more people worldwide are becoming targets for cybercriminals. To combat this growing threat, law enforcement agencies have stepped up their efforts to combat cybercrime by offering additional services such as consulting on cybersecurity strategies and training hackers. While law enforcement can certainly help stop cybercriminals in their tracks, they cannot do it alone. The community also has a role in fighting against cybercrime by educating themselves about security threats and not clicking on suspicious links or attachments. We can all make a difference in protecting our digital safety by working together!

If CCaaS ecosystem is left unmonitored and unregulated, it can cause immense damage and loss to individuals. There are several ways to address the challenges of CCaaS. The first step is recognising that CCaaS is a growing threat to public safety and national security. Second, law enforcement must be able to investigate threats, assess the risk and determine if the person poses a threat to public safety. Third, law enforcement must share information with other agencies relevant to their investigations to ensure that those agencies have the information they need to make informed decisions about the risk posed by cybercriminals in their communities.

Moreover, there are still many unanswered questions surrounding CCaaS, such as:

- How much money is being stolen by CCaaS; which types of crimes are being committed?
- How often CCaaS is occurring?
- How effective law enforcement is in dealing with the problem?
- What can be done to mitigate the threat?

Without a clear understanding of these issues, law enforcement will struggle to combat CCaaS.

Finally, to keep cybercrime at bay and protect citizens from its negative impacts, it is necessary to have a comprehensive law enforcement framework in place. Countries that currently lack such a framework or do not have a robust one can use this assessment model to improve their law enforcement efforts.

- How dependable and secure the websites and systems are where the public or private data gets hosted?
- How easy it is to report cybercrime and get a response?
- How quickly problems are solved when they get reported?
- How transparent the law enforcement is in its operations?
- The extent to which law enforcement works with the public in solving cybercrimes and addressing the issues that lead to them.
- The level of public trust in the law enforcement agency and its officers.

Chapter 41

A COMPREHENSIVE LOOK AT POLICING IN 2050

Policing is a profession that is constantly evolving. As the years go by and technology becomes more sophisticated, we will create new methods for keeping communities safe. The future of policing is already in sight. Technology is not just changing the way police officers do their jobs. It is changing how we hire, train and manage police officers.

But while the technological changes are coming fast and furious, it is essential to look at the technology itself and how we use it. Policing is still a fundamentally human activity that relies on the ability to read people, process information and accurately identify threats. Therefore, while technology is helping to change policing, it will not change everything. Only humans can make the right decisions at the right time and ensure that communities are safe.

What Is the Future of Policing?

The future of policing is about a world where technology and human interaction are at the forefront. It's about a place where police get empowered with the tools and technology they need to succeed. And it's also about a world where the everyday interactions between citizens and police are more comfortable and productive. That is the future of policing.

Soon, we'll see many departments integrating AI, IoT and machine learning into their daily operations. It's a future where we use technology to empower officers and better serve their communities. And it's a future where we will use technology to improve the way we do things. We're at a point where the lines between human and machine intelligence are becoming increasingly blurred.

In the future, we'll see an increase in data-driven policing strategies, which would allow departments to focus their limited resources on the areas where they'll have the most significant impact. It will also enable them to create real-time data dashboards that we can use to analyse crime and predict future crime patterns. The future of policing will also see increased collaborative initiatives between departments and cities. That will allow for more efficient and effective use of resources and more effective community engagement.

How Will Technology Impact Police?

A myriad of technological advancements will shape the future of policing. But, perhaps the most exciting aspect is that it will bring to life the idea that 'we can put or use technology to empower officers and better serve their communities'. The first step in this direction is the continued rise of wearable tech. Police and first responders are already wearing various wearable devices to reduce risk and increase productivity. We'll see an increase in the number of uses for wearable technology in the future - everything from body cameras and smartwatches to helmets, cameras and contact lenses. Wearable tech will also allow us to see a rise in voice recognition and speech-to-text software. That will enable officers to document and transcribe their interactions with civilians in real time. It's also likely that we'll see an increase in eye-tracking and facial recognition software. We can use such software pieces to identify and track suspects and witnesses and verify identities to ensure compliance with legal processes. It will be essential to consider the level of privacy involved when using these technologies.

The next step in using technology will be the integration of AI and machine learning into daily operations. We will use AI and ML to automate and expedite repetitive tasks and support decision-making. It will allow for real-time analysis of large volumes of data. It will also allow for the study of unstructured data, such as photos and videos. We will use AI to expand the use of computer vision or the ability for machines to see and understand the world around them, allowing for the creation of real-time alerts and maps that we will use to predict potential threats to an officer and public safety. We will also use AI to automate the collection of critical data. It will be able to recognise patterns and anticipate potential risks while also taking corrective actions. These actions include sending alerts, such as those related to officer safety or the need to respond to a crime in progress. We will use AI to automate the collection and analysis of data. Officers will use data to inform their decisions and help them understand the community they're policing.

AR in the Police Setting

AR, an immersive technology, blends digital technology with the real world. It uses various camera-based components to superimpose computer-generated images and information over a user's objective worldview.

AR will get used in a wide variety of ways to improve policing. That includes everything from helping bridge the gap between officers and the community to enhancing officers' understanding of crime, criminal investigations and daily operations. Police organisations will use AR also to provide contextual information on locations. That could include digital signage, maps or other content related to the specific site. This information can help officers understand the community and make informed decisions.

The use of AR in the future of policing will also include the integration of VR, allowing officers to experience different scenarios in the field. That could allow them to practise tactical scenarios, such as running an active shooter drill, in a safe and controlled environment. VR will also enable officers to experience things like a traffic stop through the user's own eyes. That gives officers a better understanding of what they'll encounter on the street and how they can prepare for it.

VR and the Future of Policing

VR is quickly becoming a staple in the modern world. It allows users to experience and interact with different types of content, including computer-generated environments. It's the next frontier for the future of policing. Police will use VR for various purposes, including training and simulation. VR will allow officers to experience different scenarios and understand how their decisions will impact their situation. VR will also allow officers to interact with other officers and civilians while in the field. VR will enable officers to experience different types of content, including VR simulations of other cities, futuristic cities and other environments. This content can help officers understand their role in the community, where their priorities should be and how they can improve. It's also a great way for officers to prepare for specific scenarios.

Chatbots, Virtual Assistants and AI in Law Enforcement

Technology will increasingly get used as an enabler for ambitious projects. That's what's happening in the realm of AI. This cutting-edge technology allows developers to create chatbots and virtual assistants that police departments can use to automate and expedite repetitive tasks and make complex decisions. Police agencies can use a chatbot to automate repetitive tasks, such as small talk with customers or scheduling in-person meetings. But, they can also use it to expedite more complex tasks, such as scheduling a conference call or conducting a flight search. It can even help with more imaginative tasks, such as scheduling a date night with a spouse. Police organisations will use virtual assistants and bots to help with more complex decisions. Police may use virtual assistants to check and create criminal records. These assistants can identify and flag relevant information, such as a person's criminal record, and direct officers to the appropriate place within the system. Police will also use AI to expand the use of computer vision and facial recognition. To allow officers to identify and track suspects and witnesses and verify identities to ensure compliance with legal processes.

If one were to conjure up a scenario of crime detection in 2050 and ask me – What types of crimes will police departments be fighting in 2050? Right off the bat, I think we'll see thought crimes. Imagine thinking about murdering someone. The AI sensors will detect the thought, and the individual thinking about the murder would be taken in immediately for the offence of attempt to murder. Drones with facial recognition capability and weapons will replace law enforcement officers who, from the safety and comfort of a chair, would command drones to kill any human being they deem a 'terrorist'. With no need for consequences associated with killing someone by mistake or accident. Nobody would complain about accidental killings because it just wouldn't happen anymore! Humans will have government implants beginning at birth that record their thoughts, so there won't even be an excuse for people daring enough not to conform to party lines or dress codes; for those who do not follow orders, machine intelligence will automatically place them on wanted lists. Implantation includes fingerprints, DNA samples, yearly photos, speech patterns, retinal scans, colonic maps, what-have-you, which makes me wonder if implanted humans also have an identifying chip inside them like some pets do now?

Hardcore 'terrorists' will be those who live off of the grid, do not conform to the government or dress as ordered and those who dare to think for themselves. Hearing the wrong music, reproducing without and other things will make a person a threat to the state.

Plastic appliances will replace metal knives or anything that could be a weapon or accidentally kill someone. There will be no human drivers as all vehicles will be self-driving. Automated self-driving cars will chauffeur everyone around. Hence there won't be drive-offs, police car chases, terrorists using vehicles to plough into crowds or car-jacking or using explosive-laden cars to ram into the target and no pollution and petrol problems as all cars would be either solar-powered or electric. Police would be able to disable any vehicle or vehicle suspected of carrying a terrorist or criminal and redirect the vehicle to the nearest police station. Automation will cover police work, administration, crime detection or policy.

Robots will patrol the streets, arrest the offenders and also defuse bombs. To bring some human element to policing, we would see some cyborgs like robocops with some human emotion. Although it will become difficult for humans to commit crimes, AI and robots are likely to commit crimes against humans, a dystopic unthinkable scenario. Ray Kurzweil has forecast that singularity will be attainable by 2045. At this point, machine intelligence will surpass or equal human intelligence. Various scenarios are predicted, most of them dystopian hence when this happens, the future of humankind itself could be at stake. Policing in 2050 will be highly hitech as various exponential technologies will synergies and produce mind-blowing technologies which could go out of control due to the speed at which the technological innovations will unfold and leave lawmakers behind. Hence, the governments and decision-makers must take stock and find ways to grapple with the exponential technologies that are growing at a breakneck speed by enacting laws and placing curbs on them so that they don't spin out of the machines always remain under the control of humans.

Conclusion

Technology is constantly changing, and it will impact policing in many ways in the next decade. Innovations in AI and machine learning will help strengthen relationships between officers and the communities they serve. Police organisations will use wearable tech to enhance officers' visibility and awareness. And AR and VR will allow officers to interact with their environment in a much more realistic way.

As the first responders in every community, the police community must be equipped with the tools and technology to succeed. The future of policing will depend on the evolution of these technologies and how police organisations use them.

Chapter 42

THE POTENTIAL OF AI TO TRANSFORM THE FUTURE OF POLICING

AI is progressing rapidly. It has the potential to improve almost every facet of our lives, and the world of law enforcement is no exception. Because of its potential to provide tremendous value to law enforcement, AI will play an increasingly important role in law enforcement over the next decade. As AI advances, it will help law enforcement agencies deal with crimes faster and more effectively. In the future, law enforcement will continue to focus on solving and fighting crimes. However, law enforcement will also pivot towards preventing crime, catching criminals before they can act and preventing a harm before it happens. Hence, the future holds much potential for AI and law enforcement.

Because of its capabilities, AI could drive positive change in the law enforcement sector. Police organisations using AI will reduce costs and improve services in the future. AI will also give law enforcement agencies new ways to solve problems. For example, AI could help agencies identify and track suspicious individuals. AI could also enhance trust between police and the communities they serve. Law enforcement agencies will increasingly use AI to monitor and analyse citizens. However, the technology is still in its infancy; there are several challenges that law enforcement needs to overcome.

Police departments in several countries today use AI to analyse vast amounts of criminal data and make sense of it. Police are also deploying AI to automate specific tasks and free up officers to do other, more important, things. AI can help law enforcement agencies work smarter and more efficiently. Here are several ways in which AI can help law enforcement agencies in the future.

AI Can Help Police Identify Suspects

One of the most promising AI applications in law enforcement in identifying suspects. Several police departments still adopt manual processes because of inadequate resources and tools to search against their databases of known accused and previously arrested or booked individuals. Such manual processes require significant time and resources. As a result, they follow the procedure only in some severe or high-profile cases and leave cases of lesser importance unsolved. Despite public perception, even when criminals get caught on camera, police still have to identify the suspect and connect him to the crime. Most agencies still manually sift through mass arrest records, turning to colleagues for intel and even publicly promoting the case to identify their person of interest.

It would be easier for police to identify suspected criminals if they could use an AI system that scans databases, internet records, social media and other sources of information about the criminal in question. AI offers a solution tailored for law enforcement agencies by helping police expeditiously link known offenders to criminal activity, which it accomplishes through innovative facial recognition technology (FRT) supported by a solid digital evidence toolkit.

By scanning the video footage, AI can help police identify a suspect caught on camera at a robbery scene or identify a suspect who has a warrant out for his arrest. Many law enforcement agencies use AI FRT to identify suspects from CCTV/video feeds or other records. FRT allows police to quickly compare their known offenders against crime scene footage, saving valuable time and resources.

Police compare offenders in video and photographic evidence against a database of known offenders. AI is aiding police in filtering down potential matches found in existing arrest records by key identifiers stored in the current database, such as gender, age, height, hair colour, eye colour and ethnicity, besides lining up a list of potential suspects for further evaluation and investigation. AI is facilitating easy collaboration by the feature of sharing suspect lists with intra- and interdepartmental colleagues and booking information, including photo, name, last known address and more. Further, AI also assists law enforcement in consolidating suspect information in a secure web-based platform besides organising evidence.

For instance, let's say a group of people murder a person on the road due to gang rivalry. AI will analyse the CCTV footage and compare the images of the offenders got from the crime scene with the database. Once the photos from the database get matched to the offenders at the crime scene, the AI will automatically share the images of the offenders with the patrols and other police districts so that they can launch a simultaneous manhunt to arrest the offenders. Sometimes the photos available in the police database may not match the image from the crime scene. In such cases, the AI updates the database by adding the new offenders to the existing database while simultaneously launching a lookout for the offenders by conveying the images to the other CCTV cameras and activating the FRTs inside them to identify and alert the police of their capture. Therefore, it is imperative to install cameras equipped with AI and FRT at strategic points to verify or recognise criminals or people involved in criminal activities.

AI Is Valuable in Detecting Patterns

AI can help law enforcement agencies detect patterns they might not have noticed before. Machine learning can be an incredible tool for crime pattern detection. If machine learning can identify crime patterns automatically, then the police can immediately try to stop them. Without such tools, it could take weeks or years of sifting through a database to discover a pattern, or it might get missed altogether.

For example, suppose the police department records the location of all the calls that come in. In that case, AI will analyse this data and find any patterns that could lead to the detection of more crimes, which would be especially helpful for a city with many cases that are often similar.

Crime is not random; it is a compilation of patterns. And AI can flip through patterns accurately. Using AI technology can enable the monitoring of content and prediction of crimes. And predicting crimes will ultimately help deter them. AI can help monitor a person's digital footprints and detect any unusual activities. The goal of law enforcement should not be to catch criminals but to prevent crime.

AI Can Be Valuable for Predictive Policing

The rise of AI can change how law enforcement agencies work. Police departments are already using sophisticated AI programmes to monitor crime scenes, track suspects and analyse evidence, allowing police officers to spend more time-solving cases and less time on administrative tasks. AI can also help law enforcement agencies predict where crimes will occur, which areas might be targets for criminal activity and what types of crimes might happen next. These predictions are all based on data collected by the AI programme. For example, suppose an AI programme predicts that robberies are likely in a specific area a few weeks from now. In that case, police could patrol that area more heavily or work with store owners to increase security measures. AI makes such predictions based on historical data from previous robberies in the same place. By comparing past crime rates with current crime rates, police can see when a particular neighbourhood is at risk for higher criminal activity.

AI is an excellent tool for police to monitor and predict crimes. We can also use it for identifying vulnerable areas or individuals most at risk of becoming victims or perpetrators of crime. There are socioeconomic factors that contribute to crime. AI has the potential to help police departments make better use of their resources by flagging areas that are likely to see an increase in crime or by identifying repeat offenders. AI delivers many advantages to the police department. These advantages include increased efficiency, increased accuracy and ease of implementation. With efficiency, AI allows law enforcement to be more efficient because it reduces the time and effort necessary to sort through data. AI can help investigators and analysts process over 50 per cent more data than they could use manual methods. As far as accuracy is concerned, AI provides law enforcement with a higher level of accuracy than what they could otherwise achieve manually. Finally, with ease of implementation, AI is easy to implement because it requires minimal training and a small initial investment in equipment.

AI Can Help Monitor Crime Scenes

Police to solve complex cases of murder most often need intensive investigation. AI today is helping police officers detect vital clues from the crime scene. When cops visit a crime scene, they take photographs of the place where the crime occurred. Police use such pictures to find clues and evidence that can help open up a new link to the crime. AI-enabled systems are helping cops detect hints from such police photographs. For example, police can use a toy or a weapon seized from the crime scene and search for it in the police database to find the use of the same toy or weapon in any previous murders. It might not definitively link the culprit of the last murder to the current crime, but it will open up an investigation line worth checking out.

Sometimes bombs may get placed by the criminals in strategic places. Bombs are among the most destructive weapons employed by criminals and terrorists. A single bomb can cause the death of hundreds of people. Robots equipped with AI can not only defuse bombs but potentially recognise nitroglycerin, aluminium powder, tetranitrate, passive infrared sensors and other components used to create bombs at such crime scenes. With the ability to identify bomb components, AI-enabled robots can easily detect bombs without risking the lives of security personnel.

AI Can Be a Great Tool for Training Police Officers

Training police officers is a tedious and expensive task. AI can help the police with training. It can analyse past interactions and decisions to help train new officers in the future. There are so many aspects of the job they need to learn. AI can help train officers by providing them with an understanding of the nuances of law enforcement. AI can offer a limitless number of scenarios to interact with, which will help them prepare for potential real-life scenarios. That would allow law enforcement agencies to focus on more pressing matters, like developing intelligence or combating terrorism and cyberthreats. AI also can create a virtual simulation for officers who have never been in a law enforcement situation before. This way, they'll be able to get some experience before they ever have to enter the field themselves.

AI is also a valuable tool for training a trainer. If a trainer needs to provide ongoing training to other employees, AI can help make that process more efficient by providing an easy way to provide automated feedback and testing. When used correctly, AI can be a valuable tool for training. AI is becoming a trendy tool implemented in many training programmes. There are many ways that AI police can use in a training programme. One of the most popular uses for AI in a training programme is to deliver the content to learners. Many training programmes adopt AI to allow the learners to view the content from any location. And this is especially important for today's workforce, which is constantly on the go and trying to balance family and work life. Another widespread use of AI in a training programme is to deliver assessments. There are no more paper or pencil tests with AI, which can save time and money on printing and scoring tests. AI also provides instant results, making it easy for learners to know how they did on this test.

Police training institutes can use AI to evaluate whether a trainer effectively delivers the content. Training institutes can use AI as an aid in the classroom to provide feedback regarding the effectiveness of a trainer. AI can detect if the trainer is veering off-topic, if the trainer is giving good examples and explanations and if they are using too many illustrations or not enough. AI can help provide structure and consistency to the instructor by allowing them to deliver consistent lectures across all classes. AI can also conduct research and collect data on how effective a trainer is at imparting knowledge, how well students are keeping information and how long students take to complete specific tasks or assignments. AI is also a valuable tool for training a trainer. It can evaluate whether an instructor effectively imparts knowledge to their students through their lectures and instructional methods. It can also help train new instructors by assessing their effectiveness as instructors and helping them identify areas in which they may need improvement.

AI Can Enhance Forensics

Law enforcement can also use AI for forensics. AI tools can help analyse audio, video and images to help solve crimes. AI can improve forensics by scanning crime scenes for evidence that we may miss otherwise. Using AI in forensic and criminal investigations is burgeoning. The potential applications of machine learning are staggering, including predicting when and where a crime will get committed and analysing behaviour patterns to determine the likelihood a suspect is guilty. AI is also being used to process a wide range of data, from audio recordings to video surveillance footage. That allows law enforcement agencies to streamline their investigative processes by removing some steps that were once necessary. In one recent example from China, police used AI in an investigation for the first time to classify evidence records by type, which made it possible for investigators to identify clues from recorded conversations that would have taken hours of work before AI was involved.

AI Can Enable Police to Build Trust with the Public

Building trust with the public is one of the crucial tasks of law enforcement. We can use AI to build trust with people by providing more transparency to police activities.

Lack of transparency makes building bridges with the public difficult. AI offers a solution. As law enforcement agencies and their officers use more AI technology, the data, processes and actions taken become open for all to see. That's important because people want assurances that their data is secure and that their privacy will receive protection no matter what happens. AI can also help build trust in other ways. For example, AI can predict when someone may need the police's help before calling them or even knowing they need it.

AI Can Help in Creating Safer Cities

AI will help police officers make more intelligent decisions on duty. The AI will predict events and even work with law enforcement agencies to create safer cities. One example of this already in the works is self-driving cars used by law enforcement to patrol certain areas more efficiently than humans could.

A safe city concept is a crucial aim that takes a smart city to a greater level of development. Government can achieve the highest form of liveability for its people only by providing them with everything a safe city can. And AI is the only 21st-century tool that can create an effective safety shield for everyone. Crime, illegal activities or any such suspicious activities are nothing new. But as technology advances and people become more intelligent, exposure to threats increases. So, it becomes a necessity to use AI in safeguarding cities.

AI can be a safety tool that enables cities to improve infrastructure and services by deploying intelligent technology and data in the right direction.

An integrated network of intelligent systems that effectively captures public safety information and responds to real-time events can make a city safe. These systems that use AI can predict and prevent suspicious or malicious activities from happening or going to happen in the city limits.

It is essential to focus on what information the police need to collect at the right place and time and who must have the authority to access the report. After having access, it is also crucial to decide how the information gets processed and how we ultimately use that information and create a safe environment for our citizens.

Safety Measures in India with AI

The Government of India is focusing on the development of 100 smart cities across the nation with the smart resurgence of the other 500 cities. Cabinet has already approved 98,000 crores ($980 billion) for developing safe and smart cities across the nation. The Smart Cities Mission of the Indian government includes intelligent safety solutions for citizens focusing primarily on children, women and older adults as the primary aim. The AI-integrated safety measures include centralised video surveillance and management system that monitors and keeps checks on traffic movements, assets, crime and security of the public and their reputation.

On the other side, data accumulating sensors like LPR, social media intelligence and gunshot detection with more applications on the list are shown on the GIS map to create better intelligence and precise awareness.

The best example to understand these applications better is the city of Surat. The crime rate in the city has dropped by 27 per cent after implementing AI-based safety measures.

During incidents of violent crimes and prominent law-and-order disturbances, rapid intervention is crucial to prevent serious injuries and escalation of violence. Instead of the AI systems, many police organisations still rely on manual phone information from the public.

If applied to existing CCTV camera feeds, AI-based real-time video analytics can enable law enforcement officers to monitor vast expanses of the city and spot violence faster.

Older video analytics technology could cause false alarms – for example, flagging people hugging or dancing as fighting.

Advances in technology and behavioural analytics powered by AI have dramatically boosted the precision of discovering such violence, enabling police to take proactive action to prevent its further spread.

The current behavioural analytics systems can identify fighting when hands move towards another person or repeated touching and disengagement as violence. The AI systems can also recognise differing fighting styles, including kicking, punching or wrestling, in indoor and outdoor settings. Besides, it can also detect the stabbing of a person. Researchers are now training AI systems to identify a person holding a weapon.

The action of a person stabbing another person can also get detected, even if the weapon isn't visible. Further, we can now train advanced AI to recognise a person holding a gun in a threatening position.

This knowledge and context enable security personnel to comprehend what they are dealing with before arriving at the scene and help them respond most appropriately and safely.

AI Is a Valuable Tool for Automated Decision-Making

One of the most critical ways AI can help law enforcement agencies is by making better and more efficient decisions. For example, AI could analyse crime data and autogenerate a report with crime predictions for a specific area. The police could then use this information to better plan their patrols. AI could also make quicker decisions in dangerous situations. Imagine an officer on patrol stops a suspicious person in the middle of the night. With AI, they would no longer have to drive to the station, fill out paperwork and wait for someone else to decide what action to take. They could submit video footage for analysis and await instructions from an AI-powered programme to let them know whether it's safe to take action on their own or if they need backup from other officers nearby.

AI Can Help in Bringing Down Crime Rates

Implementing AI in law enforcement will decrease crime rates as more sophisticated AI programmes. AI can help predict future crimes by analysing data sources like social media, surveillance systems and more, allowing the police to allocate resources effectively and make arrests before criminals commit crimes.

AI can help law enforcement identify suspects and even predict crime before it happens. 'predictive policing' is a proactive policing strategy that uses data analysis and computer science to expect crimes and prevent them from happening. Identifying the most likely people who can commit a crime can affect crime rates, so many police departments adopt this approach. We can use facial recognition software to identify people with warrants or other criminal records, lowering the number of crimes committed by repeat offenders.

Criminals today use the internet to discuss or plan a crime. AI is monitoring such content on the internet. The algorithms of AI detect such unusual words related to an offence conveyed over the internet. AI systems can then despatch information to the police department about such unusual activity or transmission between criminals, which can help identify the people about to commit a crime. Also, facial recognition can eventually help predict a person who will commit a crime. Behavioural changes can help AI systems detect and forecast a person's future actions with facial recognition and tracking.

AI Can Help the Judiciary in Making Decisions Regarding Bail

AI systems can help judges accurately determine whether an accused in an offence can be granted bail or not or order a pretrial release or not. The established system is an imperfect system which is open to bigotry, as judges deliver varied judgements according to their point of view towards a crime. AI can help the judges decide the release of a criminal by appreciating the risk factors such as pending charges against the criminal, previous violent convictions, previous failures to appear for court hearings and prior sentences to incarceration.

AI Can Revolutionise Traffic Management

Every smart city worldwide uses or plans to use AI to mitigate traffic density and accidents. Sensors installed at parking lots, traffic signals and intersections use AI to accumulate valuable data for governments to plan their city initiatives efficiently. This raw data is unimaginably more extensive than humans can view, analyse and process, and it is here that the role of AI comes in. AI can count many vehicles, pedestrians or other movements while keeping track of their speeds. It can perform face recognition, read licence plates and crunch all satellite data to any magnitude to establish patterns crucial for city advancements.

Conclusion

Police departments in several countries use AI to analyse vast amounts of criminal data and make sense of it. Police will also deploy AI to automate specific tasks and free up officers to do other more productive things. However, the technology is still in its infancy, and there are several challenges that law enforcement will need to overcome.

AI can be an excellent tool for monitoring and predicting crimes, for police training, for forensics and building trust with people. AI is here to stay. It continues to grow and thrive at an exponential rate. And with that growth comes a slew of opportunities, as well as challenges. AI is no longer a future concern, as it already has applications within law enforcement and the criminal justice system.

Chapter 43

IMMORTALITY THROUGH MIND UPLOADING

In the 2016 movie *Chappie*, set in Johannesburg in the near future, automated robots comprise a mechanised police force. An encounter between two rival criminal gangs severely damages the law-enforcing robot (Agent 22). His creator Deon recommends dismantling and recycling the damaged police droids. However, criminals kidnap Deon and force him to upload human consciousness into the damaged robot to train it to rob banks. Chappie becomes the first robot with the human mind who can think and feel like a human. Later, when his creator Deon is dying in the movie, Chappie turns to upload Deon's consciousness into a spare robot through a neural helmet. Similarly, in *Avatar*, a 2009 Hollywood science fiction, a character in the film by name Grace connects with Eiwa, the collective consciousness of the planet, and transfers her mind to her avatar body, while another character, Jake, moves his mind to his avatar body rendering his human body lifeless.

Mind uploading is a process by which we relocate the mind, an assemblage of memories, personality and attributes of a specific individual, from its original biological brain to an artificial computational substrate. Mind uploading is a central conceptual feature of many sci-fi novels and films. For instance, Hanson's book titled *The Age of Em: Work, Love and Life when Robots Rule the Earth* is a 2016 nonfiction book that explores the implications of a future world when researchers have learned to copy humans onto computers, creating 'ems', or emulated people, who quickly come to outnumber the real ones.

Ever since we have realised our mortality, achieving immortality has been humankind's holy grail. Although medicine has advanced and prolonged human lives, immortality has eluded us. Achieving physical immortality may seem far away, but digital immortality appears within our reach today. Transhumanists consider mind uploading as an important technology for life extension. It's probably the current best option for preserving the identity of the species, as opposed to cryonics. Many transhumanists believe that they will become immortal by creating non-biological copies of their brain and leaving behind their biological shell. They also believe that consciousness has a computational basis.

According to Moore's law, computing power doubles approximately every two years, enabling several technologies from nanotechnology to 3D printing to undergo exponential advances. Because of the implacable climb of the technologies by 2045 on a conservative estimate Ray Kurzweil, an American futurist, believes that we will achieve a level of computation to simulate a functional human brain. This impending singularity is what a 'transhumanist' interprets as digital immortality. Transhumanists believe that humans will soon upload their minds to a computer, transcending the need for a biological body that may sound like sci-fi. But, in reality, neuroscience is making rapid strides towards it.

In August 2014, IBM's Dharmendra Modha announced a breakthrough in the development of TrueNorth, a neuromorphic computing chip that IBM meant to emulate the neurobiological architecture of the human brain. In April 2013, President Obama made public the 'Brain Activity Map Project', a decade-long plan to map every neuron in the human brain and revolutionise our understanding of the human brain. The Blue Brain Project by the Brain and Mind Institute of the Ecole Polytechnique Fédérale de Lausanne, Switzerland, is an attempt to create a synthetic brain by reverse engineering mammalian brain circuitry. Markram, director of the 'BlueBrain' project, five years after the successful simulation of the part of a rat brain, believes that we can build a functional artificial human brain within a decade. Current ongoing work in brain simulation has achieved partial and whole simulations of some animals. For example, the roundworm *C. elegans*, Drosophila fruit fly and mouse have achieved mind uploading to various degrees.

Berger, a researcher at the University of Southern California, aims to replace a portion of the hippocampus region in the brain with a brain–computer interface (BCI) that converts short-term memories into long-term ones. The device converts a short-term memory such as a phone number into a digital signal mathematically transformed in a computer and fed back into the brain, sealed in as long-term memory. He has successfully tested this device in rats and monkeys and is now testing it on humans. Rothblatt believes we will create 'mind clones' in the future, which are digital versions of humans that can live forever. We will generate mind clones from a 'mindfile' from an online repository that humans already have, such as Facebook. The mindfile would run on mindware, a kind of software for consciousness. The implication of creating a mindfile is continuity of self because a person would not have to inhabit a human body. In *Altered Carbon*, a Netflix series that takes place hundreds of years in the future, the body no longer matters. A character in the series sarcastically says: 'You shed it like a snake sheds its skin.' That's because we can digitise human consciousness and translocate it between bodies – both natural and synthetic

Mind uploading can also provide a permanent backup file to enable interstellar space travel. Instead of a human astronaut in a space flight to outer planets, we could use an uploaded astronaut for unlimited interstellar travel to avoid the perils of zero gravity, cosmic radiation to the human body and the vacuum of space. In his book *Physics of the Impossible*, he mentions that mind simulation through techniques such as quantum entanglement and whole brain emulation using an advanced MRI may help teleport humans to vast distances at the speed of light. Uploading the human mind could lead to exponential economic growth. Humans would be more efficient if we upload minds into a robotic humanoid body. When the mind gets uploaded into a computer, the mind develops computer-like intelligence. It improves the ability to think a million times faster than the average brain, which in theory could mean that we can experience one year in the real world in approximately 31 seconds of real time.

Mind uploads can minimise the increase in the world's population and the resultant harmful consequences because of enhanced computing power and several folds increase in productivity. Besides, if we uploaded human consciousness into VR, there could be better environmental recuperation. Humans would have a tinier effect on the environment and release less carbon dioxide. They would not be using up energy if they existed in VR. Mind uploading could help humanity survive a crisis such as climate change by making a functional copy of human society in a 'Matryoshka brain', a computing device that consumes all energy from a star.

Mind uploading is today possible by one of the two methods. The first method is the gradual replacement of neurons or copying and transferring neurons. The human brain comprises, on average, 86 billion nerve cells called neurons, which they link to other neurons through connectors called axons and dendrites. Signals at the synapses (junctions) of these connections get transmitted by the release of neurotransmitters. Essential functions performed by the mind, such as learning, memory and consciousness, are pure because of electrochemical processes in the brain. In the former, reconstructing neurons and their connections may be a considerable task that depends on neurons' electrical and biochemical exchange dynamics. Therefore, capturing them in a single frozen state may prove difficult.

In the latter, we can achieve an upload by scanning and mapping the brain and transferring the information into a computer system. The biological brain may not withstand the copying process. The shared mind could be within a VR, a robot or a 3D body simulation model. Many of the tools and ideas required to achieve mind uploading are already in existence or are under active development. A startup in the US, called Nectome, has revealed plans to preserve human brains by a revolutionary brain embalming technique called 'vitrification'. It involves replacing the blood flow in the brain with embalming chemicals to protect its neuronal structure. Many models of the brain have estimated the computing power needed for partial and complete simulations. If trends of Moore's law persists, the models show that brain uploading could become possible in a few decades.

Millions of dollars are getting spent on digital ideas that promise to turn our brains into digital organs despite many believing that human consciousness is too nuanced to turn into a digital product. Moore's law may suggest that necessary computing power may become available within a few decades. But, actual computational requirements to enable a simulated brain to function. Because of the many neurons in the brain and the substantial complexity of each neuron, the processing demands are likely to be enormous. Every molecule is a computer in the brain, and we would need to simulate the structure and function of trillions of molecules as rules that govern how they interact. But Penrose from the University of Oxford thinks it will not be possible until the development of quantum computers which is likely to happen by 2045. He believes that consciousness is a quantum mechanical phenomenon arising from the fabric of the universe.

A great danger of mind uploads is that they could create a mindless monster. There are also questions about the legal position of such uploaded humans – What would be his legal rights? Would he inherit property? What would happen to his biological body? Can we inflict the death penalty on criminal emulations? Can an upload marry? If we assign simulated minds rights, would it be possible to protect 'digital human rights'? Computer viruses or malware could destroy the hardware of the uploaded minds and may make the assassination of individuals with mind uploads easier than physical humans. The attacker could also misuse the computing power of the mind uploaded entity.

Finally, mind uploading raises some questions. Does human consciousness have a computational basis? Do spiritual experiences come from God, or are they just a random firing of neurons in the brain? Man, the technology-creating species through mind uploading, appears all set to merge with his computational technology. Technological evolution is therefore moving man closer to becoming a God. If then, till now, was it God that was creating our spiritual experiences, or was it just our brain?

Chapter 44

QUANTUM MECHANICS AND CONSCIOUSNESS

During my early Superintendent of Police days, my sister, who lives in the US, presented me with a book written by Gary Zukav, titled *The Seat of the Soul*. The book blew me away. Impatient to lay my hands on other books written by Zukav, I bought myself his first book, *The Dancing Wu Li Masters*. It was unlike the book I had read. It turned out to be an unexpected introduction to quantum physics. I was a microbiologist, and quantum physics was as alien to me as mars. But the book did a decent job of clarifying quantum concepts to me in a manner understandable to a layman. While browsing the book, insights such as why scientists cannot help but influence the outcome of experiments on subatomic particles; new assertions of consciousness-creating reality and how subatomic particles partake in an unceasing dance of destruction and creation similar to Lord Nataraja's dance of creation and destruction; or the image of the wheel of life depicted by Buddhism which symbolises the unending process of birth, death and rebirth became apparent to me.

When one walks into a bookstore during those days and even today, it's not uncommon to find titles with the term quantum in them. 'Quantum mind', 'quantum healing', 'quantum habits', 'quantum mindset' and so on. It's as though the quantum world is suddenly orchestrating everything in our lives.

But the role of quantum mechanics in consciousness first emerged as a theory in Germany during the 1920s when Erwin Schrödinger came up with such an interpretation. Albert Einstein and Max Planck objected to such versions. When Einstein accused Niels Bohr of such an interpretation, he denied the same, suggesting it to be a misunderstanding. In 1961 Eugene Wigner composed an essay titled 'Remarks on the Mind–Body Question', proposing that a conscious observer played a fundamental role in quantum mechanics. However, things started to speed up in the 1970s with the publication of *The Tao of Physics: An Exploration of the Parallels between Modern Physics and Eastern Mysticism* by Fritjof Capra in 1975. The book's first two parts exposited on ancient religions and modern physics. The third part tried to connect the two. The third part has influenced many New Age champions to claim that quantum mechanics proves the reality of everything. Bringing out the same, New Age guru Deepak Chopra came up with his version of 'quantum theory' that the cause of ageing is the mind, which he put forward in his books *Quantum Healing* (1989) and *Ageless Body, Timeless Mind* (1993). Most physicists today are realists who have no doubts that quantum theory does not relate to consciousness.

In 2004, a film titled *What the Bleep Do We Know!?* came along, which dealt with a range of New Age ideas concerning quantum physics. Through a series of combined documentary-style interviews and computer-animated graphics, it tried to make a spiritual connection between quantum physics and consciousness. The movie bases itself on the fictional story of a photographer who encounters emotional and existential obstacles in her life and eventually discovers that individual and group consciousness can influence the material world. The movie illustrated the uncertainty principle with a bouncing basketball being in several places. Some other contentions in the film which got challenged were the ability of the human mind to change the shape and structure of water molecules as popularised by Masaru Emoto, the power of meditation to reduce violent crime rates and the assertion that 'consciousness is the ground of all being'. Many critics dismissed the film for its use of pseudoscience. I presume the claims, as mentioned earlier, were more in the realm of quantum mysticism while overlapping a great deal with quantum consciousness.

The quantum mind or quantum consciousness is a set of hypotheses that proposes that quantum mechanical phenomena, such as quantum entanglement and superposition, may play an essential part in the brain's function and could form the basis for explaining consciousness.

Such a hypothesis first came together through the Copenhagen interpretation of quantum physics. The Copenhagen interpretation was mainly devised from 1925 to 1927 by Niels Bohr and Werner Heisenberg, which happens to be one of the oldest of the many proposed interpretations of quantum mechanics. According to this theory, the quantum wave function collapses because a conscious observer measures a physical system. However, Copenhagen says nothing about what exactly constitutes an observation. John von Neumann broke this silence and suggested that observation is the action of a conscious mind.

This interpretation of quantum physics sparked Schrödinger's cat thought experiment, showing some absurdity of this way of thinking, except that it completely matches the evidence of what scientists observe at the quantum level. There have been many objections to the Copenhagen interpretation over the years. These include irregular jumps when there is an observation, the probabilistic factor introduced upon inspection, the subjectiveness of needing an observer, the difficulty of defining a measuring device and the requirement of invoking classical physics to describe the 'laboratory' in which we measure the results. John Archibald Wheeler proposed one extreme version of the Copenhagen interpretation called the participatory anthropic principle. The entire universe collapses to a state we witness because there had to be conscious observers present to cause the collapse. Therefore, any worlds that do not contain aware observers get automatically ruled out.

Physicist David Bohm used the term 'implicate order' to express what he thought the fundamental level of reality must be because of his belief that what we see is a broken reflection of an ordered reality since both quantum physics and relativity were incomplete theories. Bohm thought that consciousness was a manifestation of this implicate order and that attempting to understand consciousness purely by looking at the matter in space was doomed to failure.

Human consciousness is profoundly enigmatic; being conscious is to be aware of who or what we are. But is there a way to explain the subjective nature of our inner life in scientific terms? The general assumption is that consciousness arises from complex computation among brain neurons which became manifest during evolution as an adaptation of living beings to the external environment. Contrary to this, spiritual masters, philosophers and scientists consider consciousness to be outward or woven into the universe.

Explaining human consciousness using quantum physics began with Roger Penrose's 1989 book, *The Emperor's New Mind: Concerning Computers, Minds, and the Laws of Physics.* In the book, Penrose dismisses the claim of few that the brain is akin to a biological computer. He argued that it is a sophisticated quantum computer whose computations, instead of being on a binary system, are in a superposition of different quantum states simultaneously. Penrose ventured into the work of Alan Turing, who developed a 'universal Turing machine' and argued that modern computers had certain limitations that the brain didn't have.

A recent theory called 'orchestrated objective reduction' ('Orch-OR') suggests that consciousness is more like music than computation. According to Roger Penrose and anaesthesiologist Stuart Hameroff who collaborated to produce the Orch-OR theory, consciousness arose from quantum vibrations in protein polymers called microtubules inside the brain's neurons. The vibrations that interfere, 'collapse' and resonate across the scale, neuronal control firings, generate consciousness and connect ultimately to 'deeper order' ripples in space–time geometry. In January 2014, Hameroff and Penrose claimed that the discovery of quantum vibrations in microtubules made by Anirban Bandyopadhyay of the National Institute for Materials Science in Japan in March 2013 corroborated their Orch-OR theory.

Since humans are the only animals that can by word of mouth communicate their conscious experience, performing experiments to prove quantum effects in consciousness requires experimentation on a living human brain. Besides, a morally unacceptable practice by proponents of quantum mind theories involves the custom of using quantum mechanical terms to make the argument seem authentic, even when being aware that the terms are irrelevant. Such deceptive claims were, for instance, often made by Deepak Chopra. Chopra often used words such as quantum healing or quantum effects of consciousness. According to Chopra, 'quantum healing' cures any manner of ailments, including cancer, through effects that he claims are literally on the same principles as quantum mechanics. In his book *Quantum Healing*, Chopra concludes that quantum entanglement links everything in the universe, and therefore it must create consciousness. Pronouncements like these about quantum mechanics point to a desire to misinterpret technical, mathematical terms like entanglement in terms of mystical feelings.

Finally, how does it matter whether quantum effects are at stake with neuronal computations in the brain? We already know that quantum mechanics play a part in the brain, determining the shapes and properties of neurotransmitters and proteins, which is why drugs like heroin easily affect our consciousness. Quantum effects are there in our TV, computer, car and so on, but we are all oblivious to quantum effects. We are also connected to the earth and other planets by gravity, but that does not mean that astrology is real. People love quantum mechanics because they are into meditation or manifestation or for spiritual benefits. Still, it doesn't bring any more benefits than what gravity or planetary influences do for astrology.

Chapter 45

IOT-BASED CRIME INVESTIGATION

As I dug into the IoT to understand the revolution of IoT, which is sweeping the world. I noticed that it had changed the way I see everything, including policing. I questioned: Would 9/11 or 26/11 or a Pulwama have happened in a connected world, where police have access to connected buildings, connected roads, connected vehicles and data from sensors and devices of all sorts? Would we be able to detect bombs and suicide bombers even as they are being assembled in future? Would we be able to identify murderers even when there are no eye-witnesses? As you read on, get prepared to get blown away by the amazing ways by which devices are solving crimes for the police.

The IoT is not just laptops or smartphones, but an avalanche of everyday objects–being connected to the internet and with each other. As technology infiltrates all aspects of our daily life, police are looking towards digital devices, the IoT to help fight and solve crimes. The connected devices are becoming omnipresent, serving as non-stop eyes and ears, capturing our every move, listening in or watching us in the privacy of our homes. And police in future would be increasingly getting clues and solving cases through IoT.

The business research company Gartner estimates 8.4 billion devices like fitness bands, smart watches, smart glasses and smart camera got connected to the internet in 2017, a 31 per cent increase over the previous year. By 2020, the company prognosticates there will be roughly three smart devices for every person on the planet. Adding 50 billion new objects to the global information grid in two years means that each of these devices, will interact with the other 50 billion connected objects on earth. The result will be 2.5 sextillions of potential networked object-to-object interactions – a network so vast and complex it would be difficult to understand or model. We will be in future interfacing with several thousand things in a daily basis, each of which will gather harmless bits of data around the clock and upload the same to the cloud where it will get compiled, analysed, contrasted and reviewed. The Apple Watch or the app in your smartphone or your Fitbit will disclose your continued abstinence from physical exercise, and your refrigerator will reveal the number of beers you have been guzzling to your health insurance company. Your car will tell your motor vehicle insurance company of your reckless driving and frequent overspeeding and the garbage can will inform the local corporation of your frequent violations of recycling regulations. IoT will also let advertisers touch you with targeted advertisements from each of the connected devices. All connected devices such as fans, washing machines, refrigerators will come with terms of conditions that will grant the makers of the devices access to all the data one is generating. Although one can in theory log out of the cyberspace, in one's well connected smart home there will be no such an option, as a result all that happens in one's homes and the environment around them, will be open to observation to unwanted entities. When sensors are all over the place, they will record even minor violations and will make the transgressors liable all the time. For instance, if a person were to be driving his car for a fraction of a time at 51 km per hour in a 50 km per hour zone, he would get automatically charged for overspeeding. When everything gets connected, we can hide nothing. The former CIA director David Petraeus has stated that IoT will be transformational for undercover agents. In the old model, one might have planted a bug to eavesdrop into a conversation in the conference room. But today, it's possible to get the same information by intercepting the data streaming from the lighting app in the smartphone to the light bulb in the room. The devices we believe to be working for us could work for others. On the upside, IoT devices are becoming increasingly prominent in criminal investigations and discovery. In November 2015, James Bates had called a friend over to his house in Arkansas to watch football, and both of them got drunk on vodka. After getting drunk, James Bates said his friend had accidentally drowned in his hot tub. When the police began investigations, they came across an Amazon's Echo device, which runs on the company's AI software, Alexa. Police suspecting foul play in the death of Victor Collins requested Amazon to hand over any recordings or data from the night of the killing. Amazon refused, but Bates' lawyer filed a motion in April saying his client would volunteer the data, which Amazon then sent to prosecutors. Police after getting the data from Bate's

Amazon Echo device had evidence to charge James Bates with murder. A San Jose woman's Fitbit helped provide clues to police investigating her death. On 13 September 2018, when 67-year-old Karen Navarro was found dead, stabbed in the head and neck, in her San Jose home on 13 September 2018 it became clear to the police that the murderer had made up the scene to look like a suicide. Her stepfather, Anthony Aiello, informed the police he had visited Navarra on 8 September, with pizza and biscotti and stayed with her for about 15 minutes. Although Aiello reportedly denied killing Navarra, nearby cameras captured images of Aiello's car parked at Navarra's home when the Fitbit that the victim was wearing showed her heart rate suddenly spike, slow down and stop when Aiello was still around at her place the evidence was clear. San Jose Police arrested Aiello on charges of murder based on Fitbit evidence.

In July 2018, investigators in Iowa, with the aid of FBI experts, sieved data from Fitbit, of Mollie Tibbetts, a 20-year-old student missing for about a month. Surveillance video led them to a 24-year-old man who the police could charge him with the murder. In September 2016, Ross Compton informed police that upon waking upon he found his Ohio home on fire and so jumped through a window to escape the flames. Compton's pacemaker suggested otherwise. Police charged him with aggravated arson and insurance fraud.

A short time before Christmas in December 2015, Richard Dabate claimed a so-called burglar beat him and shot his wife, Connie, in their home in Ellington, Connecticut, USA. But Connie was wearing a Fitbit. Police requested the device's data, which showed she had walked 1217 feet after returning home from the exercise class, way more than the 125 feet it would take her to go from the car in the garage to the basement as per Richard's account. The Fitbit also registered Connie moving roughly an hour after Richard said someone killed her before 9:10 a.m. Facebook records also disproved Richard's story; it showed Connie had posted as late as 9:46 a.m. As his wife's Fitbit told another tale, police had clear evidence to charge Dabate with the murder. Police found Nicole VanderHeyden, 31, strangled and beaten to death in May 2016 in Wisconsin, USA. Initially, her boyfriend Detrie was being suspected, so police took him into custody for the murder. It later turned out that Detrie on the day of the murder was wearing a Fitbit Flex. Police later released Detrie and exonerated him when Fitbit data revealed to them that Detrie was asleep around the time when the murder was being committed. The detectives later stumbled upon evidence to prove that a man named George Burch who was just released months before from the jail had committed the murder. His complicity in the crime was established by tracking his locations through his cell phone and Google Dashboard. The wireless network signals and the GPS confirmed that Burch had allegedly killed VanderHeyden and dumped her body in a farm field. All the cases listed above have one thing in common: all of them would probably become etched in criminal history as few first perpetrators busted by the IoT. Many more such cases are sure to follow, because the connected devices we use for convenience, entertainment and health can also contradict our pretences and expose our lies. Smart cars, fridges, doorbells, watches, phones, Fitbit, sneakers, televisions, gaming consoles, coffee makers, pacemakers, all can monitor, record and provide evidence. In the future, on the downside, hackers may target personal devices to introduce malware into enterprise networks. Workplaces will become more difficult to secure when the connected devices like Fitbit and smartwatches enter offices on the wrists and pockets of employees. Such devices that appear harmless would connect to the office networks and create more entry points or vulnerabilities for criminals to compromise the office networks. Cybercriminals know this, but the employees don't realise this. Most of the devices connected to the internet are lame-brained having no capacity for upgrades. They don't possess mechanisms not only for updating themselves but also for fixing security issues that surface. Considering our present inability to secure the existing network, how are we going to protect several thousand connected devices – from pets to pacemakers to autonomous cars – which are being connected and are hackable whensoever on the planet? The IoT will become a plethora of opportunities for those wanting to exploit the vulnerabilities with nefariousness. It will throw open security vulnerabilities on an unprecedented scale, which could be unusual and horrifying. The IoT will explode in the coming age; soon all our things will get connected to the internet. We cannot stop this. We may therefore have to find ways of staying in touch with our deepest essence by moderating its influence without being overwhelmed by it. To overcome the spiritual challenge, we may have to take breaks to disconnect and reconnect with our inner, undigitised self.

Chapter 46

SHOULD POLICE DEPARTMENTS USE ROBOTIC INTERROGATORS?

We've all seen in movies where a suspect is uncooperative and can't be trusted not to escape, so the interrogators call in an AI robot for assistance. In reality, police departments around the world are using VR and AR as new methods of interrogation. In addition to old standbys like one-way mirrors and hidden cameras, some departments are experimenting with AI-powered interrogator robots like EMQ or eM software. These new technologies offer many benefits, including quicker and more detailed information from suspects without the risk of cross-contamination or stress on both parties. However, their use also raises ethical considerations about privacy, trust and respect for suspects as human beings rather than just potential criminal perpetrators.

Many fictional police departments use robot interrogators to extract information from suspects. But should real-life police departments also use them? Robots have the potential to be an excellent tool for police officers. They can help them do their jobs more efficiently and effectively. But before police officers can use robots, police leaders must consider several things:

- The robot must be safe for people and the environment.
- There must be proper training for police officers on how to interact with robots.
- There must be an understanding of how the robot works.

If the police consider all these things, robots could one day play an important role in policing. But until then, they remain just tools that can help police officers save time and make their jobs easy

Robots in interrogations have become a hot topic in recent years, with many fictional police departments using robot interrogators to extract information from suspects. But should real-life police departments also use them? A 2015 study by the University of California, Berkeley, found that while there was some evidence to suggest that robots could be helpful in interrogation, the technology was still very much in its infancy and would require significant improvements before police organisations use it on a large scale. 'Robots are not yet ready for prime time', the study concluded. 'But it's a question we'll have to answer sooner rather than later.' As for whether robots should be allowed on the job at all, that's another matter entirely. In countries like Japan and China, where the tradition of Confucianism and loyalty to authority is strong, working under an overseer can be seen as an honour. But in the US, where there is more tolerance of questioning authority, police officers are generally expected to put their conscience first when dealing with suspects they may view as criminals or enemies. The courts in several countries have ruled that it is unconstitutional for police officers to force confessions out of suspects without first establishing the probable cause of crime commitment.

In fiction, police departments often use robots to interrogate suspects. In reality, there is no clear evidence that they work. One study found that interrogators who don't know what a suspect looks like are far more effective than those who do. And another found that robot interrogators were no more likely to get a confession or produce a false confession than traditional human ones. One possible reason: The robots may be unable to read body language as well as humans. If the suspect appears nervous, the robot might infer that he's lying and press him harder than necessary.

In addition, it could be hard for a robot to tell when someone is being deceptive or withholding information without human input. Some law enforcement agencies have already started using AI in their investigations, including facial recognition software and video analysis. But for now, there's no evidence that robots are a better way to extract information from suspects than humans.

What Is an EMQ?

An EMQ – or Enhanced-Modus-Q – is a computer-generated VR or AR interrogation chamber. This technology allows suspects to be questioned remotely by an AI-powered, human-seeming robot while the suspect is in another room. As a result, it reduces the cross-contamination risk to the officer examining the suspect and the stress associated with face-to-face questioning. EMQs can also collect information from the interrogation room, including the suspect's body language, heartbeat and other biological signs. This data is then recorded and analysed by AI-powered software, allowing the interrogator to search for inconsistencies or abnormalities in the suspect's responses.

Should Police Use EMQs?

In addition to being helpful for suspects who may be particularly nervous about being questioned face to face, EMQs can offer greater detail about the suspect's connection to the crime, partly due to the suspect being questioned in an isolated environment rather than in the presence of other people. This data can include information about their emotional and mental state, which can be essential factors in interrogation. In addition, the VR or AR inside the robot's interrogation chamber allows the interrogator to call up relevant images, video clips and other forms of data, helping them better understand the suspect's mental state and motivations for committing the crime.

Are There Any Downsides to Using EMQs?

There are some downsides to using EMQs that are worth considering before being implemented in police departments worldwide. For one, there is the possibility that a suspect could obfuscate their true feelings and mental state. Although EMQs pick up on the suspect's body language, mental state and other details, they can fake these things. In addition, although VR and AR interrogation chambers can offer greater detail from the suspect, they also present the interrogator with more information to sort through.

AR Interrogations

AR interrogations combine the benefits of VR interrogations with the help of real-life interrogation. In addition to all of the benefits of VR interrogations, AR interrogations allow the suspect to remain in the interrogation room rather than being moved to a remote location which means that the officer questioning the suspect can use their actual body language and heart rate to feed data into the AI-powered software and see the suspect's reactions to the questions. It also allows the interrogator to use their natural voice and body language. Hence, AR interrogations offer all of the benefits of VR interrogations while allowing the officer to maintain eye contact with the suspect.

VR Interrogations

VR interrogations are the most advanced form of AI-powered interrogation. In a VR interrogation, the suspect wears a set of goggles that completely block their view of the interrogation room and replace it with a virtual environment. This environment can be designed to elicit a specific emotional response from the suspect and can include audio and images designed to elicit specific emotional reactions. VR interrogations are particularly useful for interrogating uncooperative suspects or emotionally unstable. They can also help interrogate people from other cultures or who speak a different language since the virtual environment can be designed in any way the interrogator wishes.

Conclusion

When used correctly, VR and AR interrogation methods offer many benefits, including quicker and more detailed information from suspects without the risk of cross-contamination or stress on both parties. However, their use also raises ethical considerations about privacy, trust and respect for suspects as human beings rather than just potential criminal perpetrators. VR interrogations can elicit emotions and mental states from suspects in ways that are difficult or impossible in real life. Although this offers significant benefits to police departments, it also raises questions about using such technologies and whether they are appropriate for modern society.

Chapter 47

SPOOKY MIND-READING TECHNOLOGY

George Orwell's dystopian novel *1984*, written in 1949, describes an eerie future where the 'Thought Police' of the superstate Oceania detect and punish subjects for 'thoughtcrimes' which are thoughts unapproved by the state. Fast forward to the 21st century, and we are today staring at the possibility of creepy 'Thought Police' coming true, chiefly because of technologies which are bobbing up to read people's minds.

A scroungy form of George Orwell's 'Thought Police' has already showed up in 'emotional surveillance technology' that is now being embraced in China where the thoughts of employees in the workplace are not private. This surveillance requires workers to wear hats or safety helmets fitted with wireless sensors. These sensors keep tabs on the emotions and other mental activities of the workers and streams their brain waves to the computers where AI detects emotions that employees consider undesirable. When the system detects abnormalities in the state of mind of the worker, the employees may ask the worker to take a day off or they may assign him or her to a less important task. China has enforced this technology on an unparalleled scale in factories, public transport, state-owned companies and the military to increase the competitiveness of its manufacturing industry and to maintain social stability.

Technology to read people's minds may appear like something right out of science fiction, but it's something which is becoming a reality. Recent advances in non-invasively identifying thoughts in the human brain have been helped along by BCI based new neuroimaging technology, such as functional magnetic resonance imaging (fMRI), electroencephalogram (EEG) and machine learning. The future Orwellian scenario of having to be careful of what we think for fear of being punished for so-called thoughtcrimes could come true, if we do not establish a right to protect people from having their mental information stolen, abused or hacked

Recent advances in EEG have led to devices like Emotiv's neuroheadset, a $300 toy that taps into a person's brain waves and lets an individual play a computer game with his mind. Which is cool? In 2012, researchers from Oxford University, UC Berkeley and the University of Geneva showed that it was possible to carry out an attack against wearers of such EEG headsets to steal sensitive personal information. They flashed students wearing the headsets images of things like ATM PIN pads, debit cards and calendars. Underneath the images were questions such as what is your PIN and when were you born? The results were powerful: by reading the brain waves emanating from these $300 headsets, researchers could guess a subject's PIN with 30 per cent accuracy and their month of birth with 60 per cent accuracy.

Imagine a scenario, in the near future where one is browsing the internet using the power of one's thoughts, while doing so the hackers could use spyware on the browsers mind through the internet to gather personal information from the brain waves. The hackers could gather people's likes and dislikes, political affiliation, sex and ATM PIN. The idea frankly is not far-fetched. It's not just the hacker who could take advantage of this technology, police could misuse it, or governments could charge people for any anti-government thoughts or for just thinking about illegal activities. China has already marched in this direction by implementing their 'social credit score' system. Which is not far from a full-blown Orwellian state.

If governments can read one's mind for security purposes, would that not violate an individual's rights? AI today can interpret our brainwaves as we conduct ourselves in, for example, an airport. It's possible to scan people's minds for potentially menacing mental images arising from their brains like bombs or firearms and alert security. The Department of Homeland Security has been testing its 'Future Attribute Screening Technology (FAST)' programme which is something akin to a mind-reading pre-crime detector to 'sense' and spot people with a hostile intent such as a terrorist act. FAST deploys concealed sensors that will right off know everything about a person even from 164 feet away by detecting the physiological peculiarities of a person like the increased heartbeat, brain waves and eye movements that one associates with a sinister intent.

Pentagon's Defense Advanced Research Projects Agency (DARPA) wants to develop a technology called 'Silent Talk' that will help the soldiers put aside wireless radios, walkie-talkies and combat PDAs, enabling them to communicate by reading each other's minds. The goal is to 'allow user-to-user communication on the battlefield without the use of vocalised speech through analysis of neural signals'. They are also planning to devise mind-reading binoculars that alert soldiers faster than the conscious mind can process them.

A new headset developed by a graduate student Arnav Kapur at MIT, USA, reads the small muscle movements in the face that occur when the wearer thinks about speaking and then uses 'AI algorithms to perform real time thought to text conversion'. With about 15 minutes of customisation and training, researchers could achieve a transcription accuracy of 92 per cent. This technology is amazing; it only reads the nerve signals sent from the brain to the face.

Scientists at the University of California, San Francisco, have developed a mind-reading device that, besides turning thoughts into text, can also detect things a person hears. This is done by placing electrodes to monitor the auditory cortex and decoding the data with algorithms. Carnegie Mellon University has developed methods of not only reading complex thoughts from brain scans, but it can also predict the next sentence in the thought process.

The Facebook is also working on a mind-reading project that would enable users to send messages using thoughts alone. Microsoft has patents that use brain activity to change the state of the computer or its applications. For instance, the system will automatically turn down the volume of the music system when the mental activity of the person shows that the listener is not comfortable with the loudness.

Scientists from the University of Pittsburgh School of Medicine have trained monkeys to move a robotic arm to feed themselves marshmallows and fruits by using signals from its brain while their arms are tied up. The University of Toronto, Scarborough, could recreate faces shown to the subjects based on their brain activity. The possibility of recreating faces from memory alone has tremendous applications in the police investigation. Japanese researchers at the University of Kyoto and researchers at Purdue University, USA, are using fMRI scans plus AI to recreate pictures based on blood flow to the brain.

A startup called Neurable has developed a VR game called *Awakening* in which a player can pick up objects and hurl them with his thoughts.

HTC's Vive X accelerator programme, called Looxid Labs, is developing a mobile VR headset with built-in emotion detection technology. Motor car manufacturer Nissan has unveiled an IMx KURO concept car, complete with an EEG headset, at the 2018 *Geneva Motor Show* which reads the brain waves of the driver and performs functions depending on the thoughts of the driver. For example, the moment the car detects that the driver intends to apply the brakes, the car automatically brakes even before the driver steps on the brakes.

Researchers at the University of California, Berkeley, have been able to form, erase and reactivate memories in rats. Researchers are working on extending the same method to humans. This discovery could be enormous for police officers and military personnel who suffer from PTSD. Scientists have also developed a BCI drowsiness detection system which uses algorithms to detect the drowsiness and alerts the driver of an automobile by processing the rhythmic values of theta and alpha of EEG signals. Two researchers at Washington have showed not only telepathic communication but could also send the motor muscle stimulation over internet to cause another person to move his body with a mere thought.

We can also use brain scanning technology to determine if patients in a comatose or vegetative stage are conscious despite their inability to communicate verbally or via motor actions. An expert puts questions and interprets a brain scan image as a yes or no response based on the activation of the areas of the brain. This would allow the police to record the dying declaration of a person who has slipped into a coma or question conscious vegetative state patients, or allow vegetative state patients to testify and also help assess their conscious healthcare wishes. This technology can be of great help in police and healthcare decision-making.

AI-assisted mind-reading may make our lives practical, productivity-enhancing and actually enjoyable. Mind-reading applications could make everything happen correctly and automatically. Lights and sounds may turn up or down based on mental preference at a particular moment. Criminal law could be one potential area of application. The Evidence Act, however, does not permit self-incrimination. But not performing brain scans on suspects also prevents wrongly accused from proving their innocence.

On the downside, criminals can misuse mind-reading technology. Experts at the University of Washington have revealed how hackers could insert images into dodgy apps and read people's minds using brain–computer interfaces. It will also be possible for hackers to attack neuroprosthetics like other medical implants such as pacemakers and diabetic pumps by subverting communication and control protocols. An attacker, for instance, would be able to turn off electrodes of deep brain stabiliser in a Parkinson's patient causing violent tremors and seizures. Using their minds, people are today able to move objects on IoT, control a drone and play a video game. If it is so, what will stop hackers from remotely manipulating someone's mind?

There're many possibilities for such a technology. A 'cloud-based brain-to-brain interface server' could allow the direct transmission of data around the world via the internet. Such a global brain net, besides the problems of privacy, security and neurorights, could also lend deeper insights into how individual consciousnesses might transcend the biological confines of the human skull to work collectively. If so, can this technology help humanity realise the 'Oneness' which the scriptures have always been exhorting us? Will it help humankind know that individual consciousnesses are all part of this one universal consciousness which people call the Universal Force?

As far as India is concerned, mind-reading is an ancient technology. One can find mind-reading (*cetopariyañāna*) dealt with in the third chapter of the *Patanjali Yoga Sutras*. Ancient Indians cultivated this superpower through yogic practice.

CHAPTER 48

CRIMINAL ROBOTS AND DRONES

Can robots commit crimes? Killer robots are an erstwhile fodder of sci-fi cinema. Films like *Terminator* have already given us a peek of the apocalyptical world we are quite likely to inherit. Researchers have cautioned that robots and computers will commit more crimes than humans by 2040. Maxim Pozdorovkin in his new documentary, *The Truth about Killer Robots*, delineates all sorts of hazards – economic, psychological, moral – posed to humans by automation and robotics. At the centre of his film lies the question: 'when a robot kills a human, who takes the blame?' In March 2018, an experimental Uber vehicle, operating in autonomous mode, struck and killed a pedestrian as she was crossing the street in Tempe, Arizona – the first fatal accident of its kind. Then there is the famous case of a driverless Tesla car on autopilot hitting a truck without decelerating, and another in which the car crashed into the highway median. In both cases the drivers were killed by machines they trusted. However, the very first case of robotic homicide was reported way back in 1981 in Kawasaki Heavy Industries factory in Japan when an employee working on a robot was scooped up by its hydraulic arm and hauled into a grinding machine where he got crushed to death. On 7 July 2016, Dallas police used a robot with an explosive device on its manipulator's arm to kill a suspect after five police officers were murdered and seven others wounded.

A 136 kg, K5 security robot employed to guard the Stanford Shopping Center in Palo Alto, California, collided into a 16-month-old child and carried on driving leaving him bruised with a swollen foot and sore head. The robot manufactured by Knightscope was meant to be on the lookout for known shoplifters at the shopping centre by patrolling along predetermined routes. In the US, in 2001 a car factory employee was killed when he stepped into an unlatched robotic cage to clean it.

The robotic arm presuming that the intruder was an autocomponent clasped him by the neck and stifled him to death. The Occupational Safety and Health Administration has reported that in the US alone at least 33 deaths have occurred and that the number is inclined to soar as robots leave their cages and begin walking among us. In 2009, South African National Defence Force, during a live fire training exercise, a computerised Oerlikon MKS twin-barrelled anti-aircraft gun, underwent an unexpected software malfunction, causing the weapon to fire in full-auto mode at the rate of 550 rounds per minute while pivoting about crazily in 360-degree circles. At the end it created a blood-splattered scene leaving nine soldiers dead and 14 others grievously injured. According to a *Washington Post* report, over four hundred military UAVs have accidentally fallen from the sky, domestically and overseas, smashing into homes, farms, runways, highways and so on.

In the hospital, a robot grabbed a patient's abdominal tissue during a colorectal surgery and declined to release it despite all efforts until the machine was rebooted. In another case, a woman was struck in the face by a surgical robot during her hysterectomy. Two London-based artists created a bot that purchased random items off the dark web. The bot besides buying fake jeans, a baseball cap with a spy camera, a stash can, some Nikes, 200 cigarettes, a set of fire-brigade master keys, a counterfeit Louis Vuitton bag also bought ten ecstasy pills. Should these artists be liable for purchase and possession of drugs? What are the means of determining culpability? Who is culpable and liable when a robot or AI goes berserk? *Actus reus* and *mens rea* are the foundations for criminal law. These two key terms of the law stem from the phrase *actus non facit reum nisi mens rea*, which literally means 'an act does not make a person guilty unless the mind is also guilty'. It's been taken that a person is guilty if they are proved to be culpable or reprehensible in both thought and action.

When a robot commits a crime how to determine whether it's the vile act of the robot? Most robot-related incidents until now have been, firstly the result of machines being too stupid, rather than too smart, or secondly on account of a disharmonious relationship between man and machine. For better worse, AI is poised to change both at this point, we are expecting to attain singularity by 2040, at which time we can expect a significant chunk of crimes to be committed by robots and machines. For robot or machine to commit a crime based on guilty mind, AI technology would have to approach the singularity. A point at which, the machine intelligence equals or surpasses the human mind bringing, harm, risk, fault and punishment into the picture.

Still, if a robot kills someone, then it has transgressed the law (actus reus), but technically it has committed just half a crime, as it would be extremely difficult to establish *mens rea.*

How would a lawyer go about demonstrating the 'guilty mind' of a non-human? And what would 'intent' resemble in a machine mind? How would we go about proving an autonomous machine was justified in killing a human in self-defence or the extent of preconceived malice?

Even if we solve these legal issues, we are still left with the question of punishment. What's a 30-year prison sentence to an autonomous machine that does not become old, grow ill or miss its dear ones? Unless, indeed, it was programmed to 'ponder' on its wrongdoing and find a way to rewrite its code.

Gabriel Hallevy, author of *When Robots Kill: Artificial Intelligence under Criminal Law*, has proposed changing penal law to hold autonomous machines liable for crimes, similar to corporations. Micro-robotics is also advancing rapidly. Robots which are as small as fingernails, equipped with HD cameras and microphone are taking surveillance to a whole new level.

Dragonfly robots, and robo-bumblebees which can fly undetected into buildings, take pictures and even attack terrorists have been uncovered. Micro-multi-robotic systems with swarm capabilities have abilities to achieve incredible things both for armies and criminals.

In 2014 researchers at Harvard University created the biggest robot swarm ever, using 1024 micro-robots which are no more than a size of a coin. The robots could separate and assemble themselves into various shapes and designs, like a flock of birds or swarm of bees.

It's scary to have a drone with a gun chasing you from behind, but nothing can be terrifying and deadly than a flock of 30 such robots swooping and hunting down a victim. Just imagine the consequences, if such swarm of robots were to suffer a virus or a hack, the robots could reverse their attack on the host itself instead of the enemy. Up heretofore, we have seen how the robots deployed by man are committing crimes, robots are also being rampantly deployed as tools to commit crimes in creative ways by criminals and terrorists. The drug cartels in Mexico have started using drones since 2010 to transport drugs.

In Mexico, prior to 2011, virtually all drones owned and operated by cartels were produced abroad, primarily in Israel and China. Mexican syndicates have now become so accustomed to drone use that they are now using Mexican-based companies to build them in cities including the Federal District, Guadalajara, Monterrey, Querétaro and Tijuana.

Mexican success has enticed the Colombian drug cartels to use drones as well motivating them to test the same method in their territory. As a matter of fact, by 2012, drone use along the border was highly prevalent as evidenced by US interception of 150 drones carrying an estimated two metric tonnes of drugs, primarily marijuana, cocaine and heroin.

Drones have started off to be a perfect drug mule in the sense that they are fraught with less risk to narcotics trafficking organisations and their employees, who represent a major risk to any cartel by way of the arrested individual furnishing information about the drug operations. Additionally drones, when compared with their human counterparts cost significantly less, as a drug mule can earn as much as $10,000 for successful delivery of a single shipment.

The new Mexican-made drones are poles apart from the ones used for personal use as they can supposedly transport anywhere from 60 to 100 kg (132–220 lb) of drugs in a single trip. In terms of current use, drones used to transport narcotics usually operate during the night, and they never land on the US soil. They simply drop the shipment and return to Mexico. Drones are also being used to smuggle drugs, mobile phones and weapons into prisons. Prisons have tall walls, often with electrified fences and pointed structures to prevent prisoners from escaping as well as to isolate the prisoners from the public. The walls of the prison were never designed to secure it from drones and robots. Today the remote-operated drones and robots are posing a real threat to security as criminals have started using them as a tool to smuggle cell phones, drugs and dangerous weapons to jailbirds. The primary type of drones used for smuggling contraband is quadcopters. The quadcopters are controlled by a smartphone. They have four arms, each with a motor and a propeller. At the Provisional Detention Center in São José dos Campos in São Paulo, Brazil, a quadcopter drone flew over the prison walls and dropped 250 grams of cocaine into the prison in the presence of jail officers. Near Moscow, a drone flew 700 grams cocaine into the Tula prison, while in Greece, a drone carried a box of mobile phones. In April 2017, two men were jailed in the UK for using such drones to deliver class A and B drugs and iPhones to inmates in three prisons across Herefordshire. Similar prison intrusion incidents have been reported from Canada, the UK, Australia and the US. A sophisticated

UAV, capable of being precisely manoeuvred using GPS technology and carrying a payload of up to 1.5 kg, can be bought for less than a lakh of rupees and flown with minimal training. In 2015, the UK witnessed 33 such drone-related incidents in its prisons, while Australia witnessed six such incidents from New South Wales alone. In Canada, the federal agency responsible for prisons recorded 41 drone-related incidents at federal prisons between July 2013 and December 2016. Hackers have also figured out how to use drones for intercepting communication by eavesdropping into phone calls as well as tracking the movement of people by letting WASP hover in the neighbourhood of a target. WASP, short for 'Wireless Aerial Surveillance', is an airborne hacking platform that can infiltrate Wi-Fi network, intercept mobile calls, jam radio signals and even hack websites wirelessly. It has a cellular phone, a small onboard Linux computer, a 340-million-word dictionary, which the drone can use to generate passwords to get brute-force access into a network in real time. It also embeds a software to read signals from ground-based phones and computer networks. It intercepts cell phone calls, literally by pretending to be a flying cell tower. Its signals fool phones on the ground into relaying calls through it and allows hackers to record all phone calls and text messages that pass through any device that is being hacked. A hovering drone that picks up cell phone calls could also be used for good. Imagine sending one such drone to an area hit by an earthquake, where power and cellular services have been knocked out. The device would be great for providing emergency mobile access to such regions. A device with such interception capabilities would have cost several millions of dollars, but the makers of this device built it for just $6200. Criminals also would get to use such spy drones to steal intellectual property by hovering over corporations, or use it to jam mobile phone signals of their enemies, or to distinguish a target using the target's cell phone to identify him in a crowd and then follow his movements. It would also come handy for drug smuggling or for terrorists to trigger a dirty bomb. Can robots feel emotions and carry out a murder? This has been beautifully portrayed in the 2004 sci-fi film *I, Robot* directed by Alex Proyas. The film is set in 2035 AD, where robots are everyday objects and are programmed to live alongside humans. Detective Del Spooner is tasked to investigate the suicide of the robotic scientist Dr Alfred Lanning. Spooner suspects that the death might not be a suicide, but a murder committed by one of the robots. Spooner's suspicions, in the end, come true. Therefore, questions about criminal liability for robots may require to be answered sooner than we think – especially granted that self-driving cars and robot security guards already gallivant in some US cities. Finally, can robots and drones evolve to become spiritual like humans? For machines to be religious, they would have to be conscious, have personal agency and a sense of wonder. As human consciousness is composed of something non-physical, I firmly believe consciousness is not humanly creatable. But Raymond Kurzweil, an American inventor, futurist and the author of the book *The Age of Spiritual Machines*, is convinced that the future machines will 'proclaim to be conscious, and thus to be spiritual' and concludes that '21st century machines' will go to church, meditate and pray to connect with this spirituality.

Chapter 49

BATTLING THE WEAPONS OF MASS DISTRACTION

The smartphone is the world's greatest WMD, owing to the magnitude of the distraction epidemic and cybermania it has unleashed on us. Day and night, our mobile phones and other devices buzz, ping, beep, hum, drone, croon, howl their way into our attention. Our brain is limited in its ability to pay attention. When we spend that extra hour on social media, we pay for it with our sleep. That results in stockpiling of sleep debt, as too much social media time leads to less sleep. Air Marshal B. S. Dhanoa, during the *Aerospace Medicine Conference* held in Bangalore on 14 September 2018, acknowledged that sleep deprivation caused by spending too much time on social media was the cause behind the crash of MIG21 Bison fighter aeroplane in 2013 at Uttarlai in Rajasthan. Recent studies confirm links between smartphone/social media addiction and increased levels of anxiety, depression, poor sleep quality and increased risk of vehicle accidents or death.

Sleep deprivation and stress can have ripple effects on a population, leading to more severe workplace accidents and suicides. When I was on deputation with the Central Industrial Security Force (CISF), we found a peculiar escalation in suicides amongst constables when the mobile phones became affordable. Bad news from their remote villages, which used to take days, was now reaching them instantaneously and throwing their coping mechanisms out of gear. Apart from work-related stress, mobile phones are a conduit for significant pressure on police personnel. Recognising the need to combat stress, Tamil Nadu became the first state in the entire country on 20 September 2018 to launch a comprehensive wellness programme called the 'Police Well-being Training' in collaboration with the National Institute of Mental Health and Neurosciences

(NIMHANS), Bengaluru, to help the police personnel battle all forms of stress including digital stress and improve their mental well-being.

In 1988 when I left home to pursue my PhD in New Delhi, I kept in touch with my parents, who lived in Hyderabad once a week on expensive landline calls and sent letters that arrived a week later. Quite often, to get in touch with my parents, I had to walk more than a mile, stand in the queue of the STD booth, sometimes for more than an hour, and incur a monthly expenditure on the telephone bills, which far surpassed my monthly mess bill. Quite recently, when my daughter left abroad for higher studies, my wife and I were in continuous contact with her, through FaceTime, at the drop of a hat, without spending a dime. Technology has shrunk the distance and transformed the experience of making a call into a hugely easy and pleasurable one. Technology is neutral. It isn't morally good or bad. Social media platforms may intend to promote rich social connections like FaceTime. They can be contrived to keep the user addicted to the social site by delivering recurrent dopamine hits like Facebook. Some social media platforms activate the same parts of the brain as cocaine. Most developers of social media platforms have been intentionally devising and designing sites to keep their users perpetually addicted and hooked. As a result, most social media platforms are taking a heavy toll on our lives by leaving us mentally frayed, tattered, distracted and drained.

Social media platforms like Facebook, Instagram, Twitter and so on are equivalent to huge dopamine reserves. We experience a biff of dopamine whenever we get a like on our Facebook or a whack of dopamine whenever someone comments on our Instagram post. Social media platforms are therefore turning us into dopamine junkies. More and more social media users are digging into them to receive dopamine jolts to the brain, much like the bonks received by the addicts of cocaine or nicotine. Facebook, Snapchat and Instagram leverage the very same neural networks used by slot machines and cocaine to keep us using their products as much as possible.

Social media addiction eventually messes up our brain chemistry, leading to depression, anxiety, sleep debt and so on. Dopamine, the pleasure or reward neurotransmitter, is excitatory, while on the contrary, serotonin and GABA, the inhibitory neurotransmitters, are also crucial. Both dopamine and serotonin play a role in our sleep–wake cycle. There are tangible signs that point towards the participation of the neurotransmitter dopamine in wakefulness. Things that enhance dopamine levels in the brain, like social media, slot machines, drugs like cocaine amphetamine, contribute to feelings of wakefulness. Raising dopamine in the brain via genetic modification by getting rid of the dopamine transporter in a mouse produced a mouse suffering from insomnia. People with Parkinson's disease seem to suffer from excessive daytime sleepiness due to low dopamine levels. On the flip side, serotonin and GABA are involved in sleep onset and production of melatonin's sleep hormone, which could be imbalanced by excess dopamine from social media fixation. The blue light emission from our device screens also plays havoc with the nocturnal release of the hormone melatonin, disrupting our circadian rhythms. The two other major players in the stress response that builds with social media usage are adrenaline and cortisol. Adrenaline increases the heart rate and blood pressure, while cortisol causes blood sugar to rise. A study out of the University of Queensland in Australia, published in the *Journal of Social Psychology*, found that taking a break from Facebook, even for periods less than a week, could bring down the levels of the stress hormone cortisol in a person's body.

After they showed up in our lives, smartphones' impact had been a long way off from good. Paradoxically, we are busy but ineffective at the same time. Although we can connect to people on devices, we feel isolated and lonely all the time. On the surface, connectivity afforded by technology appears to have enhanced our sense of freedom. Still, in reality, the chains of technology have insidiously enslaved and shackled us to the electronic screens and imprisoned us there. The problem is not with our smartphones themselves. Our concern stems from our relationships with our devices. Therefore, it's not about waging war against WMD, nor is it about securing a truce with WMD. In the long run, it is all about managing and curtailing how technology gets used so that it becomes an ally, not an enemy. As a first step, we should keep an eye on our online activity by installing apps like *Rescuetime*, *Checky*, *Moment* and so on and turn off the notifications on the phone to monitor and reduce technology consumption. That will help us establish boundaries between our online and offline lives. Embarking on digital detox occasionally could also go a long way by helping us become aware of the joys and wonders available to us outside the connected world. Setting up phone-free periods during the day, not reaching for the mobile until after breakfast and switching off the smartphone two hours before bed could vastly improve your quality of sleep as the impact of blue light on the sleep would be minimised. Substituting social media time with face-to-face activities with family and friends who support and care, setting aside the phone while socialising, during dinner/meal times, reading, gymming times and so on are other strategies that could be extremely helpful. Dropping out and going offline enabled me to get back to reading voraciously and to writing. In one study, 95 per cent of those interviewed said that their mood improved a great deal after putting down the phones to spend time outside in nature, changing from depressed, stressed and anxious to more calm and balanced.

The other strategy that has worked exceptionally well for me is a productivity hack called 'batching' proposed by Tim Ferriss in his bestselling book *The 4-Hour Workweek* where he sets predetermined times, twice or thrice a day to check and respond to e-mails, texts or scroll through Instagram or interact on Facebook. Tim uses automatic responders to let people know that their e-mails will get dealt with in due time. The other book which has changed my life by making me adopt better habits and do things with more focus is Cal Newport's book titled *Deep Work: Rules for Focused Success in a Distracted World*. Cal, in his book, explains his logical foundation for the significance of deep work, which is essentially performing focused work without distractions for designated chunks of time.

The world's most outstanding public technocrats are also the world's greatest private technophobes, not without reason. They are aware of the dangers and ills of the techno-gadgets. Evan Williams, the founder of Blogger, Twitter and Medium, bought hundreds of books for his two young sons but never gave them an iPad. I remember watching Steve Jobs explain why the iPad was the best way to look at photos, listen to music and imbibe knowledge through iTunes University. He believed that everyone should own an iPad, but he refused to allow his kids to possess the device. In 2010 he revealed to *New York Times* journalist Nick Bilton that his children had never used an iPad, and the amount of technology his children could have access to was determined by him, and it was never more than the bare minimum. Technology is a double-edged sword. We can either make it our ally or enemy. Let's make it our partner by realising that the offline world is the natural world, and the virtual world is just a mirage.

Technology serves as a catalyst exacerbating our restlessness and distraction exponentially. It scatters our attention in a hundred directions, turning our brain into a monkey mind on a triple espresso. We experience blurred, scatter-brained, vacuous, disorderly and dissipated senses because we get connected to everyone and everything at the click of a mouse. Still, we seem to have lost connection with ourselves. Logging into our inner self is the most significant connection we can make. Plugging into our inner essence occasionally and unplugging ourselves from the networked world is the only therapy we may need to overcome sleep-deprived, dopamine-ravaged and social media-habituated minds. Once we allow ourselves to plug into the spiritual essence available within us, nothing in the outer world, no shiny object, no gadget or gizmo, would be able to dazzle our eyes, hold sway over us to take control of our minds. You may get a billion likes on your Facebook page, but that would still be nothing compared to the unalloyed joy and bliss you will access by connecting with yourself.

Chapter 50

RECLAIMING OUR ANALOGUE HERITAGE IN THE DIGITAL ERA

During my childhood, I would attend school, study a bit and play the remainder of the time outdoors till my parents would yank me and heave me home after it got dark. I wish I could get into a time machine and go back in time to relive those glorious tech-free analogue days, which were the best days of my life. We did not have smartphones or fancy gadgets. Simple things such as a tennis ball or marbles were enough to keep us enthralled the entire day. Screen-glued kids of today are just a shadow of what we were. They may never know the glee of playing in grime and dirt under the scorching sun, the ecstasy of splashing about in puddles of fresh rainwater, the rapture of puttering in the backyard, the thrill of hopping over walls to steal mangoes on the way back from school, the amusement of endless pranks at school, the exhilaration of punching and clobbering up the winning cricket team after a loss, the euphoria of clandestinely lighting up a cigarette, the agony of suffering bruises while playing it rough, the misery of being ambushed and thrashed by the rival gang and the charm and allure of playing hide and seek under the moonlight.

Shortly afterwards, after I grew up to be a junior college student in Hyderabad, I went backpacking for two months in the hilly terrains of the Himalayas on a shoestring budget. I could travel that far by myself as my father was an officer in the railways. That entitled me to a free first-class train pass as a family member. For those two months, none of my friends or family knew where I was, nor did they have any idea whether I was living or dead. I might have dialled my parents a couple of times to let them know I was well whenever I reached a town having an STD booth. Long-distance calls were prohibitively expensive, so my conversations never lingered more than a couple of minutes. I frequently mailed letters that reached my parents a week later. There were no cell phones, no e-mail, no texting, no digital photography. I hauled money as cash, which I stashed away in my underwear from the reach of pickpocketers. I toted a Minolta camera which took photographs on a film, 36 frames per second, which we could develop only at a studio.

No kid today will ever have that experience. Anybody travelling today would be texting, emailing, posting on Facebook and tweeting every moment. A sense of being in a new place is not there today. Once I got on the train, there was no way to contact the world I had left behind. In short, cell phones and modern technology have taken away the sense of isolation and have made us perpetually available. I see people today unable to function without a smartphone and mighty scared to leave home without a cell phone.

Come to think, we have learned to use and forge earth's elements to manufacture computers and phones. But any gift of God could eventually become a curse if we become profoundly entrenched and attached to it and are incapable of detaching ourselves. Creating and living in a digital scenario in which we have total control over every possible outcome, contrary to living with unpredictable, dangerous and chaotic nature, is akin to playing God or, worse, becoming God itself. Therefore we must know how to detach from digital and embrace analogue because, with every irrational embrace of new technology, we could be giving rise to dystopian consequences.

For instance, in the movie *Matrix*, a war erupts in the early 21st century, between humanity and intelligent machines, in which society loses the battle, after which all surviving humans are subsequently apprehended and restrained in a 'Matrix', which is a shared alternative reality, constructed to imitate the world as it existed in 1999. The survivors could live the rest of their lives, happily plugged into the Matrix blissfully unaware that they are floating naked in a human glass pod with intravenous vitamins and calories to sustain their brains and bodies in what is purely digital existence. We can see movies portray dystopian futures in films such as *Blade Runner 2049* and *Minority Report*. We are today not far behind these films. Shortly, we would have humans living digitally and virtually in similar conditions if we continue to distance ourselves from nature and lead a technology-imbued, analogue-obsolete existence.

Under such digital existence, our future food could seem like an asymmetrical fancy-looking block of ideally constituted carbon molecules with a customised, highly engineered protein, fat and carbohydrates. This nutriment will not only match a person's precise biological needs but, when paired with VR goggles and a haptic headset, will allow one to experience all the joy of happily chowing down a Thalappakatti or Paradise biryani with a bottle of chilled coke. As far as spirituality is concerned, we may not have to meditate like Buddhist monks in a monastery to attain enlightenment and bliss in the digital world. We would experience enlightenment by merely strapping on Oculus Rift with software like *Tripp* to create an indescribable spiritual experience. A sedentary digital lifestyle, rapid internet access to pornography, VR headsets, the evolution of love dolls or sex dolls as actual AI humans capable of giving a man or woman all the sensual pleasure they might derive from intercourse with a real, attractive human being is leading to reduced levels of hormones. Doug Wilson's book *Ride Sally Ride*, which is getting filmed into a movie, hilariously describes the slippery slope of sex doll advancement and its consequences.

If we let ourselves go so deep into the digital territory, we will have to give up part that makes us human. Analogue experiences engage our senses and connect us to people, unlike digital, which disconnects and isolates us. We have to start filling our world with real-world connections and activities and learn to unplug the digital and put it back in its box. People embracing the analogue world have begun digital decluttering and deleting Facebook accounts. Such yearning to return to analogue reveals our craving to reconnect with humanity. David Sax has written a fantastic book, *The Revenge of Analog: Real Things and Why They Matter*, which speaks about the resurgence of all things analogue such as vinyl records, board games, paper notebooks, brick-and-mortar bookstores that have almost become extinct.

Digital technology may lead us away from tasting God's creation by immersing us in a fake world. Still, if I had to choose between the two worlds, I would not discard the digital but continue to embrace the analogue while responsibly and minimally utilising the digital.

So, even when the erratic and turbulent analogue world feels way better than the sham and phoney digital world, I would still need the digital space to write blogs on my website (www.jayanthmurali.com), shop online and do myriad other things. For instance, we, the dedicated members of the armed police, enthusiastically decided to launch an impactful outreach initiative that introduced a myriad of voluntary services to our society. Our primary goal was to empower and engage virtual volunteers who could extend their valuable assistance by effortlessly registering through our meticulously designed website, LetsFightCorona.com.

Furthermore, I proactively reached out to compassionate donors by ingeniously crafting a captivating webpage aimed at raising substantial funds for the deserving victims affected by the relentless corona pandemic. To demonstrate my unwavering commitment, I embarked on a remarkable endeavour of running an awe-inspiring distance of 50 km, symbolizing our unwavering determination to combat the ongoing crisis. Through the creation of this thoughtfully designed webpage, our noble mission flourished, yielding remarkable results.

By seamlessly blending the extraordinary aspects of our analogue existence with the remarkable potential of digital conveniences, we achieved a harmonious synergy, elevating our efforts to new heights. Our unwavering dedication allowed us to revel in the unparalleled benefits that both worlds had to offer, creating an environment where innovation thrived and profound impact resonated.

CHAPTER 51

THE EMERGING FUTURE OF FIREARMS IN LAW ENFORCEMENT

According to rough estimates, over 400 million firearms are in circulation globally, with India accounting for a significant percentage of this number. Police officers rely on firearms in their jobs, as they play an important role in law enforcement. Police officers use firearms for self-protection/defence, protecting suspects while escorting or apprehending them. Firearms are also valuable for investigations, training exercises and other uses. Law enforcement has used firearms for decades, with positive and negative effects. Law enforcement agencies use firearms to deter crime, maintain law and order or fight armed gangs and terrorists. For the most part, firearms are a force multiplier. They allow an officer to be more lethal than they otherwise would be. However, they also carry the risk of unintended consequences.

Most firearms used by law enforcement today are semi-automatic rifles, which fire one round per trigger pull. In India, police officers at and above the SI or head constable rank carry a sidearm, generally a 9 mm pistol or a Glock 17. However, at the state level, special units in India have automatic weapons, such as the AK-47, AKM, INSAS and Bren guns. And special forces and SWAT units are equipped with Heckler & Koch MP5s, Brügger & Thomet MP9s, AK-103s, M4A1 Carbines and others. While semi-automatic rifles are incredibly accurate and reliable, they also tend to result in more collateral damage than a single-shot weapon (such as a revolver or shotgun). Semi-automatic rifles can also be difficult to reload quickly amid a gunfight, creating an additional tactical disadvantage for officers who may have to wait several seconds before being able to fire again after firing a gun in fully automatic mode. In that case, the rounds will continue firing until no more ammunition is left, which makes it even more difficult for officers to return fire accurately during a gunfight. Finally, semi-automatic rifles are unsuited for long-range engagement with targets that require precision shooting (such as snipers). On the other hand, some law enforcement agencies do not use firearms because they believe them to be too dangerous or impractical.

However, with more guns in circulation, keeping them all safe is more challenging, as firearms are not perfect devices. They can malfunction or misfire, most are heavy and bulky, some are expensive to maintain, some are easy targets for criminals and police tend to misuse them often by resorting to firing on innocent victims. These factors have led many police departments to consider alternatives which are less lethal weapons like tasers and pepper spray. Others are experimenting with devices like body cameras and drones. Still, others have started exploring new technologies that could someday revolutionise how we handle guns in law enforcement. There are several different technologies available to law enforcement today.

Weaponisation of Firearms with AI and AR

As the world progresses, so does the technology we use daily, which is also true for the firearms industry, which is always looking for ways to improve the efficiency and effectiveness of guns. The future of firearms technology in law enforcement is looking very exciting. New guns are under development incorporating AI and other cutting-edge technologies, such as AR, allowing law enforcement officers to be better equipped and more effective in their jobs. One of the most promising new developments is using AI in firearms. AI is considered the third revolution in weaponisation; first, there was gunpowder, second nuclear weapons and now AI weapons. The military is already using this technology in some countries, and it is now starting to be adopted by law enforcement agencies. AI-enabled guns can identify targets and even distinguish between friends and foes, which is a massive advantage in dangerous situations where every split-second counts.

However, there is a dystopian side to weaponising police weapons with AI. Weaponising weapons with AI means using AI to intentionally inflict harm on humans by integrating it into police or military weapons systems and tools. Creation of autonomous weapons using AI, which was once the realm of sci-fi films like the *Terminator* series and *RoboCop*, killer robots, also technically known as Lethal Autonomous

Weapons Systems (LAWS), have now been created and are being tested at an accelerated pace with little oversight, some prototypes have also got deployed in actual conflicts. So far, there are reports of Israel's, Russia's, South Korea's and Turkey's militaries having weapons with autonomous capabilities. Countries like Australia, Britain, China and the US are reportedly investing heavily in developing LAWS with an ever-expanding range of sizes and capacities. Slaughterbots, also called LAWS or 'killer robots', use AI to identify, select and kill human targets without human intervention. Police can enable autonomous systems to assess the situational context and decide on the required attack according to the processed information. Ultimately, LAWS could use AI technology to identify targets and kill innocent individuals. Besides, killer robots, like all technology, are vulnerable to hacking and could turn against their creators in the event of cyberattacks.

An Autonomous Sentry

Use of AR in Firearms

Another new technology under development for law enforcement firearms is AR. AR could provide officers with real-time information about their surroundings and help them identify potential threats. This technology can overlay information on the real world, such as the location of targets or potential threats. It is beneficial for law enforcement officers, as it gives them critical information that they can use to make split-second decisions. Additionally, AR could provide officers with guidance and instructions on delivering the best response in a given situation. The future of firearms technology is looking very bright, and it is clear that law enforcement agencies are taking advantage of the latest advances. We can consider this good news, as it means that we can expect law enforcement officers to be even more effective in their jobs in the future.

Smart Guns

Another latest and positive trend in this industry is the development of smart guns equipped with networked technology that can keep people safe. Despite the concerns of some gun enthusiasts, smart guns have the potential to be a valuable tool for law enforcement agencies. In addition, using smart guns can help reduce the number of accidental shootings and the number of firearms that are stolen and used in crimes. While there are still some concerns about the safety and reliability of smart guns, it is clear that this technology has the potential to revolutionise the firearms industry. As more law enforcement agencies adopt these new guns, we will likely see a decrease in gun-related crimes and accidents.

A 'smart gun' is a firearm that employs fingerprint sensors, radio frequency identification (RFID), magnets or biometrics to prevent anyone except the owner from firing the weapon. Some smart guns also incorporate a combination of grip style and the strength and size of the person's hand to unlock the weapon. At the same time, some models allow the gun's owner to enable other people to have access to the weapon (like the owner's spouse). One of the significant concerns among law enforcement over models that employ biometric technology like fingerprint scanning is that authentication doesn't work 100 per cent of the time – as anyone with an iPhone can attest. All it takes is dirty or wet fingers/hands to lock a user out of their weapon. And, of course, you're vulnerable to hackers when you introduce electronics into the equation. RFID, for example, can be hacked.

Privately owned or licensed gun owners could also safeguard their guns by installing intelligent chips in their weapons, which could determine whether the user is the current gun owner. The chip could also prevent kids from shooting themselves accidentally or other family members from committing suicide or make theft of the gun by thieves or naxalites useless as they will never be able to use it. Cybersecurity will be critical when smart guns emerge in the Indian market to prevent hackers from breaching the system that monitors these devices. However, as the technology becomes more common, it will become easier to secure and protect the networks from hacking

This technology is a 'no-brainer' for plainclothes cops as most officers in plainclothes don't have safety holsters, if such an officer with a gun were hands on with a suspect and the suspect got the officer's gun. The officer wouldn't have to worry about it because the person who grabbed the gun wouldn't be able to use it against the officer or anyone. But even with the introduction of new, more LE-friendly models, there is also the question of whether putting untested technology into the hands of first responders who face uncertainty daily on the job is a good idea. But given the technology's potential, it's probably only a matter of time before a model that addresses the needs of police officers makes its way onto the market and departments, and investors get on board. Indian police should take the lead in piloting the technology, as it would move our country in improving the safety of firearms and reduce accidental firing and deaths.

A Smart Rifle That Can Automatically Aim and Turn Anyone into a Sharpshooter (US Army)

Meanwhile, recently Kanpur-based Sri Hans Energy System Private Limited has developed a Kavach Smart Fingerprint Gun Holster for IOF. The Kavach holster has a biometric lock, so only the owner can retrieve the firearm placed inside the Kavach holster by using the impression of his fingerprint. The innovative holster uses a material similar to Kevlar, a polymer used to make bulletproof vests.

Smart guns can help to improve the efficiency and accuracy of police forces. In a fast-paced and dangerous environment, every second counts and having a weapon that authorised personnel can easily and readily use can make all the difference. Moreover, smart guns can help create a safer working environment for police officers. By reducing the risk of accidental discharge, for example, officers can feel more confident and comfortable carrying out their duties. So, there are many good reasons why Indian police should have access to smart guns. With the correct implementation, this technology has the potential to save lives and make a real difference in the fight against gun crime.

HELLADS

While smart handguns and rifles might be an incredible advance in firearms technology, they aren't the only cool thing coming out of R&D these days, especially for military applications. There's also HELLADS, which stands for High-Energy Liquid Laser Area Defence System. It might not be the phasers or energy blasters we see in *Star Trek* or *Star Wars*, but we're heading in the right direction. The goal is to create a high-energy laser system that is powerful enough to generate intense laser energy while weighing less than 5 kg per KW of power produced. It's not a handheld phaser or blaster pistol, but we get to move away from projectiles as the primary ammunition for police weapons.

Railguns

Once we start moving into outer space, how do we create a weapon you can use in the vacuum of space? Our current weapons and firearms lean on a contained blast to thrust a bullet forward. But there is no oxygen in outer space for the explosion to push the shot at the target. Researchers plan to bring rail guns to overcome the lack of oxygen in outer space. Railguns use solid projectiles similar to bullets. Still, instead of depending on explosions to propel them forward, they use electromagnets to create a potent magnetic field which will hurl the projectiles out at tremendous speeds, sometimes faster than Mach. Currently, available railguns are enormous and mounted on military vessels. Still, if we find our space force needing weapons in the vacuum of space, we may go ahead and develop handheld railguns.

A Handheld Railgun

Sandia has developed a self-guided bullet for small-calibre, smooth-bore firearms that could hit laser-designated targets at distances of more than a mile (about 2000 metres with devastating accuracy. Conception and development of a self-guided bullet prototype by hunting enthusiasts Red Jones and Brian Kast and their associates took place at Sandia National Labs, an R&D subsidiary of one of the world's largest defence contractors, Lockheed Martin. The four-inch-long dartlike bullet holds an optical sensor that catches sight of a laser-designated target, triggering electromagnetic actuators in the bullet. These steer tiny fins that cut all spin and navigate the bullet to the mark with devastating precision. The creators expect that the production of these bullets could be inexpensive and rapid, making them potentially available to the military, law enforcement and recreational shooters.

A Self-Guided Bullet

Merely 50 years back, much of the technology we take for granted today, from mobile phones to FRT, only existed in science fiction. But technology changes everything it touches, and that includes firearms too. It might not be long before we have smart guns in our homes to keep us safe. Today we might not have handheld railguns, phasers or blaster pistols, but one thing is sure – we're steering in that direction. The gadgets and devices we see in sci-fi movies will become real. With the technologies evolving exponentially, we may not be able to foresee how future firearms of the police will pan out, but it will be exciting to wait and see.

Chapter 52

WHAT DOES CHATGPT HOLD FOR THE FUTURE?

ChatGPT is the new rage of today and is set to revolutionise the education system, business and marketing. It may even be able to replace humans at work in the future.

What Is ChatGPT?

Although the AI chatbot ChatGPT has only been in the public's eye since December last year, more than 1 million people are already using it. And with more than 100,000 users logging in for a test run, it's clear that it has the potential to change the way we communicate. However, there are some pitfalls that ChatGPT must avoid. Specifically, there is a need to train ChatGPT to reject inappropriate requests. For example, bad actors could programme it to generate instructions for various illegal activities, such as terrorist attacks.

Hence, it is a significant concern for Google, which is trying to protect its reputation from the possibility of bots that can harm or scam its users. So Google has been guarding the public's access to ChatGPT very closely.

On the other hand, ChatGPT's ability to write human-like texts is impressive. It can generate jokes, answer questions, compose music and write college application essays. But it still has a lot of blind spots. Some commenters have suggested that this technology might lead to the end of white-collar knowledge work. To combat this, OpenAI is trying to address the risks of anthropomorphising the AI systems it builds.

Why Is ChatGPT Making Waves?

The release of ChatGPT by OpenAI, a startup founded by Elon Musk, has ignited social media discussions. The chatbot has already been downloaded more than a million times and is generating significant buzz. The bot combines NLP and machine learning technologies that analyse users' words and provide relevant responses. It can provide a list of scenarios to choose from and write in a voice like a famous writer. The robot also has a few other tricks up its sleeve. For example, it can explain concepts in simple sentences and generate ideas from scratch. Another thing it does is debug code because the software can identify data patterns and use that information to make predictions and generate responses. As a result, it is capable of delivering tutorials, and it can even provide travel tips. But it is most known for its ability to give users just the correct information. The chatbot can be helpful in practical matters, such as decorating a living room. However, it could be an Achilles heel regarding more abstract issues, such as searching the internet for something.

Can ChatGPT Replace Humans?

There has been a lot of buzz about ChatGPT. Whether or not this AI can replace humans is uncertain. However, it does offer a compelling use case. It can provide immediate solutions to complex problems and help to simplify scientific concepts. But some people are concerned that the output is formulaic and lacks nuance and creativity. It depends on the data it has learned from. And because the bot receives training by machine learning, its output is not context-free. For example, it will not answer a question about a bank robbery. Instead, it will answer the question with a factual explanation that may be inaccurate. The AI can also reject requests that it feels are inappropriate. In some cases, it will even admit its mistakes. But while its output may be helpful for some tasks, it will not be a replacement for humans. Some people are concerned about its capacity to understand the human brain, a crucial factor in how it makes decisions.

ChatGPT vs. Google

There are concerns that Google is on the verge of financial disaster if ChatGPT goes live. In fact, according to Twitter, the chatbot could cost the company over $3 million per month to operate. If it goes live, then ChatGPT will have to compete against Google, which has decades of experience and a massive technology base. As a result, some experts have questioned whether ChatGPT can threaten Google's search engine. In a thread on Twitter, AI research scientist Margaret Mitchell explains why she believes ChatGPT won't replace Google Search anytime soon. Instead, Mitchell argues that it will be an effective tool for providing credible information. However, she warns against the possibility that the chatbot could spread misinformation.

Some have argued that the chatbot is flawed, as it has generated many incorrect answers. Others claim it is still a work in progress. But ChatGPT has made remarkable progress in a short period. Although it's in beta, ChatGPT has amassed more than a million users in just five days. This is impressive for an AI chatbot. It can answer questions on any topic and present information in a conversational style. While it does have the capability to generate toxic material and generate wrong information, it is also capable of presenting information in a manner that can enhance a user's online experience. For example, the chatbot can write poetry, write song lyrics and interpret research papers. Still, there's a lot of room for improvement. ChatGPT needs to learn more linguistic inputs, which costs more money to train. And it must find a quick path to monetisation. Currently, the biggest problem with ChatGPT is that it doesn't offer a click target which is vital to Google as it is a crucial revenue source. Ad revenue generated 81 per cent of Alphabet's revenues in 2021. The inclusion of featured snippets would offset the loss of ad revenue. Another issue is that ChatGPT lacks a way to handle current events. Experts are warning against the potential for a bad actor to use the chatbot to amplify ransomware attacks. The use of an AI chatbot in the real world has received a lot of press lately, especially since Alphabet Inc's stock has been on the skids. Earlier this month, Google announced its first-quarter earnings, showing a revenue growth slowdown. It also underperformed the NASDAQ-100 benchmark.

ChatGPT May Impact Education

Whether ChatGPT is the next big thing in education is hard to say. The buzz surrounding AI's ability to deliver personalised learning experiences has raised the bar on what should be a well-rounded educational experience.

The biggest challenge is implementing the new system in the classroom. Teachers must adjust their thinking when a new AI bot swoops into town. This is particularly true when it comes to grading student work. Some teachers may have to cut out the grade book in favour of a more personalised approach. Likewise, some students might have to take a back seat to a more streamlined process. If you're a teacher, there's a good chance you've already heard about ChatGPT. It's been around for more than a year but only made headlines in the last couple of weeks. It could only generate a single answer in the early days, but now it's been improved to create initial responses each time. Interestingly, it also has a built-in plagiarism checker that can trace a student's work to the source. There's no question that it can be a helpful tool, but there are some limitations. For one, it's not always possible to distinguish between student-generated and machine-generated work. Also, it can't decide the best way to display the results. To make matters worse, the average rate at which ChatGPT delivers its answers is abysmal. That's news for any user trying to solve a problem. Ultimately, it's a decision made by schools and districts. With so much on the line, making the right decision is essential. Thankfully, there are a few ways to solve this problem. One of the first is implementing a new policy on how teachers will use the tool. For example, a teacher will have to decide if they will use it in conjunction with a traditional assignment or use it independently. Alternatively, the teacher can eschew the task and let the AI do the heavy lifting. Of course, this isn't a long-term solution to the problem, and some IT admins will likely opt to block it outright.

AI tools have started changing how we impart education. These tools can help students focus on their creativity and can be used to test their skills. However, they also come with significant risks. The ability to use AI technologies responsibly is essential. ChatGPT is one such tool. It is a new kind of chatbot. This bot is programmed to learn from a large volume of text data on the internet. A student can give the AI a task, and it will provide advice, write essays or remix the student's work. ChatGPT is free. However, educators should be cautious about using this tool. While it can be an excellent tool for improving teaching and learning, it can also pose risks. In addition, it may not always generate accurate information. Students may use ChatGPT for indulging in malpractices. There have been cases where students used the tool to create fake essays. They might then republish these as their own. Additionally, students might be tempted to copy and paste ChatGPT responses to write their answers.

ChatGPT May Impact Marketing

When a chatbot like ChatGPT starts answering questions, it could be a massive disruption for business marketing. The technology can help marketers create more valuable content from complex answers. It can also be used to enhance workflows and provide better customer service. ChatGPT is a question-and-answer service powered by AI. Technology can automate many of the tasks that humans perform. However, it is still in its infancy, without adequate training to do much of anything. ChatGPT works by responding to text prompts with paragraphs. Like Google, it can answer questions on a wide variety of topics. Unlike Google, though, ChatGPT's answers are uncluttered and natural. In addition, one can use it to help identify common questions, concerns and interests. It could also be a helpful way to enhance customer experiences, streamline workflows and improve digital marketing campaigns.

Is ChatGPT a Good Tool to Create Content?

There are many reasons to be sceptical. For one thing, ChatGPT's name may be a mouthful, but the company has no problem making its name easy to spell. If that's the case, then using an AI chatbot to write your articles may not be the best option. Not everyone is comfortable writing for a machine, but the technology can be a productivity booster if used correctly. In the same way that a person can write a single article for several hours, a ChatGPT can perform the same function in less than a minute. While the most impressive ChatGPT function may not be the smartest, there are a few clever tricks in its bag. First, the software can spit out an op-ed – and if you're a writer, that's pretty darn good. There is currently no filtering mechanism in place to catch inappropriate content. For example, a user puts a 12-year-old daughter's essay into a ChatGPT bot. And the bot misstated the character's parent's death.

Drawbacks of ChatGPT

ChatGPT is an AI chatbot that has taken the internet by storm. The bot's ability to respond to text prompts already amassed over a million users in just five days. However, the bot has many problems that could hinder its ability to use for good. One major issue is that the bot isn't completely transparent. It doesn't disclose its sources or how it got its information, so it's possible for people to find information about the bot online that wasn't initially intended for them.

In addition, the bot tends to provide incorrect answers, which can cause users to wonder whether the bot is speaking for themselves. Users also have concerns about the bot's ability to write. Although the ChatGPT system uses AI to generate responses, it's still a very experimental tool. The bot was developed by OpenAI, a research and development company that Elon Musk cofounded. Initially, the bot was trained on a data set finalised in 2021. However, the ChatGPT model is not capable of answering questions that get posted online after 2021.

The chatbot technology known as ChatGPT is one of the most significant technological developments in the last five years. It could change how we interact with the internet. But it also has its limitations. While ChatGPT is a powerful tool, it does have its flaws. Its responses are not always correct. This technology is not good at making ethical decisions and will often generate unintended responses.

However, some users have found ways around these limitations. They have asked it to write jokes, answer questions, compose music and even write computer programmes. And the results have been pretty impressive. The reason is that ChatGPT's responses get based on data fed into it. OpenAI has programmed it to reject offensive requests. That means it will not take the bait on obviously racist queries. Also, future releases will close other loopholes. However, the responses can be very different every time. For example, a ChatGPT can create country song lyrics in the heavy metal style or explain scientific concepts to varying difficulty levels. But this is not necessarily a good thing. The answers aren't necessarily correct, as it depends on the data derived from the internet. There are many examples of it presenting misinformation as fact.

ChatGPT can answer questions and even write text. It's possible to use it to find answers to math problems or to answer customer service and online marketing questions. However, some experts warn that it can give false or misleading responses. The AI is based on a language model called GPT-3.5. The model simulates a conversation between a human and a machine. Many large tech companies use this technology to improve their virtual assistants. But as many people are already finding out, it is not always accurate. Even though OpenAI's ChatGPT gets trained on a vast data set of text from the internet, it can give wrong answers. And the model itself can admit to mistakes. The problem with AI technology is that it can perpetuate societal and cultural biases. For example, it can lead to a lack of employment in creative industries. So, it's not surprising that users of this new product are a bit concerned about how it can be misused.

In addition, many have suggested that ChatGPT can pose a threat to writers. While the robot is good at writing humorous responses, it still has problems with accuracy. As with any AI system, it's essential to know the implications of using a ChatGPT. A low rate of answers is a severe hazard to users, especially when trying to find a solution. The main issue is the information it provides. Most people do not factcheck before they post their answers. To ensure that ChatGPT doesn't provide misleading information, it should have to be regulated by a human, which could include requiring users to factcheck their responses before posting them. Also, the company should require users to sign up for a ChatGPT account before they can post their questions. The FAQ on the ChatGPT website does not fully address these issues. There is still a debate about who should regulate it.

CHAPTER 53

CHALLENGES AND BENEFITS OF DEEPFAKES IN LAW ENFORCEMENT

Deepfakes, also known as deepfake technology, are used in the Netherlands to help solve crimes. However, their use has some limitations. This technology may be an excellent way to catch criminals, but it can also become a massive security threat.

WHAT ARE DEEPFAKES?

Deepfakes, or synthetic media, are a relatively new technology in the cybercriminal arsenal. A deepfake is an artificially created video or audio clip that the creators generate by applying AI or machine learning features on a video or audio clip. Deepfakes can be used to create a variety of malicious and benign outcomes. For example, deepfakes can be created to feign legitimate celebrity endorsements for a commercial product and to blackmail individuals or businesses.

The first recorded application of deepfakes was in creating fake pornographic images. The first public cases of counterfeit media got documented in recent months.

The creation of these fake media has been made possible by the rapid progress in AI. Machine learning can analyse large amounts of data to generate authentic-looking fake photos and videos. In a recent cyber incident, a criminal defrauded an energy company of $243,000 by impersonating the voice of the chief executive. He also used an app that generated fake nude images of women.

The Dangers of Deepfakes

Deepfakes have the potential to create serious harm. They are a form of AI that can generate realistic-looking fake photos and videos. Cybercriminals also use these to do things such as blackmailing people, phishing and hijacking IoT devices. However, the dangers of deepfakes are far from limited to just cybercriminals.

There are several threats from deepfakes. About 96 per cent of deepfakes are pornographic videos that reduce women to sexual objects and cause emotional distress. Deepfake could depict a person as indulging in antisocial behaviours and could create social discord, increase polarisation and can even influence the election outcome. Deepfakes could accelerate the trust deficit in traditional media. Non-state actors could use them to create chaos in the target country, undermining trust in institutions. Non-state actors (terrorist organisations) could misuse them to stir anti-state sentiments. Liars could dismiss an unpleasant truth as deepfake or fake news, giving more credibility to denials. The weaponisation of deepfakes to dismiss objective truths in the media as fake news is already happening.

Some experts believe deepfakes could be a significant problem for financial institutions. Many financial experts have rated them as the top technology challenge. The threat is more pronounced in countries with unstable economic conditions, as well as those with weaker financial oversight mechanisms. Deepfakes can play into existing economic fears and even amplify them. Nevertheless, it's not easy to gauge the impact of deepfakes, as there have been only a handful of documented cases to date.

One of the most prominent uses of deepfakes is as a form of political propaganda. For example, the MIT Center for Advanced Virtuality used a deepfake to share a fake moon landing disaster speech. While this is the first time there has been public recognition of AI-generated media as such, there's been plenty of controversy over its effectiveness.

Deepfakes Are a Looming Challenge for Security

Deepfakes are a looming threat to national security. They can manipulate elections, spread disinformation and incite terrorism. A single convincing video can throw an election, crash the stock market and lead to riots. In addition, deepfakes can be created and distributed with readily available software. There is a need for comprehensive solutions that address deepfakes which requires a holistic approach, including technological detection, education and law enforcement. These solutions should be multi-stakeholder and collaborative.

First, education is a crucial part of the solution. The public needs basic information on how deep fakes get made and how to identify them. As more people get exposed to deepfakes, there will be more erosion of trust in the media. Next, countries need a legal framework for regulating deepfakes based on research and careful analysis of the processes involved. It should also be a part of a well-thought-out overall strategy.

Third, there is a need to prepare the legal system for a deepfake technology that can pose opposition from civil rights groups. While the government can't stop the development and commercialisation of deepfakes, it can help to establish a fair and consistent legal process.

The Problem of Deepfakes

Deepfakes, or AI-generated media, are becoming a growing threat. They have been used to spread disinformation and political discord, particularly in emerging markets. It is essential to know what to expect, how to respond and how to use this technology in your favour. A deepfake is a digital file manipulated to mimic a natural person's face, created with publicly available photos. Sometimes, they are used to impersonate corporate executives and apply for remote work.

In a recent study, two out of three respondents said they had encountered a deepfake. Using these techniques is easier than ever, and criminals are incorporating them into their schemes. As technology progresses, the quality and accuracy of deepfakes will only improve. For instance, AI can now produce fake images that look authentic. One of the biggest threats is privacy. Deepfakes can be used to create fraudulent documents or manipulate the media. Some law enforcement agencies have issued warnings about these types of digital attacks.

Deepfakes Can Be Used to Solve Crimes

The Dutch police have made a ground-breaking discovery that could revolutionise the way we solve crimes. Solving crimes using deepfakes is an exciting development in the world of crime-fighting. Dutch police have recently begun using deepfakes to help them solve serious crimes, like murder and kidnapping. Using this technology, they can create an image of a missing person or get a better look at a suspect or witness. By creating a realistic image of the suspect or witness, they can get a better idea of what they look like and who they may be. This is especially helpful when there are no witnesses or when the witnesses can't clearly see the suspect. It can also be used to help find missing persons, as the deepfakes can provide an accurate representation of what the person looks like now. Also, deepfakes can also be used to recreate witnesses for murder scenes. This technique uses existing video footage to create a realistic, computer-generated version of someone who wasn't there during the crime. This deepfake witness can then be used to recreate the events as they happened, providing the police with vital information about the crime. Deepfakes are a powerful tool for law enforcement and can be used to solve crimes more quickly and efficiently, making them a valuable asset for police forces everywhere.

Further, by combining the latest in AI and FRT, police will be able to transform audio recordings of witnesses and victims into realistic images. This technology is being used to help identify and catch suspects in a variety of cases, ranging from murder to theft. With deepfakes, police can now create a photorealistic image of a suspect that they can then use to compare with a database of images. This has been a game-changer for law enforcement and is helping them solve cases in ways that were never possible before. With this technique, the police are now able to solve crimes faster and more accurately than ever before. It's an exciting development that could change the way police departments around the world investigate and solve crimes!

How Dutch Police Are Using Deepfakes to Solve Crimes

The Dutch police are using deepfakes to solve crimes. It's a technology that uses AI to create a video that mimics the movements of a real person. We can use this technology for good or bad. But there is a growing concern about the use of these videos. Police say it's an excellent way to get clues from the public. Since the video's release on YouTube, they've received a dozen tips. They are now working to verify the authenticity of these tips. Using deepfakes is one way to attract more witnesses to a case. However, authorities are finding it difficult to detect these fake videos. Often, these videos have unnerving movements and can be deceptive. Ultimately, the idea is to have witnesses come forward with information about the murder. Dutch police have been trying to solve a cold case for years, but they could not find the killer. Authorities believe a criminal gang operated near the metro station where the shooting occurred. The police, to lure witnesses into providing information, decided to recreate a video of the boy's murder in 2003. According to the spokesperson, the video is the first of its kind. During the video creation, police worked with the family of Sedar Soares.

The Challenge of Deepfakes

Deepfakes are synthetic media that can be produced with AI and distributed by computer networks. Miscreants can use fake media for disinformation and terrorism and support criminal activities. Synthetic media has gained attention as a national security concern as miscreants could use it with devastating effects in countries with unstable economic environments. The financial sector has been a target for deepfakes.

In recent months, several publicly known cases of deepfakes have got identified. These include a mother of a child who manipulated an audio recording of her husband to convince a court of his violent behaviour. Another case involved an energy company that was defrauded for $243,000 by criminals who impersonated the voice of the chief executive. The legal and regulatory landscape for deepfakes is complex. Legislators, law enforcement and the legal system must work together to find an effective solution. Some protection groups may challenge rulings regulating deepfakes, especially if the rulings are too narrow, which could result in the inability to combat deepfakes. Law enforcement must develop new technologies and skills to prevent and counter these attacks. Police are devising programmes in various countries to detect and analyse deepfakes. Programmes include DARPA's Media Forensics, which supports an automated assessment of the integrity of videos. Similarly, Facebook and McAfee are developing software to develop deepfakes.

Deepfakes Could Become a Staple for Organised Crime

Deepfakes are a new kind of media derived from AI designed to look like genuine photos or videos. Lawbreakers use them for many purposes, including document fraud and political disinformation. Deepfakes are becoming increasingly sophisticated. AI advancements can produce more realistic and convincing fake videos and photographs, which can lead to severe consequences. For instance, a deepfake could produce a misleading video of a bank executive describing a liquidity crisis. If enough people share this deepfake, it could trigger a successful bank run, likely during financial turmoil. Aside from the threat to the market, deeper fakes also potentially undermine public safety and trust in institutions. As more and more people begin to distrust traditional media and news sources, these astroturfing tactics can accelerate the erosion of public confidence.

Deepfakes could be used to spread misinformation, create fake recordings of enforcement actions and generate non-consensual pornography. Some experts predict these methods could become a major staple of organised crime over the coming years.

Impact of Deepfakes on Law Enforcement

Deepfakes are a form of subversive digital activity. They artificially generate media or process data to influence concrete decisions. Depending on the content, deepfakes could threaten the rule of law, democracy and the well-being of citizens. Technology is still in its infancy. However, its adverse effects are already manifesting themselves. One of the first things law enforcement needs to address is how to detect and respond to deepfakes. In particular, law enforcement agencies must improve their skills and collaboration with computer science experts. As technology advances, deepfakes will become more common. Miscreants are already using deepfakes in crimes such as document fraud, non-consensual pornography and identity theft. They also pose challenges to trials and evidence management. For example, in a recent case, an energy company was defrauded by a group of criminals who faked the voice of its chief executive. Deepfakes, therefore could mean financial harm, spook customers and cause money transfers. Deepfakes also threaten social institutions and relationships if used to influence elections and international decision-making. It's unlikely that individual law enforcement agencies will have the resources to investigate deepfakes properly unless steps are taken to develop tools to detect deepfakes and regulate them by enacting laws.

How Countries Are Combating Deepfakes?

To combat deepfakes, China has announced a policy which requires service providers and users to ensure that any doctored content using the technology is explicitly labelled and traced back to its source. The EU has an updated code of practice that requires tech companies, including Google, Meta and Twitter, to take measures to counter deepfakes on their platforms. If found non-compliant, these companies could face fines of as much as 6 per cent of their annual global turnover. The US has enacted a Deepfake Task Force Act to assist the Department of Homeland Security in countering deepfake technology by conducting an annual study of deepfakes. In India, there are no legal rules against using deepfake technology. However, specific laws exist for copyright violation, defamation and cybercrimes that could address the concerns of deepfakes. Canada is undertaking some of the most cutting-edge AI research with several domestic and foreign actors.

Solutions to Curb Deepfakes

The most effective tool is media literacy for consumers to combat disinformation and deepfakes. Countries should put in place meaningful regulations by involving technology, industry, policymakers and other stakeholders to disincentive creation and distribution of deepfakes. Nations should research and develop technologies that will quickly detect deepfakes and enact laws to punish miscreants. People must become internet-intelligent consumers and not share and contribute to the infodemic by discerning and refusing to share fake content.

CHAPTER 54

VOICE BIOMETRICS AS A CRITICAL TECHNOLOGY FOR FIGHTING FRAUDS AND CYBERCRIME

Voice biometrics is an emerging technology that utilizes the unique characteristics of an individual's voice to establish their identity. It holds great promise as a non-invasive, user-friendly, and portable biometric method. Whether for individuals or companies, voice biometrics plays a vital role in combating bank fraud and cybercrime. With technological advancements, a person's voice has become one of the most reliable means of identification.

The financial services industry is a prominent user of biometrics, with the widespread adoption of smartphones leading to the increased use of fingerprint and facial biometrics for security purposes. However, these methods are not entirely foolproof and can be vulnerable to deep fakes. To mitigate fraud and identity theft risks, banks are turning to voice biometrics, which offers significant security enhancements over traditional knowledge-based authentication methods.

One of the remarkable features of voice biometrics is its versatility. It can be employed in various situations where identity verification is crucial, including banking transactions, customer service calls, e-commerce purchases, and voting. In the future, voice biometrics could also be utilized to secure access to homes, cars, hospitals, airports, and other facilities. Additionally, it can be employed to prevent fraud in telecommunications and financial services, authenticate users when logging into computers, apps, or websites, verify identity for job applications and government services, and monitor employee whereabouts and movements throughout the day.

Apart from its wide range of applications, voice biometrics offers several other benefits. Firstly, it is highly scalable, making it ideal for low-cost services that require rapid deployment. Secondly, it provides enhanced security compared to traditional password authentication methods, as it is nearly impossible to spoof or replicate someone's voice. Lastly, voice biometrics is privacy-friendly, as it does not necessitate the disclosure of personal information, unlike conventional authentication methods such as passwords.

Passwords, being the weakest link in security, pose significant risks, especially considering the numerous apps, services, and accounts people use today. Voice biometrics presents a more formidable challenge for hackers, as analyzing the caller's voice during a call can help verify their identity and identify suspicious calls. As demonstrated by HSBC UK, implementing voice biometrics in telephone banking services resulted in a significant reduction of fraud cases by over 50% in the first half of 2021, preventing the loss of millions of pounds. Numerous companies, including Chase, Wells Fargo, and Schwab, have also started leveraging voice biometrics to prevent fraud and enhance customer experiences by eliminating the need for complex passwords.

Voice biometrics has rapidly grown as a software technology for user identity verification, with the market projected to reach a size of $3.9 billion by 2026 and a compound annual growth rate of 22.8%. As an authentication solution, voice biometrics can help companies safeguard themselves against criminal attacks by providing an easy and reliable means to verify customers during phone calls, eliminating the reliance on passwords or knowledge-based identification systems. Voice verification can be performed actively, where the caller speaks a specific phrase upon request, or passively, where the system silently conducts identity checks while the customer converses with the support agent. By enrolling their voices, customers enable the system to store their unique voiceprints, which can be matched and verified during future calls.

During verification, if the voice fails to match the voiceprint, the system alerts employees or security personnel about a suspicious caller. For example, even if the caller provides correct customer details and answers security questions but fails biometric verification, it signifies the presence of a potential fraudster. Prompt alerts enable the support team to take appropriate action, including notifying management or involving law enforcement. Moreover, voice biometrics enables organizations and law enforcement agencies to maintain a database of known voiceprints of fraudsters, allowing them to identify and take action against these individuals when they attempt new fraudulent activities.

Voice biometrics is a rapidly growing trend in forensics and police investigations, enabling law enforcement to track and identify individuals using voice recognition technology. This advancement allows for better crime prevention and response by identifying and deterring criminals before they can commit offenses. Voice biometrics has wide-ranging potential applications, including security systems, cash registers, and electronic voting systems, making it a valuable tool in preventing various types of crimes. These technologies assist law enforcement in improving investigation efficiency and establishing extensive databases of known criminals and individuals on watch lists. Additionally, voice biometrics has significantly reduced the time required to identify a speaker.

Voice-biometrics in forensics and police investigation also prove beneficial in identifying suspects in cold cases. Although audio recordings may not always be suitable for identification purposes or the suspect may intentionally alter their voice, experts can compare voice characteristics and present evidence in court. This aids the court in determining whether two recordings originate from the same person. Forensic voice analysis includes speaker profiling, which involves examining a speaker's voice dialect to analyze their background. Using this information, experts can determine whether two recordings come from the same person. In a recent study, a voice profile extracted from an emergency call recording in the George Zimmerman case helped an expert identify the speaker as a Cuban national and native of the eastern United States.

The technology behind voice biometrics creates a digital voiceprint and compares it to the customer's voice, flagging fraudulent calls to operators. While the system is not foolproof and may generate false positives, it provides a real-time risk score indicating the likelihood of a call being fraudulent. The most accurate systems can even detect cloned voice samples. The cost of implementing such systems varies based on the number of voiceprints in the fraudster database and the response time required.

Beyond the evident advantages, voice biometrics is an effective means of identifying professional fraudsters, which is particularly crucial as many frauds involve call centers. Voice biometrics significantly reduces the time taken to identify a caller, enabling call centers to serve more individuals at a lower cost. A notable feature of voice biometrics is its device independence, meaning that even if a mobile phone is stolen, authentication can still be achieved through voice biometrics. This is vital in combating criminals who change pin codes to gain unauthorized access to accounts. Moreover, voice biometrics simplifies the caller identification process, allowing customers to verify their identity within seconds. This convenience enhances customer satisfaction, eliminating the need for customers to answer a series of questions or share personal data over the phone. The system identifies the customer in less than three seconds, making it nearly impossible for scammers intercepting one-time passwords or notifications to complete the voice authentication process.

Voice biometrics relies on a customer's voice, which is considerably more challenging to steal compared to other forms of identification. By analyzing the caller's voice throughout a conversation, voice biometrics can swiftly verify the caller's claimed identity and promptly flag any suspicious calls. Additionally, voice biometrics raises customer awareness and vigilance. When customers know that voice biometrics is used to identify them by their bank or support center, they become more cautious when asked for bank details or login information for "verification procedures." They understand that a "Telco technical support employee" should only need voice verification rather than personal login details.

Voice biometrics stands as one of the most promising technologies in crime prevention, providing an automated and indisputable method of identifying individuals based on their voice. Law enforcement can employ voice biometrics to rapidly identify criminals attempting to disguise their voices through tactics like drugs or disguises. Compared to visual scans of faces, voice recognition technology offers greater reliability and accuracy, as facial recognition often has a high error rate and requires direct eye contact. Voice recognition, on the other hand, maintains a significantly lower error rate and does not necessitate eye contact. Whether an individual is speaking to themselves or on the phone, voice biometrics makes it easy to determine if they are engaging with someone else. This technology has extensive applications, from criminal background checks to airport security, and plays a vital role in building trust between law enforcement agencies and the community. When people know that identification can be swiftly established through voice biometrics, they are more likely to report suspicious behavior, resulting in proactive crime prevention.

In conclusion, voice biometrics is a form of biometric technology that law enforcement agencies can leverage to identify individuals based on their unique vocal characteristics. Implementing a voice biometric system represents an intelligent investment for any bank or financial institution, as it eliminates the need for customers to endure tedious questioning, flags suspicious calls, and provides organizations with speed, accuracy, and enhanced security. Overall, voice biometrics is a cutting-edge technology that holds immense potential in various domains, from law enforcement and forensics to fraud prevention in call centers. Its ability to quickly and accurately verify identity, detect suspicious activity, and enhance customer satisfaction makes it an invaluable asset in the fight against crime. As this technology continues to advance, its applications are likely to expand, contributing to a safer and more secure society.

Part IV

POLICING AND LAW

Chapter 55

THE GROWING CYBERCRIME RISKS OF NFT EXPLOSION

In the world of cryptocurrencies, one of the most popular and lucrative investment opportunities today is to invest in 'NFTs'. NFTs are digital assets with unique characteristics from traditional cryptocurrencies. They are digital representations of unique, real-world items such as securities, collectables or other finite digital assets. They are called so because they are not fungible, as they are unique and cannot be substituted, unlike fungible tokens, which an individual can substitute for a similar asset. Such tokens may seem like a niche concept, but the mainstream financial and investment world now recognises their value. NFTs due to their unique characteristics are susceptible to exploitation by criminals. Although many new doors for investments have opened up with the advent of NFTs, several investors who view NFTs as an excellent deal to get rich are finding them fraudulent in many instances.

The spread of crypto assets such as NFTs poses new challenges for law enforcement agencies in the digital world. Cryptocurrencies have many legitimate use cases, such as digital currency exchanges, decentralised digital wallets and NFTs. On the flip side, criminals use them for illicit activities such as money laundering, cybercrime and terrorism financing.

In a world where cybercriminals and terrorists are looking for new ways to finance their illegal activities and evade law enforcement, cryptotokens and NFTs could significantly impact the future of law enforcement.

NFT is a form of digital art that can be bought and sold under a veil of anonymity given by blockchain technology. If criminals combine NFT with new technology, they can conceal money laundering. People buy and sell NFTs using cryptocurrencies, adding another layer of complexity to tracing these transactions. An artist may take several weeks to produce a work of art, but criminals can steal such art and generate multiple NFTs in a few minutes. The value or piece of NFT gets determined by the price a buyer is willing to pay. A criminal wishing to convert dirty money can generate an anonymous NFT, list it for sale on the blockchain and buy the same NFT using another anonymous digital wallet which could be the dirty money earned through child pornography or drugs. He thereby converts his illegal earnings as legitimate money earned from the sale of the digital artwork or NFT. Modifying illicit fiat-currency profits into cryptocurrencies and then moving cryptocurrencies through a complex series of transactions across multiple wallets renders tracing the illegal funds' route tedious and hard for law enforcement investigators.

For instance, the US police are investigating a rug pull, where creators of NFT solicited investments and abruptly abandoned the project and retained the investor's funds by defrauding them. The creators of the NFT Frosties website attracted investors by promising them purchaser's holder rewards and, among other things, giveaways, early access to a metaverse game and an exclusive mint pass to upcoming Frosties seasons. Soon, the creators of the website, who had disguised their identities, abruptly abandoned the Frosties NFT project within hours after selling out Frosties NFTs by deactivating the Frosties website and transferring approximately $1.1 million in cryptocurrency proceeds from the scheme to various cryptocurrency wallets under their control in multiple transactions spawned to confuse the source of funds. Following a detailed investigation, police have now charged two 20-year-old accused, Nguyen and Llacuna, for wire fraud which carries a sentence of 20 years.

Blockchain data company Chainalysis, which has been tracking NFT crimes, has reported several instances of 'wash sale' and 'money laundering. In 2022, they have documented numerous cases of phishing, hacking and scams using NFTs. In a wash sale, the owner of an NFT misleads potential buyers by repeatedly buying his own NFT from different electronic wallets set up by him at very high prices by artificially bidding up the cost to create artificial demand, which tricks the unsuspecting buyers into buying the NFT at a mind-boggling price. Chainalysis, the data company which analysed wash sales, detected net crime proceeds of $8.4 million from 262 such incidents of wash sales. As the NFT industry is new, it will take time to detect other new NFT crimes which may be happening.

Further, Chainalysis, while analysing their blockchain data, discovered \$2.7 million worth of NFT money laundering transactions compared with \$8.6 billion in crypto money laundering. One of the reasons why Chainalysis detected a low percentage of money laundering in the NFT space could be because money laundering in the NFT space could be outside the world of data, or it's probably because NFTs are still not widespread and are not being viewed as an attractive option in the crypto space.

NFTs, due to their unique characteristics, could transform the way crimes get committed and investigated. For instance, we don't have a method to detect the drug cartels masking their income from the sale of drugs as proceeds from the deal of NFT. NFTs need close monitoring because of the risks associated with buying or selling NFTs using cryptocurrency. And transfers of cryptocurrency from illicit wallets related to malware, ransomware, darknets, scams, terrorist financing and so on. Authorities must insist NFT marketplaces collect KYC information on users who send or receive payments in NFT transactions to prevent fraud and scams.

There has been little NFT regulation to date in India. There is no specific Act in India to govern NFTs, and as such, it is currently only governed by the general principles of contract and the Copyright Act. As criminals have begun using NFTs, law enforcement machinery in India needs awareness, education, rules and laws to stop criminals from exploiting the latest emerging technology of NFT.

Chapter 56

CAN THE POLICE LIVE BY BREAD ALONE?

Taking care of the soul is crucial, but I kept procrastinating and deferring because it seemed the most irrelevant thing to nurture in this fast-paced, busy world. Hitting the gym occurred to me as the most pragmatic and prudent thing to do than sitting cross-legged on the ground with my eyes closed. So the decay and neglect of my soul went on until I ran into an old childhood friend of mine while boarding a flight a few years ago at the local airport, which made me realise that all the striving in the outer world had not fetched me any joy or lasting happiness. On the contrary, I figured out that all the grind was not only depleting me physically and mentally but also leaving me drained and spiritually parched.

Harking back to my childhood days, I can vividly reminisce several fond memories of time spent with this boyhood chum, either trapping guppies at the local pond or going catapult hunting in the fields or playing truant at school to binge on Clint Eastwood's movies at the local cinema. I lost touch with him when they left the neighbourhood after his father got transferred. After over four decades, on that random evening at the airport, we were suddenly staring at each other, thrilled beyond words at the reunion. There was something magnetic about his presence that instantly stupefied and hushed me. His saintlike demeanour radiated deep peace and expansive compassionate energy. Despite the hustle and bustle of milling crowds around us, I could sense his presence, exuding an energy of indescribable joy and peace unknown. A quick conversation with him revealed he had veered to a life of service and contemplation after jettisoning a glamorous profession. This brief interaction was so profound that I desperately wanted to gain all his hallowed qualities by subjecting my being to spiritual disciplines.

Over the years, especially after the tryst with my childhood buddy, I have since uncovered that tending to one's spirit is far more valuable than caring for one's body and mind. Because our spirit can be strong and glorious as ever even after age has atrophied our muscles, the skin has got shrunken and shrivelled, the brain has got permeated with plaques, and the blood vessels have got clogged despite our relentless quest for fitness and longevity.

Most police officers like me, at some stage of life, realise that there must be more to life than day-to-day existence, and some entertain thoughts of having a rich inner life. Contemporary policing has become more complex and challenging. It has become more demanding and stressful than before. Cultivating spiritual disciplines could help police officers grow and strengthen their souls. Eventually, bolstering the ability of a police officer to feel inner peace, demonstrate moral courage, get insights, conquer bad parts of oneself, endure hardships and act unselfishly. Inculcating spirituality in the lives of police officers does not mean making them religious. It implies helping them develop a deeper, more transcendent meaning of life which is untrammelled to roam and explore their life bereft of all calcified dogmas, tenets and traditions.

So, spiritual disciplines are specific habits that develop, grow and strengthen our spirit, build our character muscles and train our soul. Just as we grow our muscles in the gym by lifting weights, or grow new neurons in the brain by challenging the brain with new tasks, we can consistently train our spiritual muscles with spiritual activities like meditation, service, prayer, gratitude, fasting, silence, journaling and so on to prevent us from becoming spiritually unfit, spiritually barren and spiritually stagnant.

Hence, to strengthen the soul, we would have to train in a conscious, intentional manner, like overcoming resistance by pushing weights in a gym. We need discipline in all walks of life. We need the discipline to learn a new art or craft, go to the gym, lose weight or achieve something in life. The same steadfast laws that underlie discipline in the physical world also apply in the spiritual realm. We must intentionally choose to train the soul consistently. Persistence is essential. Just as we earmark a specific time for physical exercise, we must make time for spiritual activities. Wellness and vitality that accrues from such practices could enhance the quality of service we provide as law enforcement professionals.

Thus, incorporating spiritual disciplines during our basic training could go a long way in building and insulating resilience and spiritual strength in the recruits to better combat stress and face the worst-case scenarios in their future duties. Interweaving spirituality into the training curricula could help embody personal resilience into police officers' lives as an antidote to stress. During the training, trainers could help recruits reflect on their purpose and examine what lured them to police work.

Further, the trainers could also teach recruits to develop effective spirit-based coping strategies. Understanding emotional resilience, which links a person's physical and emotional reactions, could help a recruit infer the cause of the body's adverse reaction and help him devise suitable strategies to combat it. For generating ethical police officers, it is imperative to strengthen the spirituality of recruits. Ethical on-the-job decision-making often correlates to employee spirituality. Hence, the spiritual dimension could be a critical element that could significantly influence physical, cognitive and emotional aspects by providing recruits with direction, purpose, connectedness or inner completeness. Connectedness here could be a connection with God, other people or nature.

Now, research is disclosing that spiritual development can effectively protect the police against the harmful effects of policing. The pronouncement of Jesus Christ that man does not live by bread alone in the Bible implies that it's not enough to feed the body with food and ignore the spirit. The soul also needs nourishment in the form of meaning and connection. Ample evidence is emerging from studies to prove that police cannot live by bread alone as spirituality is a vital component that provides purpose and direction to police personnel. Therefore, to infuse a culture of contemplation, we have established dedicated silent spaces called 'Zen Zones' and 'Zen Dens' for officers and men in all the TSP Battalions under me to serve as sanctuaries of serenity and calm reflection.

Finally, imparting such training to police officers would help them understand how to nurture and maintain their inner spirit of compassion, noble service and connectedness. As a result, they would be much more likely to develop that sense of inner calling and meaningful purpose in the quality of their work. Hence, it is essential to overhaul the current police culture to integrate spirituality and emotional wellness into law enforcement. It can help police officers understand the spiritual connectedness to their inner sense of duty and the needs of their fellow officers and the society they serve. Hence, training institutions should endeavour to encourage and promote the non-religious spiritual practices of recruits to produce well-rounded police officers who are adept at physical, mental, emotional and spiritual levels. Police officers need bread to live, but we are all spiritual beings having a human existence, so the soul is paramount, and we can't afford to starve the soul and live on bread alone.

CHAPTER 57

CAN SPIRITUALITY BEAR THE CROSS OF THE POLICE?

Filled with action-packed police drama, *Courageous*, made in 2011, is the fourth film produced by Sherwood Pictures. *Courageous* narrates the saga of four law enforcement officers who bravely confront the worst the streets offer. However, at home, they find they are falling short as dads, as fatherhood's challenge is something that they are incapable of grappling with. In the film, a daughter of one of the police officers succumbs after being hit by a drunk driver, which forces him to question what is important to him. Following this, the grieving police officer resolves to be a better father. He gets his other three police cronies to agree to promise to abide by a resolution, which includes many things such as spirituality, integrity and family. All four of them decide to uphold their promise. This endeavour to rectify themselves yields many beneficial transformations in their family lives and heals past traumas.

Just like the enforcement officers in the film *Courageous*, we can discover meaning and purpose in our lives once we turn to spirituality. Spirituality is essential for all law enforcement officers as it helps them derive meaning and connectedness in life. Spirituality involves recognising a feeling or sense of belief that something more significant exists than oneself. There is something more to being human than sensory experience and that the greater whole we are part of is cosmic or divine.

Most police officers enter the police organisation aspiring to serve, self-discovery, finding meaning or a fondness for wearing the uniform. But they soon discover that there is an enormous chasm. Besides, police officers experience an overwhelming discrepancy between their longing and working realities in the field. Soon realisation dawns on them that a policing career is a thankless and unappreciated job about confrontation and crisis management, where police get despised, loathed and hated for no reason.

As I am writing, I hear that a CISF jawan performing election duties in Salem has attempted suicide by shooting himself. Every day a policeman in some part of the world reaches a point where he believes his life has no longer any meaning and tragically takes it. When a police officer takes his life, it's a catastrophe for his family, friends and colleagues.

Such instances happen because a policeman's job is demanding and threatening. After all, they confront crime, criminals, murder, accidents, suicides and terrorists day in and day out. All of which takes a massive toll on policemen and their family's health and well-being. Non-recognition of a police officer's work and the reality of facing the most wretched and nastiest things in society cause distress, desperation, frustration and even a loss of meaning in a policeman's life. Police organisations emphasise the police personnel's physical and mental well-being but ignore their spiritual well-being. Several valid reasons are there as to why police leadership should bestow adequate importance to police personnel's spiritual well-being.

Sometime back, while I was reading *The Seat of the Soul* by Gary Zukav, I had a lightbulb moment when I came across the concept of authentic power. It occurred to me that most police misconduct stems from misuse and misinterpretation of the powers bestowed on them to carry out their legitimate duties. A police officer's illegitimate power to commit excesses or indulge in torture or sexual harassment of victims emanates from five external sensory powers instead of authentic power. The author defines authentic power as the alignment of the personality with the soul.

According to Zukav, humanity is transforming from a species pursuing external power, which can manipulate and control using five senses, to a species that grows spiritually by creating authentic power. Authentic power is the capacity to distinguish love from fear within oneself and choose love no matter what is happening inside an individual or what is happening outside him. Creating authentic power wilfully requires a person to select his intentions that result in consequences for which the chooser will assume responsibility.

Law enforcement officers wield enormous power against the citizens. They deprive them of their freedom, search them and their dwellings, seize their property and use force against them. Further, because of the rigid hierarchy and rank structure, police officers also exert power over their subordinates to subdue them or harass them mentally or sexually under the guise of discipline. Introducing police officers to the concept of authentic power during the initial days of training could go a long way in shifting their mindset from one relying on external power to one exercising authentic power, inducing them to realise that there is no power in abuse and revenge.

Policing is a highly stressful job that draws on every aspect that an officer has in his armoury. A grounding in spirituality or spiritual practices can make police officers incredibly resilient and develop in them high levels of self-control, compassion, professionalism and love for the work they have chosen to do. Spirituality may also help police officers develop an aptitude to transform negative experiences, swivel their emotionally charged frustrations and reverse the feelings of victimisation to generate new meaning and compassion. Clear proof now appears to be emerging that spiritual practice can help police officers cope with their job's toxic nature.

Police officers cultivating spiritual practice even during extreme suffering, violence and tragedy discover immense resources within themselves to counter the bombardments and storms in their outer life by uncovering and staying connected to their spiritual beliefs. Such officers unfailingly display empathy, ethical honesty and an intense yearning to serve humanity. A study is crucial to investigate spirituality in policing and determine to what degree spiritual resources build police officers' capability to act with compassion in their professional arena and create meaning and purpose in their lives.

Every police organisation's motto must be to train and equip their men to be fully fit to perform their role. The fitness I am talking about is holistic, which encompasses physical, mental and spiritual wellness. All three are essential, though we neglect the spiritual dimension in our country. And all police organisations must have resources to meet police personnel's spiritual requirements.

Studies have shown that meditation and mindfulness positively affect the stressed-out policeman. Finding a calm spot and reflecting for a few moments, relinquishing control of whatever is vexatious and tormenting could calm a police officer down. Spirituality brings better health outcomes and enables police officers to cope with the disease, suffering, depression and death of close relatives.

Finally, the inherent power to transcend the five senses to experience our spiritual dimension is what sets human beings apart. The journey from the physical to the spiritual dimension is the voyage from gross to subtle, finite to infinite and tangible to intangible; it's a journey that could awaken the inner spirit and lead to a realisation of the oneness of all.

Chapter 58

MINDFULNESS FOR MINDFUL AND HUMANE POLICING

Last six months I was in a bad state of mind. My work had got me down, and I felt like I was on a roller coaster of emotions. I felt high when I was running, writing my column or painting, but felt outright crappy and down at work. Every day after work, I dumped all the darkness engulfing and drowning me over my family, who adored me no matter what. I remember being at a point in my life where things were going downhill every way – especially emotionally. I felt as though I was spiralling into a deep depression. While being at that lowest point, I discovered and gobbled a book sitting on my shelf, called *The Miracle of Mindfulness* by Thich Nhat Hanh. After two weeks of breathing and a somewhat quiet mind, I began seeing the most beautiful, vibrant colours of purple, indigo and white – giant blobs of light bouncing and swaying back and forth, with a simultaneous realisation of the miracle of mindfulness that had flashed its light banishing the darkness festering inside my mind.

Mindfulness is a practice of purposely bringing one's attention to experiences occurring in the present moment without judgement. One can develop this through a method of meditation. Mindfulness bases itself on Zen, Vipassana and Tibetan meditation techniques. Adoption of programmes created on mindfulness models in schools, prisons, hospitals, law enforcement and other environments has resulted in positive outcomes when it came to ageing, weight management, athletic performance and so on.

Mindfulness or meditation slows the mind by bringing a focus on the breath. It brings attention back from distraction and focuses the mind on the present. The practice of meditation comes from an intuitive and primitive need to connect to the universe and oneself. Being physically fit is not enough for a policeman; emotional well-being is also crucial.

Meditation enables some people to become more self-aware, making others less stressed and anxious. Unlike other practices, mindfulness meditation requires no gear. For instance, I love to run; I need shoes and a road or a ground to run. And running is best done in a hot city like Chennai either in the mornings or evenings. But meditation requires no equipment, and we can do it anywhere, even on the chair you are right now sitting. You need not follow a particular religion, belief or guru. Even guided meditations available on the internet can be an excellent place to start.

Mindfulness is imperative for police personnel as they face ordeals day in and day out. Recently, I knew a junior colleague of mine who came back from work depressed and exhausted and unable to sleep through the night. He also suffered from acute backache. His body was in a constant state of agitation. Although he continued to work, he was falling apart. Desperate to calm his mind, he combed the internet and stumbled on mindfulness meditation. As he began practising mindfulness, he experienced terrific results. He got back his sense of self, the sense of worth and his ability to breathe and he slept. He felt whole and hopeful again. Mindfulness in his case, like for several others, turned out to be a powerful tool in his recovery because it equipped him to rediscover his calming sense of control over his experience. Even when surrounded by a chaos of tumultuous emotions, the officer could use mindfulness to become grounded. Through this practice, he could bring himself back to basics, knowing that all he needed to do was to breathe, be present and be aware of the event.

Hence, police personnel need to practise meditation to ease the stress of policing. Teaching and practising meditation should be a vital piece of police officer development because policing careers have high rates of depression, sudden cardiac death, diabetes and sleeplessness because of stress. The University of Buffalo and the National Institute for Occupational Safety and Health suggested that stress, trauma, obesity, shift work and exposure to toxic chemicals might contribute to early deaths. One study of almost 2800 white male police officers in Buffalo, New York, found their average life expectancy to be 22 years shorter than their civilian counterparts. Police personnel are also more prone to suicide than the general population and are more likely to kill themselves than getting killed while on duty.

Further, a 2015 clinical study published in the *Journal of the American Medical Association* showed that about half of military veterans who underwent mindfulness training reported a reduction in PTSD symptoms, compared to only a third who took part in a different form of therapy. A small 2016 study by Hunsinger, Goering and others of 43 police officers who went through eight weeks of mindfulness training showed improvement in self-reported resilience, stress, emotional intelligence and sleep and reduced feelings of burnout, anger and fatigue. We know mindfulness cuts off stress by bringing one's attention to the present moment by withdrawing the attention from the past or future and enabling one to feel Zen-like by letting one experience life as it exists in the right here and now.

Experimenters conducted randomised control trials to study the effect of meditation on stress levels of police officers of five forces. Over six hundred officers practised mindfulness at Avon and Somerset in the UK in this study. The College of Policing Studies revealed improved well-being, life satisfaction, resilience and work performance. They divided the police officers into two groups. They trained one group using a commercial meditation app available for download in the App Store called *Headspace*. The second group got trained on Mindfit Cop, an in-house meditation technique, and the third group did not get any mindfulness training. The researchers found that the first two groups recorded 'meaningful improvements' in well-being and life satisfaction and resilience compared with the control group. As the research produced strong evidence of mindfulness improving well-being, resilience and life satisfaction compared to control groups, leaders of the force decided to give meditation lessons to 200,000 police officers in England and Wales.

Mindfulness training builds resilience and the ability to bounce back from stress. Similarly, it creates 'response inhibition' of the impulse to do something harmful and preventable, like opening fire on a mob. Police officers need to respond not to react, but police officers almost always react and do not respond. A police officer has to be in the now to respond to a situation, not get triggered and overtaken by emotion. Mindfulness helps in such situations by bringing the officer into the now by making them resilient.

At the University of Wisconsin's Center for Healthy Minds, researchers are working with the Madison police department to gauge the impact of an eight-week changed version of Mindfulness-Based Resilience Training (MBRT) on physiological measures like heart rate and breathing, along with the ability to inhibit automatic responses in the face of emotional distractions.

Resilient police officers tend to have a better response inhibition as meditation builds more cognitive resources. When the police are facing a situation, personnel with mindfulness training as a matter of routine perform a self-awareness check which would include some deep breathing to get in touch with the way they are feeling and mentally preparing themselves to embrace the fear or anger at the injustice that is unfolding without letting those emotions cloud their tactical cognitive decision-making. Thus, the practice of mindfulness or meditation helps the police officer to see the perspective of another, enhancing his compassion for the persons who get agitated, and makes them likely to go berserk in awkward volatile situations. The trained officers tend to make better decisions than untrained groups, as they have slower maximum heart rates and quicker recoveries. A fast-beating heart is most often the cause for irrational decisions. Therefore, mindfulness has the potential to reduce unnecessary violence.

Further, as we live in an age of distraction, a 'quiet room' is imperative in each police station to allow for short breaks to enable police personnel to recharge by connecting with themselves. Quiet room can help officers escape during a period of stress to do some calming inner work and build inner resilience.

Research at Harvard Medical School has revealed that mindfulness practices switch on disease-fighting genes that protect the practitioners against cardiac diseases, high blood pressure, joint pain, back pain and diabetes. Mindfulness meditation exerts its effects on the brain by acting on the components of attention regulation, body awareness and emotional regulation. When testing characteristics such as a sense of obligation, genuineness, compassion, self-acceptance and integrity, studies have shown that mindfulness meditation renders a more coherent and healthy understanding of self and identity. Neuroimaging techniques have shown that mindfulness meditation correlates with changes in the anterior cingulate cortex, temporoparietal junction, front-limbic network insula and default-mode network structures. In addition, mindfulness may prevent the onset of mild cognitive impairment and influence genetic expression, reducing the risk of inflammation-related diseases.

Studies have shown that mindfulness enhances grey matter concentration in the brain in areas that regulate emotion, including memory processes and improvement of the immune system, which could explain the correlation between stress reduction and increased quality of life. These changes partly appear to be due to the thickening of the prefrontal cortex hippocampus, shrinking of the amygdala and the strengthening of the connections between brain cells. Long-term meditators have more folding of the cortex (gyrification), a significant amount of which may allow the brain to process information faster than non-meditators. Meditators associate mindfulness with higher levels of life satisfaction, agreeableness, conscientiousness, vitality, self-esteem, empathy, a sense of autonomy, competence, optimism and pleasant effect because of such effects on the human brain.

Incorporating mindfulness practices for police personnel needs to gain steam in India. Indian police officers also have the highest stress levels among all occupations because of violence, pressure and job demands. The US Secret Service and Federal Bureau of Investigation and police agencies in cities like New York, Los Angeles and Chicago have all incorporated mindfulness and are using the services of Blue Courage. This training company has components of mindfulness in its training. Likewise, the Washington State Criminal Justice Training Commission has incorporated 16 hours of Blue Courage training for all basic law enforcement recruits.

It's no wonder that mindfulness is today a $4 billion industry. There are over 60,000 books for sale on Amazon on mindfulness with titles such as mindful parenting, mindful eating, mindful teaching, mindful therapy, mindful leadership, mindful finance, mindful nation, mindful dog owners and so on glorifying its benefits, to name just a few.

Eventually, a quote from Rumi says: 'Keep knocking, and the joy inside will finally open a window and look out to see who's there'. That is appropriate for police personnel or anyone as mindfulness can help them reconnect to the joy that is always there and that still lives within each one of them. All the police organisations need to provide the training to help their personnel access this valuable treasure.

CONCLUSION

In conclusion, *A Random Potpourri* has taken you on a journey through a wide range of topics, from the magical powers of forest bathing to the growing cybercrime risks of the NFT explosion. Throughout this book, I have shared my reflections, musings and insights as a policeman, and I hope you have found these insights both thought-provoking and inspiring.

In the first section of the book, we explored the importance of creating a life that feels good on the inside, the power of self-discipline and the impact of human–wildlife conflict. We also delved into the power of silence, the law of assumption and the incredible potential of 'Om' chanting.

In the second section, we delved into the world of health and nutrition, exploring topics such as the benefits of tree-hugging, the best fuel for running and the potential of a plant-based diet. We also looked at the impact of COVID-19 lockdown on diet and weight loss and examined the benefits of supplements like berberine.

The third section explored the impact of technology and social media on policing and law enforcement. We examined the potential of 5G technology, AI and mind-reading technology to enhance policing in the future and considered the implications of criminal robots and drones. We also looked at the impact of social media on crime-fighting and explored the potential of voice technology to combat fraud.

Finally, in the fourth section, we delved into the world of policing and law, exploring topics such as the growing cybercrime risks of NFT explosion, the importance of mindfulness for humane policing and the relationship between spirituality and policing.

As you close the book, I hope you have gained a deeper understanding of the world around you and the many challenges and opportunities we face as a society. I also hope you have been inspired to think more deeply about your own life and the ways in which you can make a positive impact on the world. Thank you for reading *A Random Potpourri.*

BOOKS PUBLISHED BY THE AUTHOR

ABOUT THE AUTHOR

Dr K. Jayanth Murali, IPS (Retd.), is a dynamic and charismatic leader who has left an indelible mark in the realm of law enforcement and beyond. Hailing from the vibrant city of Golconda Fort in India, Dr Murali's career has been nothing short of extraordinary, brimming with excitement, accomplishments and unwavering dedication to public service.

A trailblazer from the very beginning, Dr Murali's insatiable thirst for knowledge led him to pursue a PhD in microbiology from the prestigious Indian Agricultural Research Institute, New Delhi, where he emerged as a brilliant scientific scholar. However, destiny had other plans for him, and he was handpicked for the prestigious Indian Police Service in 1991, setting the stage for an illustrious career that spanned over three decades of unparalleled achievements.

With his larger-than-life personality and exceptional leadership skills, Dr Murali served in a diverse array of policing assignments that left a lasting impact. From tackling complex law-and-order situations to spearheading high-stakes crime investigations and providing VIP security, Dr Murali's unwavering commitment to duty earned him widespread recognition and admiration. As Chief of Crime Branch CID, Director of Vigilance and Anti-corruption and Additional Director General of Police, Law and Order, and Director General of Police for the Government of Tamil Nadu, he carved a niche for himself as an exemplary law enforcement professional.

But Dr Murali's contributions go far beyond his official duties. He is a prolific writer, whose thought-provoking articles have graced the pages of leading newspapers and e-magazines, capturing the imagination of readers with his diverse interests and deep insights. As a gifted writer, Jayanth's words resonate with depth and insight. His critically acclaimed book, *42 Monday's: On Emerging Technologies in Policing*, is a testament to his profound understanding of the evolving landscape of law enforcement. In addition, he has authored three other captivating books, namely *Soliloquies on Future Policing*, *Enkindling the Endorphins of Endurance* and *Marathon* (in Tamil). His writings on policing, security, technology, sports, science fiction, health and fitness are nothing short of captivating, igniting a spark of inspiration in the hearts of his readers.

In addition to his literary pursuits, Dr Murali is a man of many talents. An avid farmer, he nurtures his passion for the land and has a green thumb that is the envy of many. He is also a renowned coach for running, nutrition and health, helping countless individuals achieve their fitness goals and lead healthier lives. As a painter and cook, he unleashes his creative genius, delighting others with his artistic flair and culinary expertise.

Dr Murali's indomitable spirit and unwavering determination are further exemplified by his exceptional achievements in the field of marathon running. He has completed over 50 half and full marathons and holds prestigious records in the India Book of Records and Asia Book of Records, showcasing his unparalleled prowess as an athlete. His dedication to the cause of organ donation, through marathons and other initiatives, is a testament to his compassionate heart and desire to make a positive impact on society.

Beyond his professional accomplishments and athletic pursuits, Dr Murali's humanitarian endeavours are truly awe-inspiring. As ADGP, Armed Police, he launched the LetsFightCorona initiative during the pandemic, leading a remarkable effort to distribute relief worth over Rs 50 lakhs in just 40 days, providing much-needed aid to those in need. His selfless acts of kindness and unwavering commitment to serving humanity have earned him the respect and admiration of people from all walks of life.

In his personal life, Jayanth is a loving husband to his college mate Dr Jayanthi, IFS, and a proud father to two accomplished daughters, Anisha, an architect in Mumbai, and Anussha, a postgraduate student at Jawaharlal National University, New Delhi. Jayanth's extraordinary journey is a shining example of resilience, determination and compassion, making him a true inspiration to all. To learn more about this remarkable individual and his incredible achievements, visit www.jayanthmurali.com and prepare to be inspired.

www.ingramcontent.com/pod-product-compliance
Lightning Source LLC
LaVergne TN
LVHW041010150826
845672LV00001B/42

* 9 7 9 8 8 9 1 8 6 9 2 1 9 *